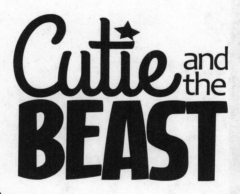

Cutie and the BEAST

story & art by
YUHI AZUMI

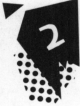

2

Contents

▶

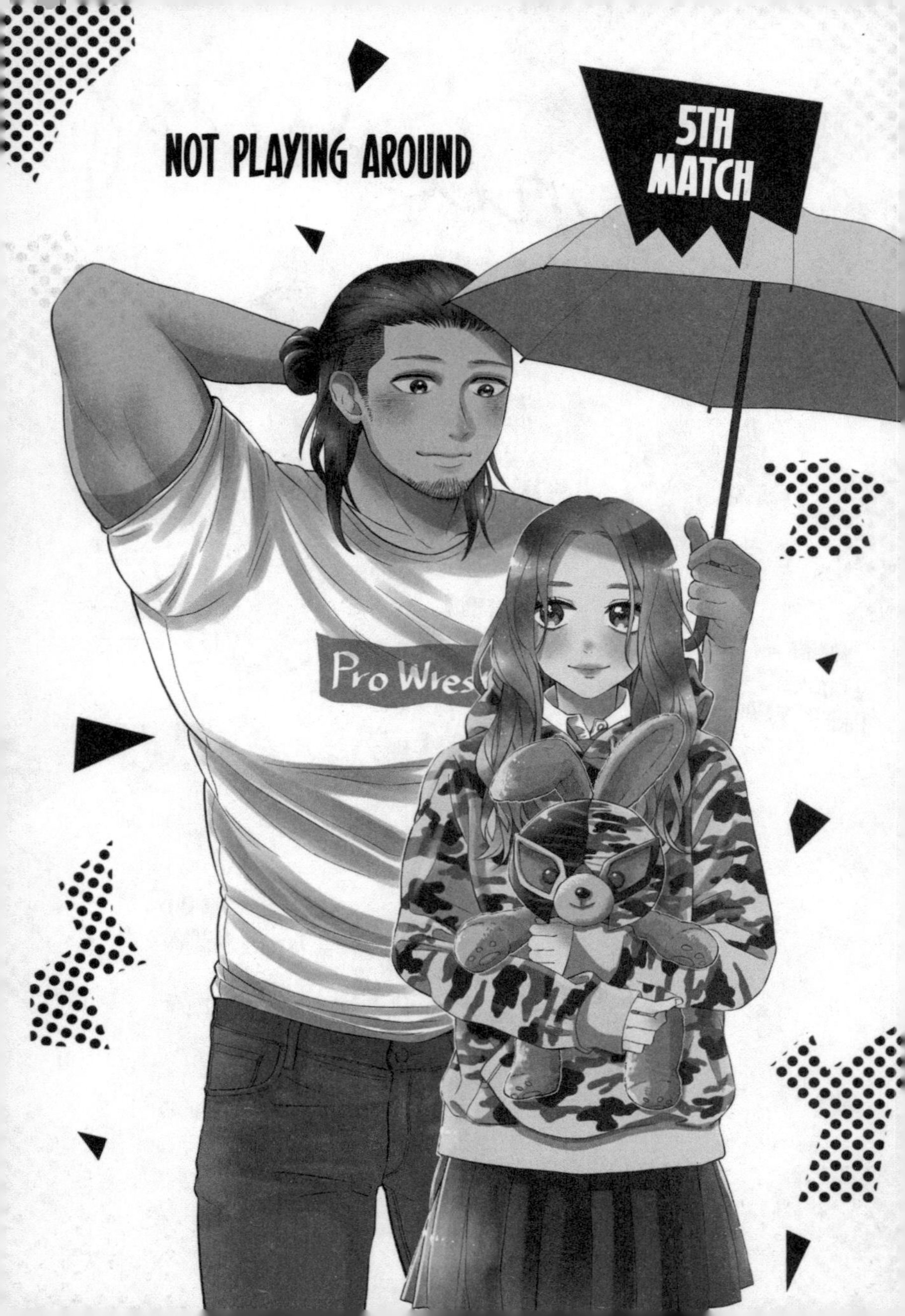
5TH
MATCH
NOT PLAYING AROUND
Pro Wres

Story

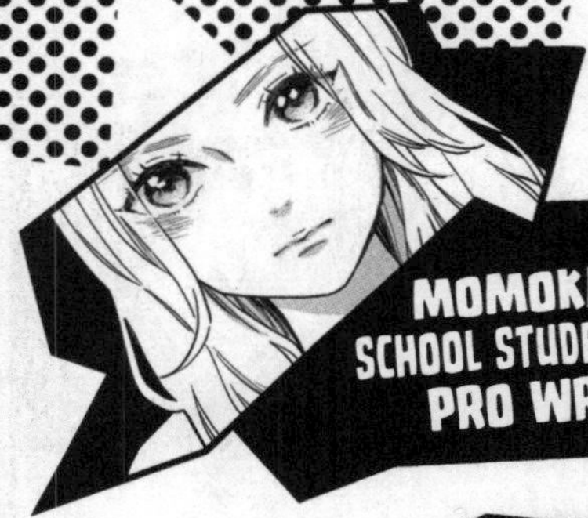

MOMOKA IS A HIGH SCHOOL STUDENT WHO LOVES PRO WRESTLING.

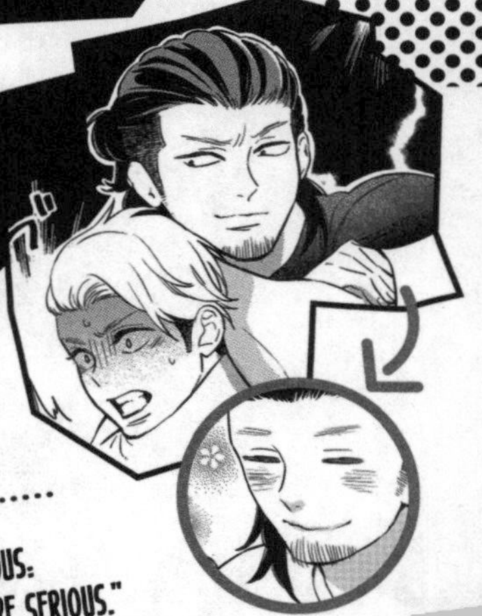

SHE'S A HUGE FAN OF A WRESTLER NAMED KUGA!

MOMOKA AND KUGA MEET UP AT THE STADIUM AFTER A MATCH, WHERE HE RECOGNIZES HER FROM HER FAN LETTERS. WHEN SHE'S ABOUT TO LEAVE, HE KISSES HER ON THE CHEEK?!

ON THEIR FIRST PHONE CALL, KUGA'S NERVOUS: "I NEED YOU TO UNDERSTAND THAT MY FEELINGS ARE SERIOUS."

BUT HE DIDN'T REALIZE THAT SHE WAS STILL IN HIGH SCHOOL!

AFTER MOMOKA DROPS THAT TRUTH BOMB, KUGA PANICS AND CUTS THINGS OFF. AFTER GETTING A BIG TALKING-TO FROM MOMOKA, KUGA INVITES HER TO A MATCH, WHERE SHE CHEERS HIM ON. AFTER THAT, IN THE VERY SAME SPOT WHERE THEY KISSED, HE ASKS HER TO MARRY HIM SOMEDAY.

WHICH IS OF COURSE THE EXACT MOMENT WHEN MOMOKA'S PARENTS SHOW UP. UH-OH.

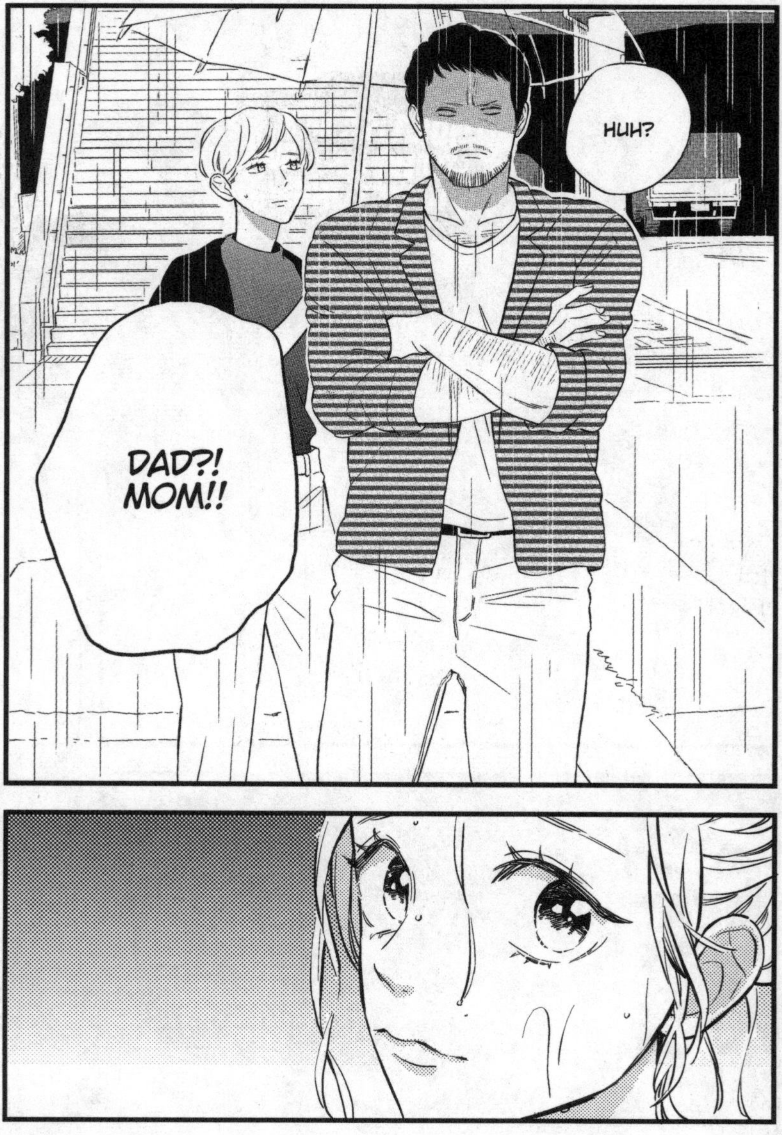
HUH?
DAD?! MOM!!

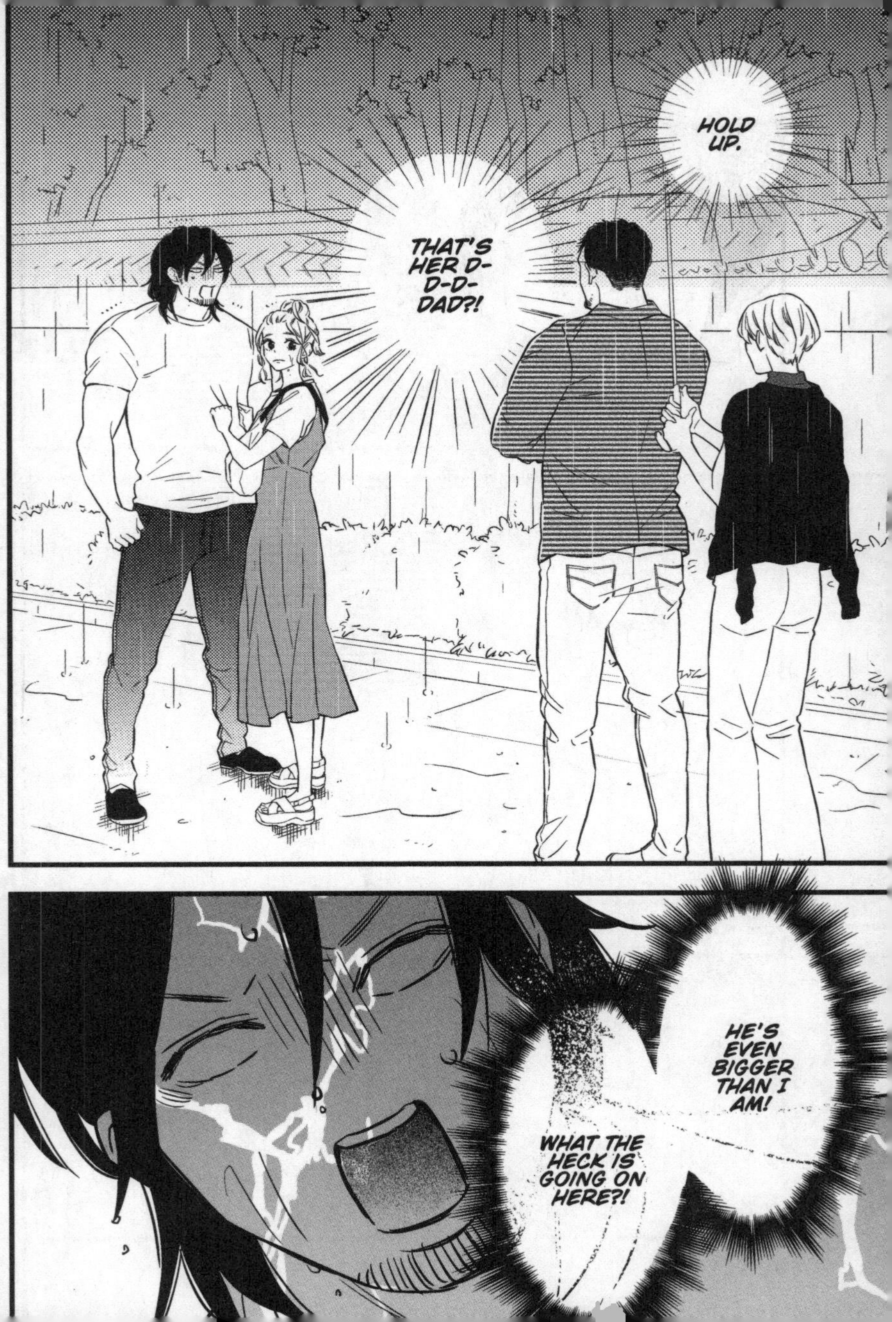
HOLD UP.
THAT'S HER D-D-D-DAD?!
HE'S EVEN BIGGER THAN I AM!
WHAT THE HECK IS GOING ON HERE?!

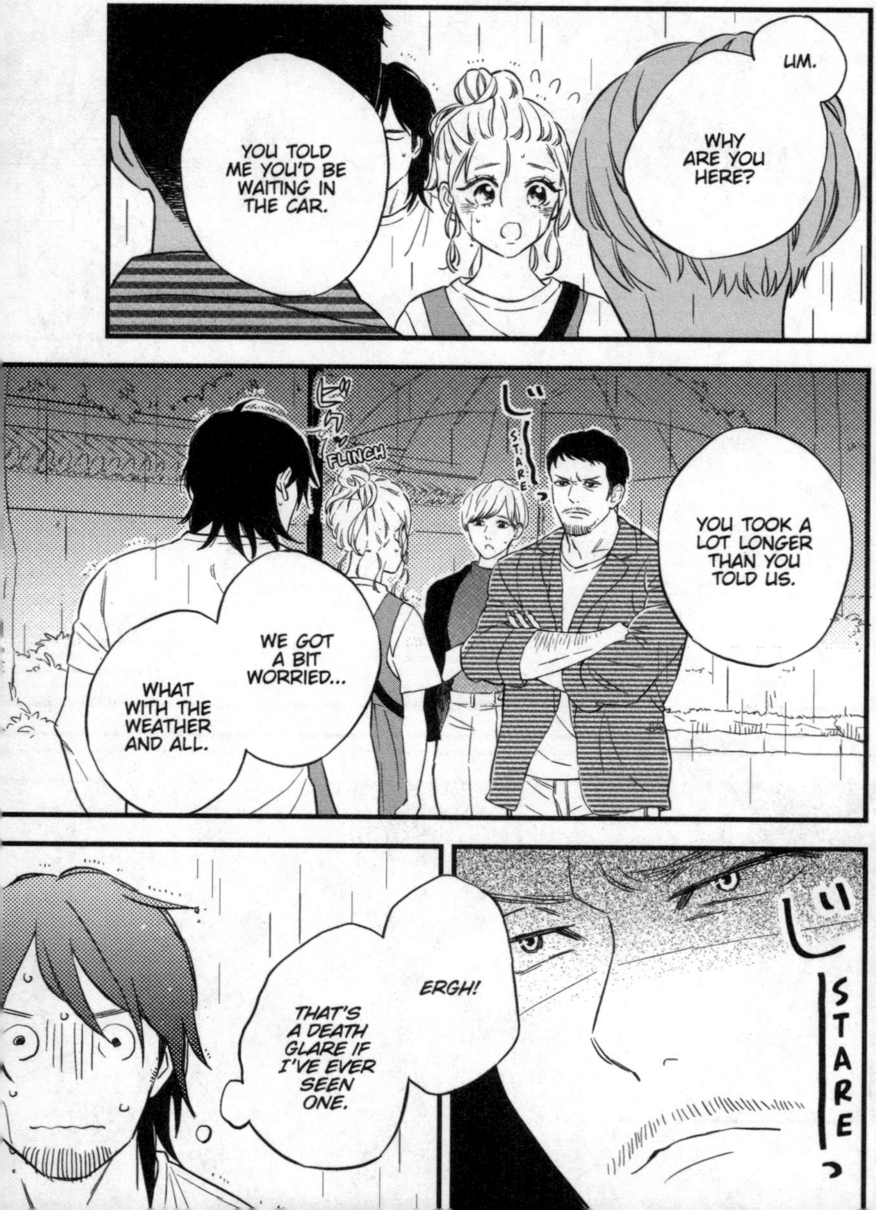
UM.
WHY ARE YOU HERE?
YOU TOLD ME YOU'D BE WAITING IN THE CAR.
YOU TOOK A LOT LONGER THAN YOU TOLD US.
STARE
FLINCH
WE GOT A BIT WORRIED...
WHAT WITH THE WEATHER AND ALL.
STARE
ERGH!
THAT'S A DEATH GLARE IF I'VE EVER SEEN ONE.

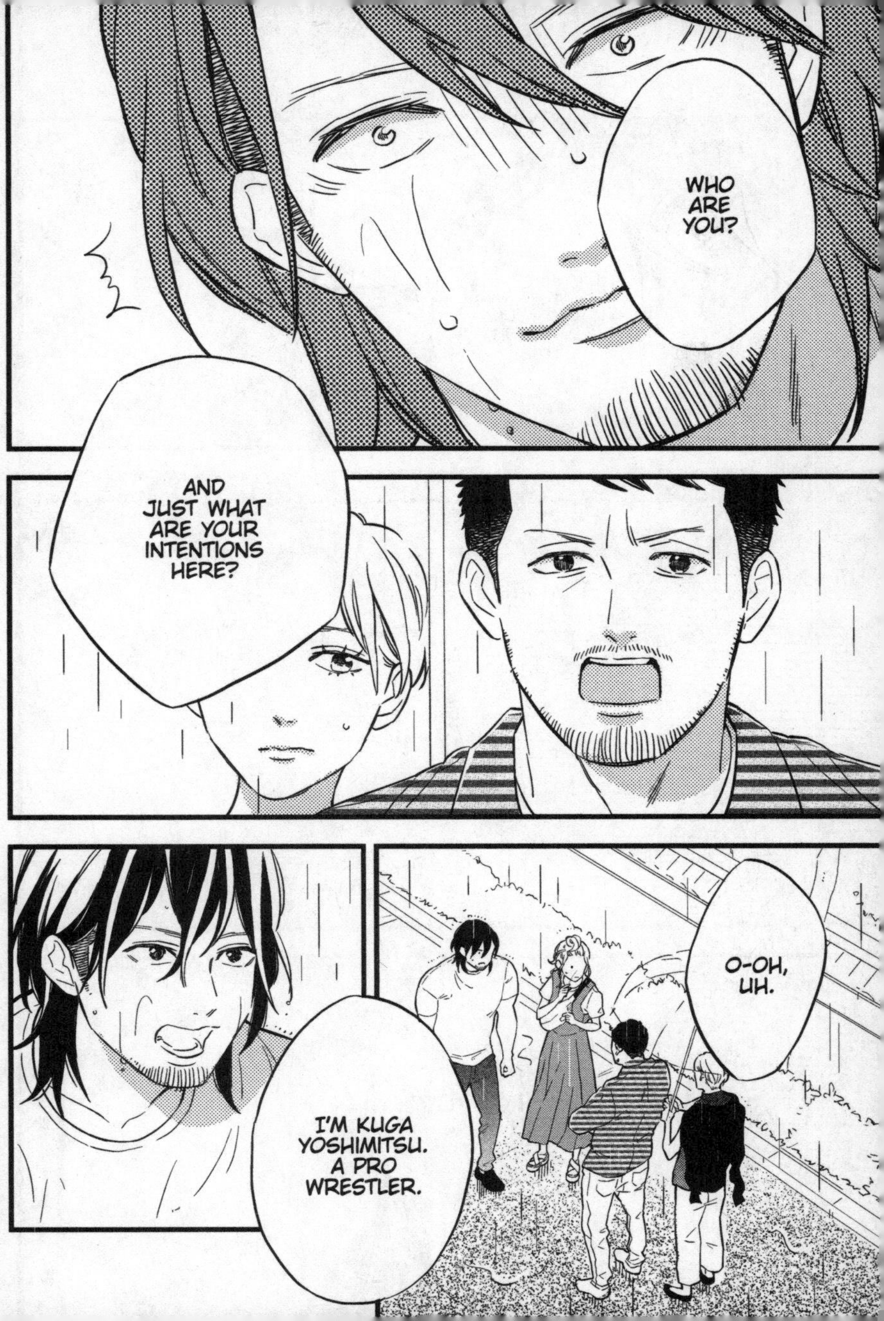
WHO ARE YOU?
AND JUST WHAT ARE YOUR INTENTIONS HERE?
O-OH, UH.
I'M KUGA YOSHIMITSU. A PRO WRESTLER.

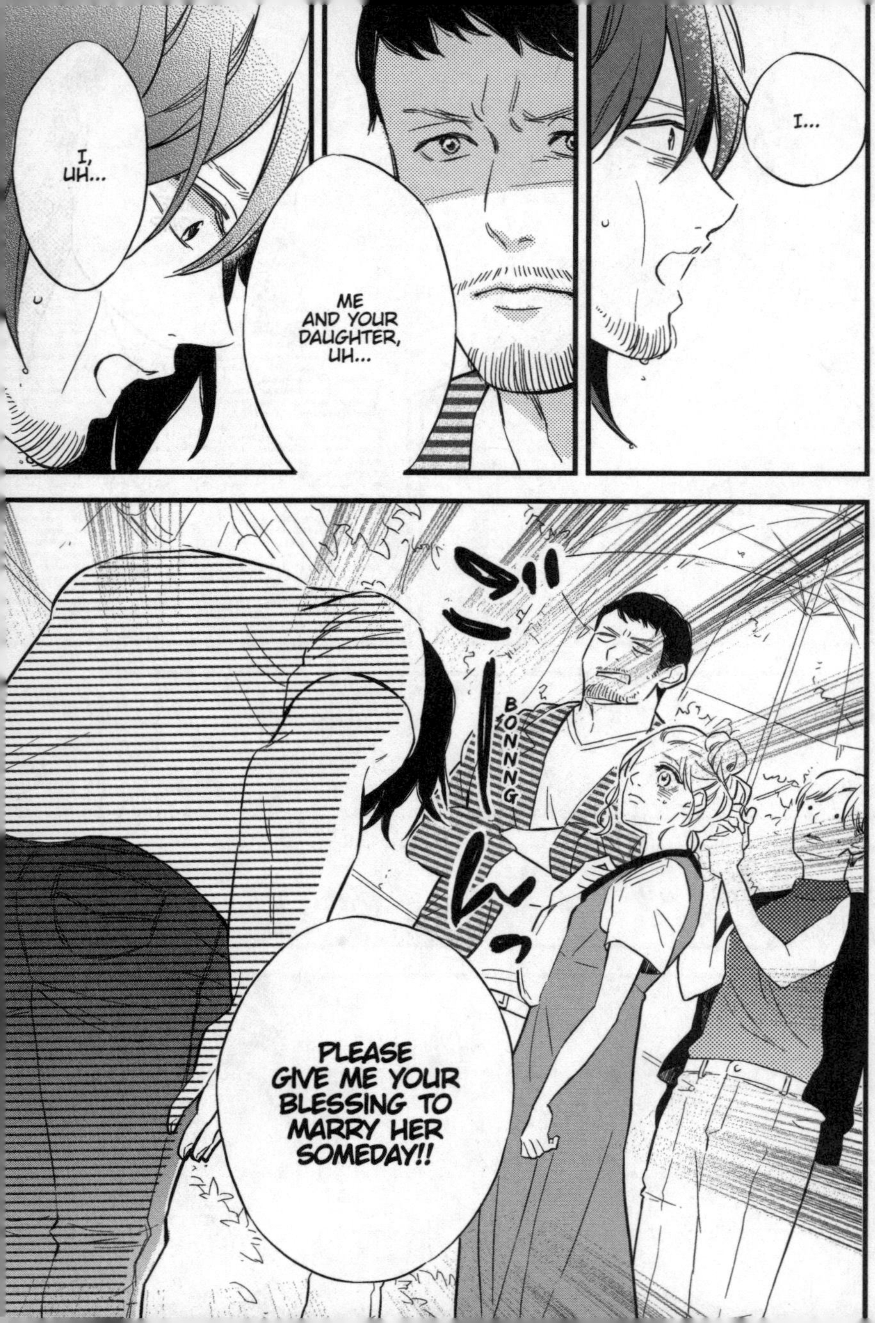
I...
I, UH...
ME AND YOUR DAUGHTER, UH...
BONNNG
PLEASE GIVE ME YOUR BLESSING TO MARRY HER SOMEDAY!!

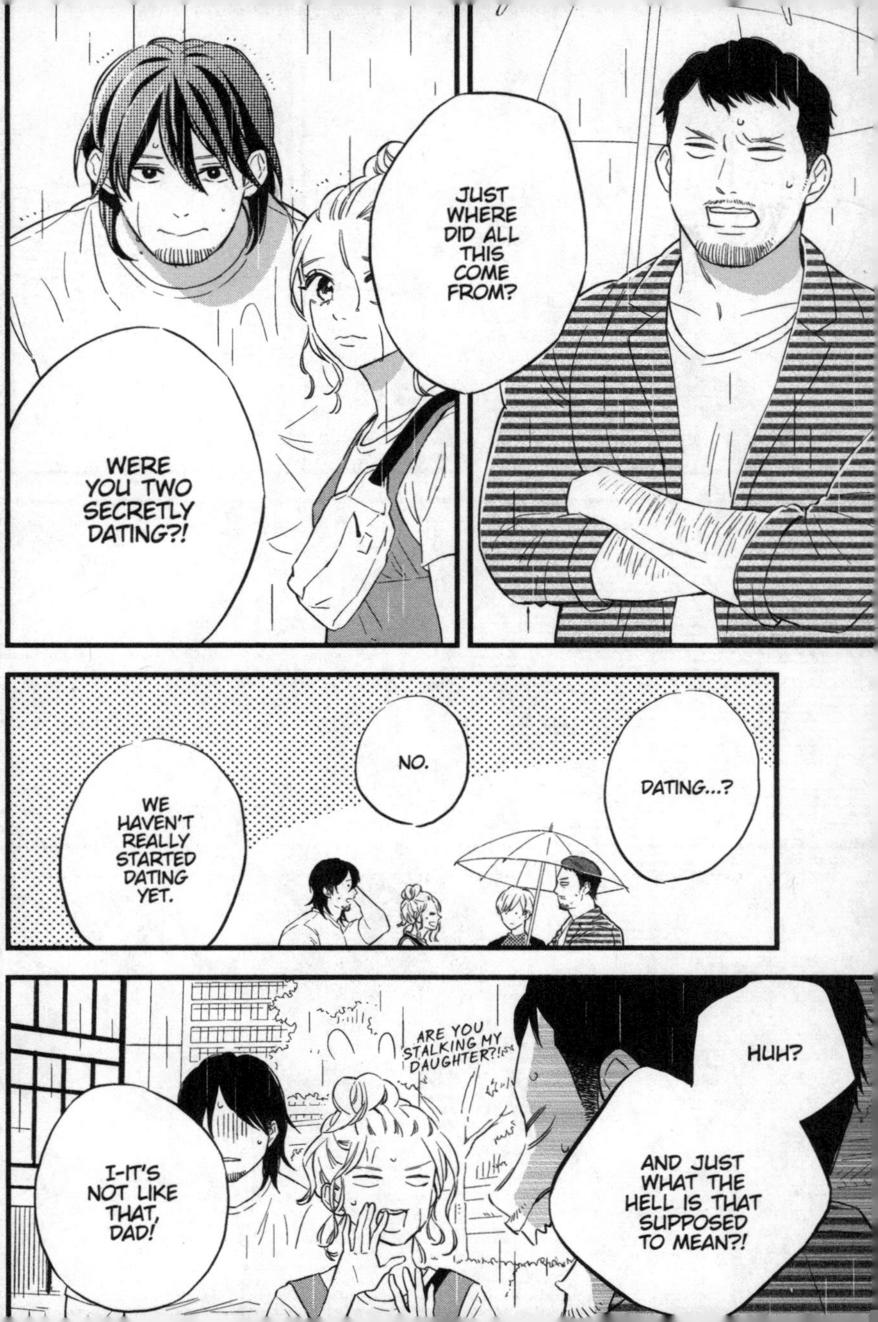
JUST WHERE DID ALL THIS COME FROM?
WERE YOU TWO SECRETLY DATING?!
DATING...?
NO.
WE HAVEN'T REALLY STARTED DATING YET.
HUH?
AND JUST WHAT THE HELL IS THAT SUPPOSED TO MEAN?!
ARE YOU STALKING MY DAUGHTER?!
I-IT'S NOT LIKE THAT, DAD!

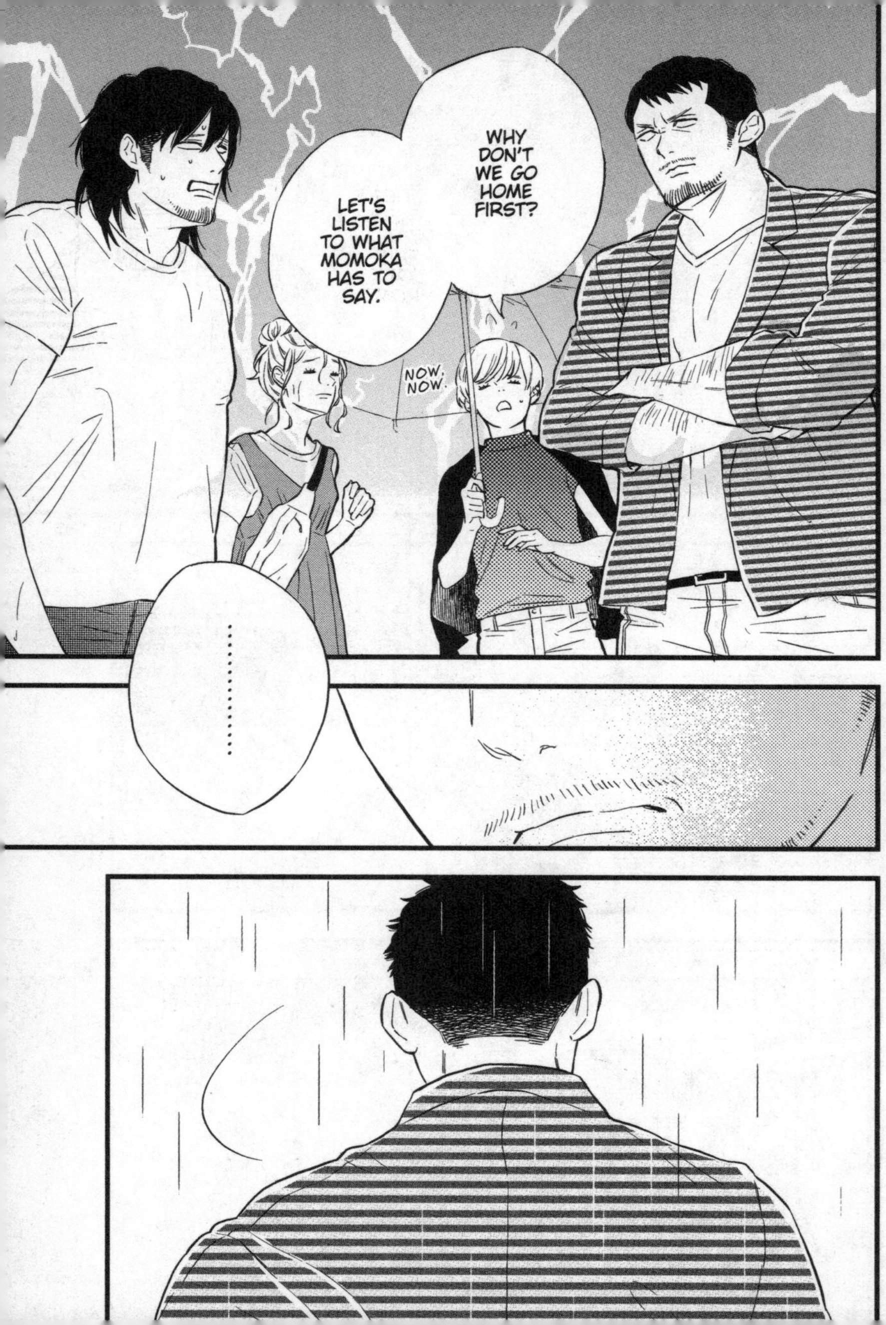
WHY DON'T WE GO HOME FIRST?
LET'S LISTEN TO WHAT MOMOKA HAS TO SAY.
NOW, NOW.
......

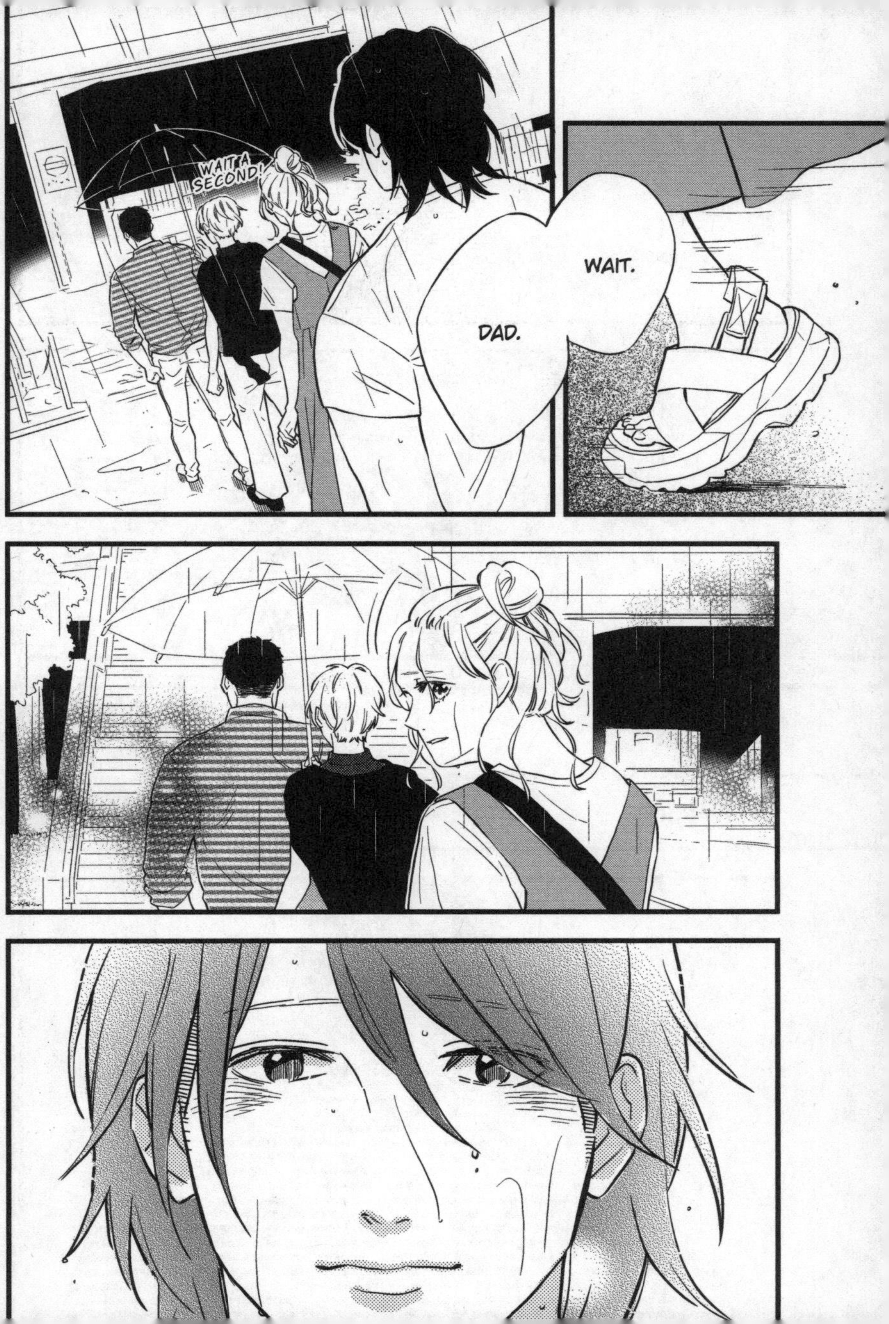
WAIT.
DAD.
WAIT A SECOND!

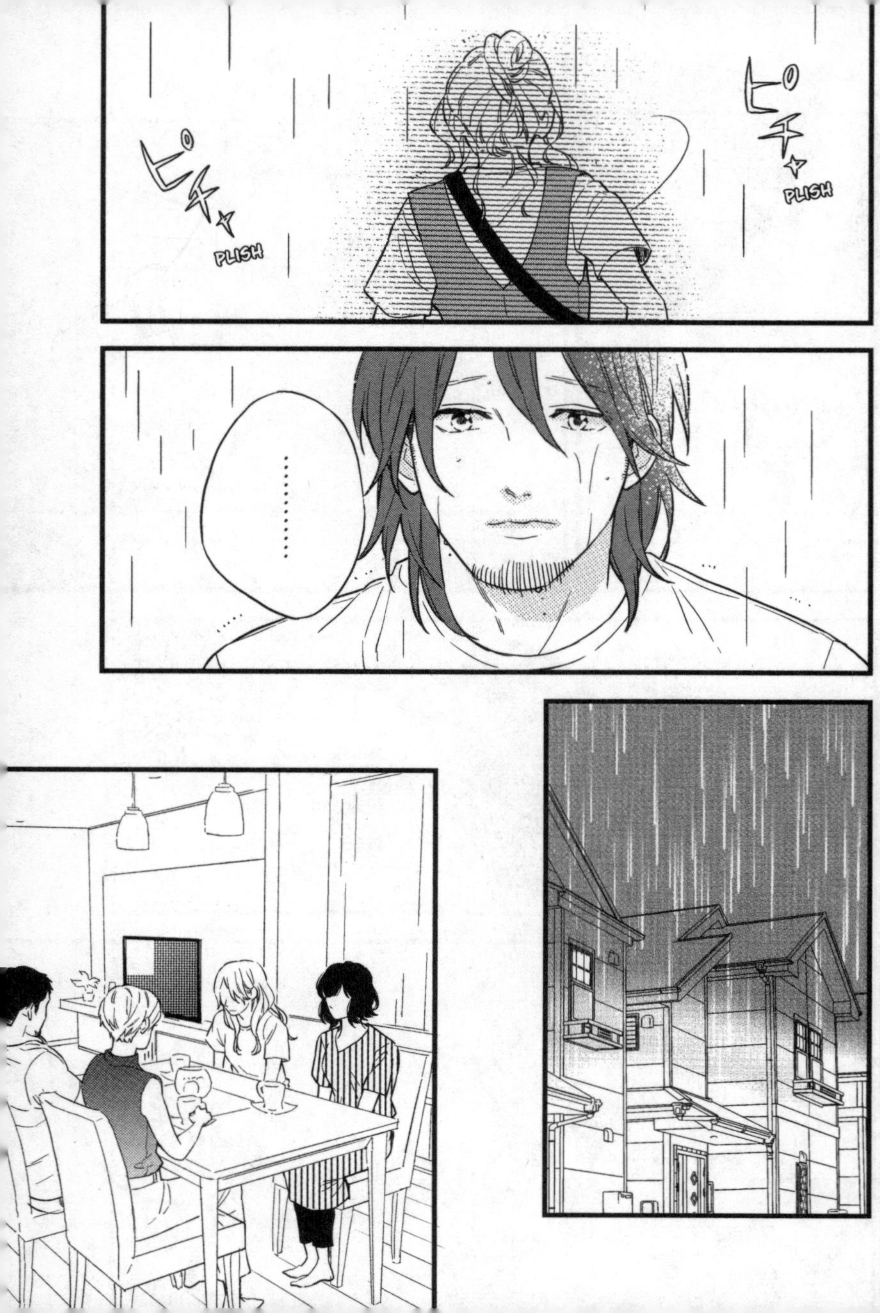
ピチャ
PLISH
ピチャ
PLISH
......

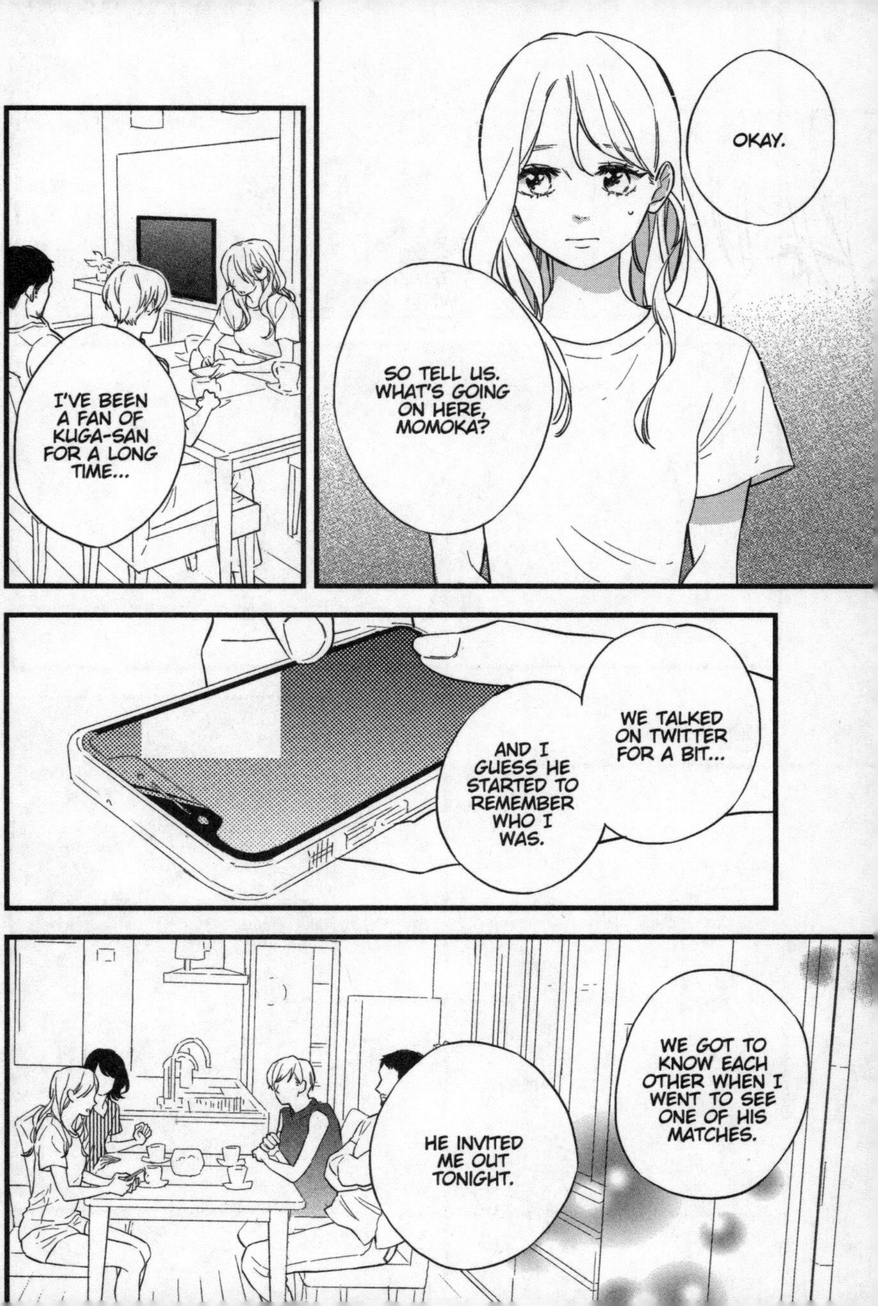
OKAY.
SO TELL US. WHAT'S GOING ON HERE, MOMOKA?
I'VE BEEN A FAN OF KUGA-SAN FOR A LONG TIME...
WE TALKED ON TWITTER FOR A BIT...
AND I GUESS HE STARTED TO REMEMBER WHO I WAS.
WE GOT TO KNOW EACH OTHER WHEN I WENT TO SEE ONE OF HIS MATCHES.
HE INVITED ME OUT TONIGHT.

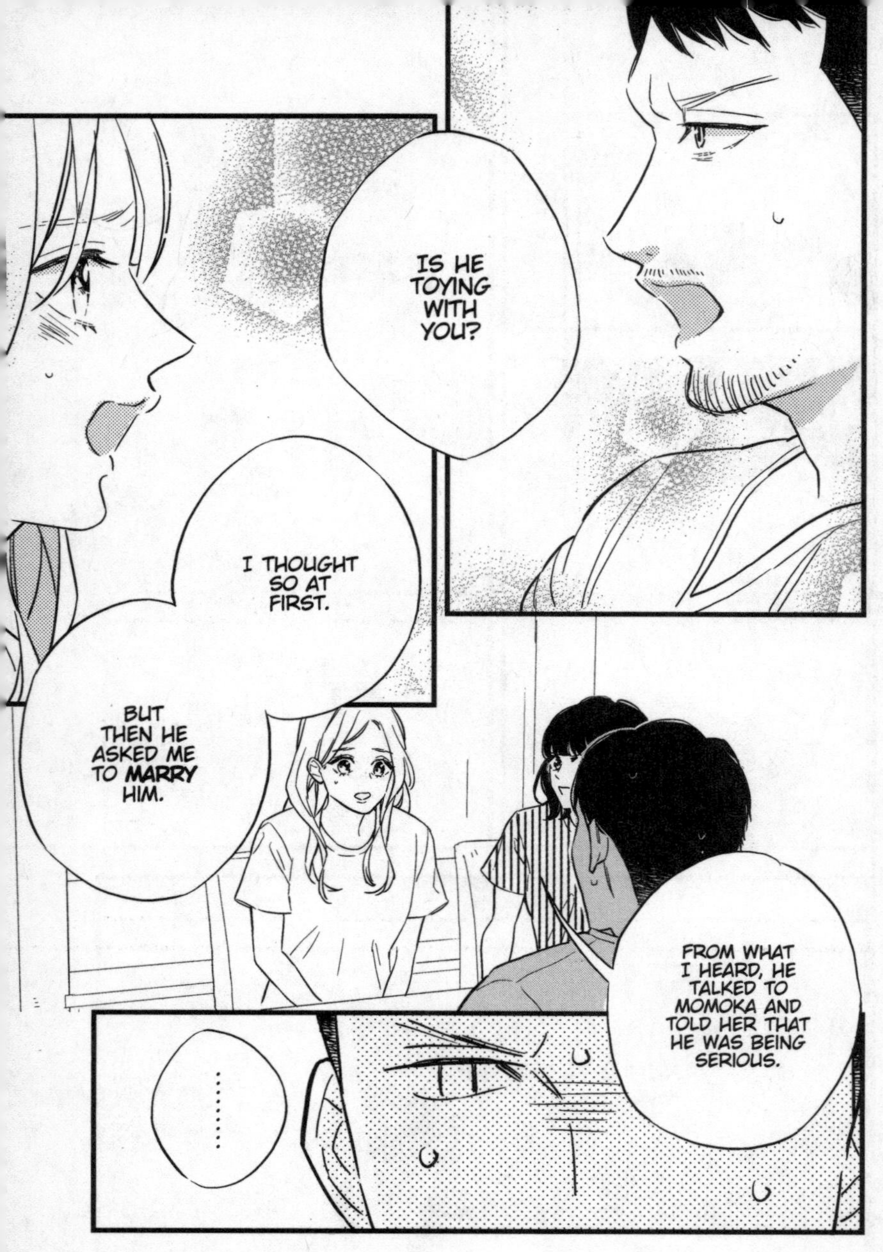
IS HE TOYING WITH YOU?
I THOUGHT SO AT FIRST.
BUT THEN HE ASKED ME TO **MARRY** HIM.
FROM WHAT I HEARD, HE TALKED TO MOMOKA AND TOLD HER THAT HE WAS BEING SERIOUS.
......

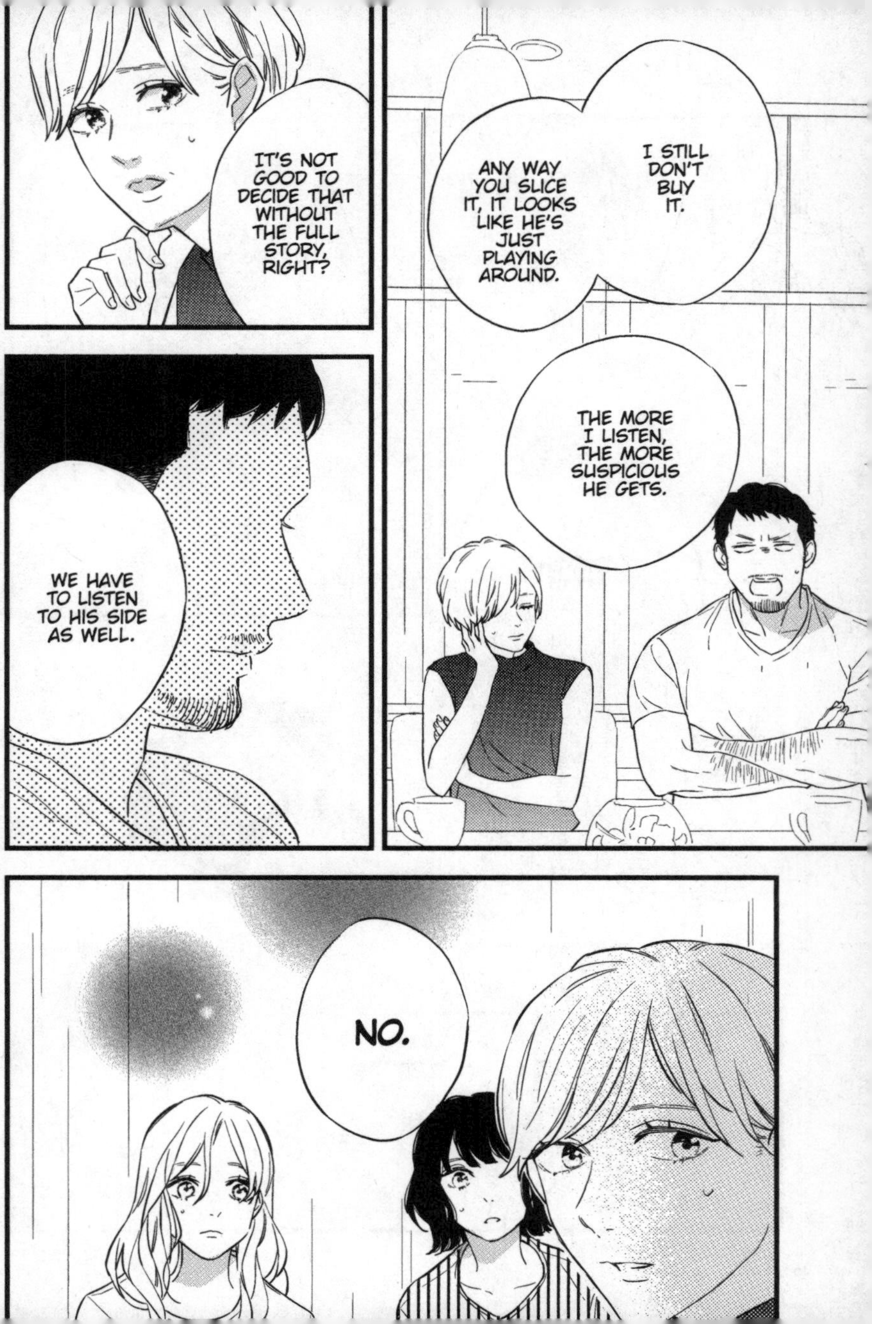
I STILL DON'T BUY IT.
ANY WAY YOU SLICE IT, IT LOOKS LIKE HE'S JUST PLAYING AROUND.
THE MORE I LISTEN, THE MORE SUSPICIOUS HE GETS.
IT'S NOT GOOD TO DECIDE THAT WITHOUT THE FULL STORY, RIGHT?
WE HAVE TO LISTEN TO HIS SIDE AS WELL.
NO.

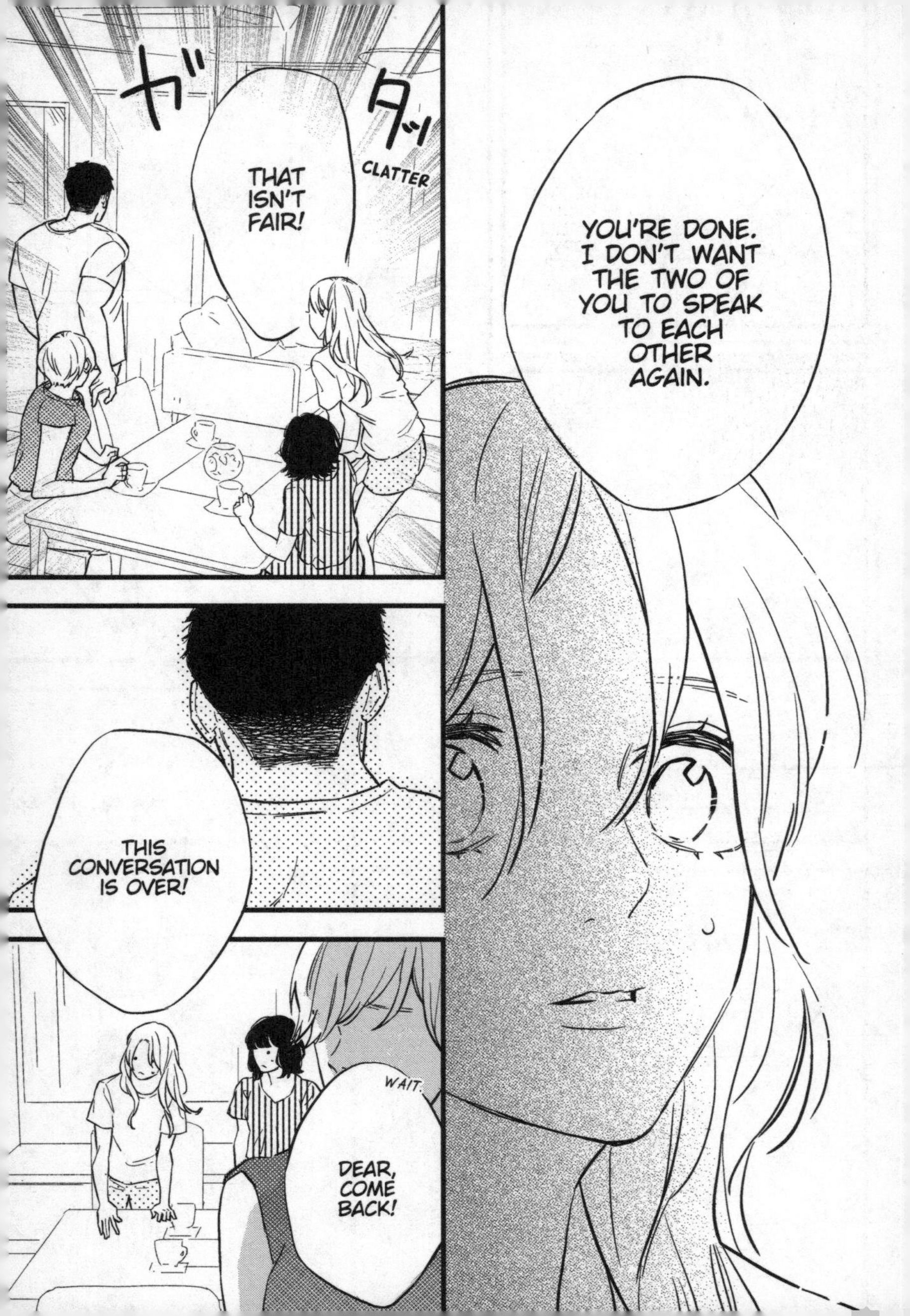
YOU'RE DONE. I DON'T WANT THE TWO OF YOU TO SPEAK TO EACH OTHER AGAIN.
CLATTER
THAT ISN'T FAIR!
THIS CONVERSATION IS OVER!
WAIT.
DEAR, COME BACK!

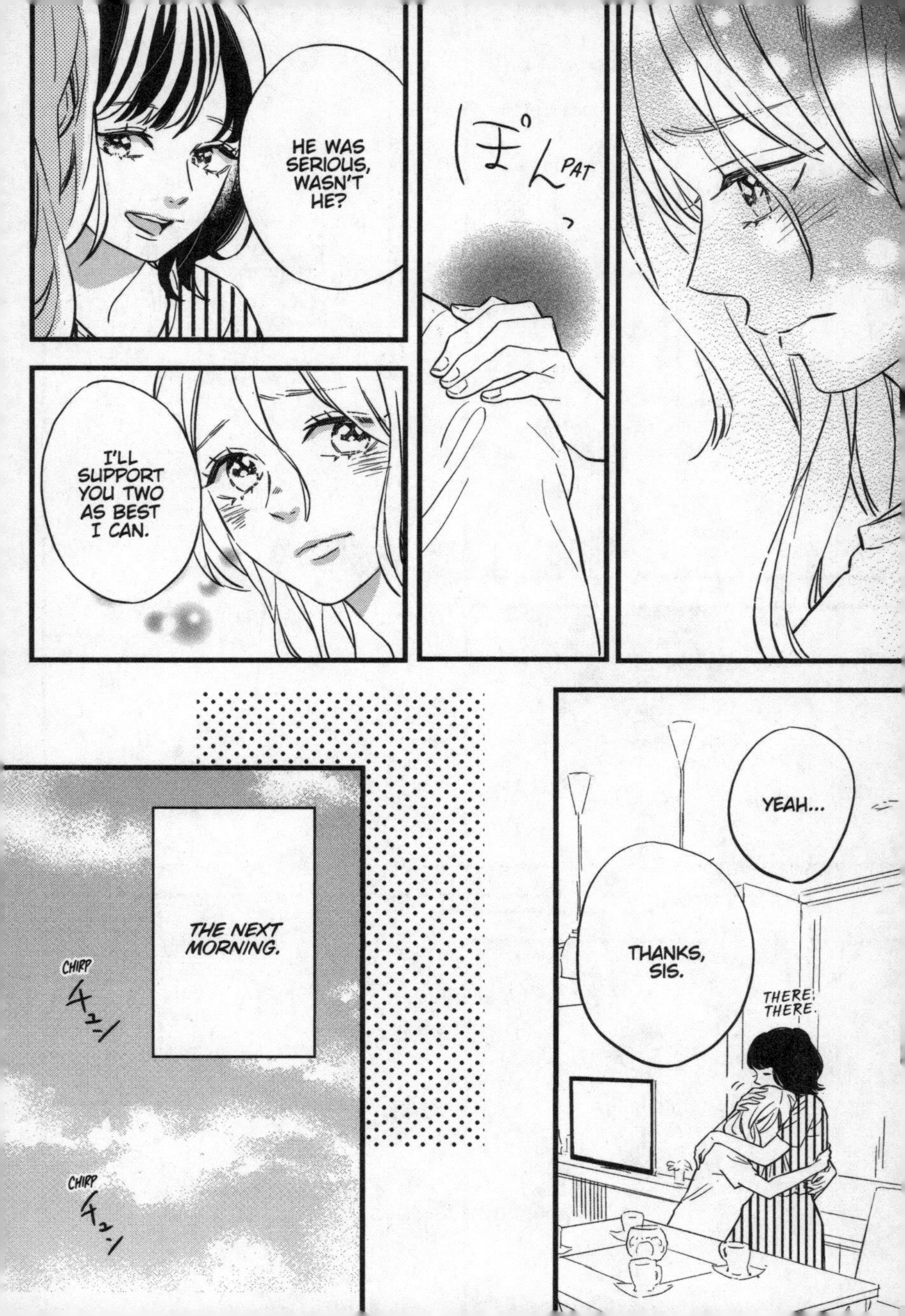
ぽん PAT
HE WAS SERIOUS, WASN'T HE?
I'LL SUPPORT YOU TWO AS BEST I CAN.
YEAH...
THANKS, SIS.
THERE. THERE.
THE NEXT MORNING.
CHIRP チュン
CHIRP チュン

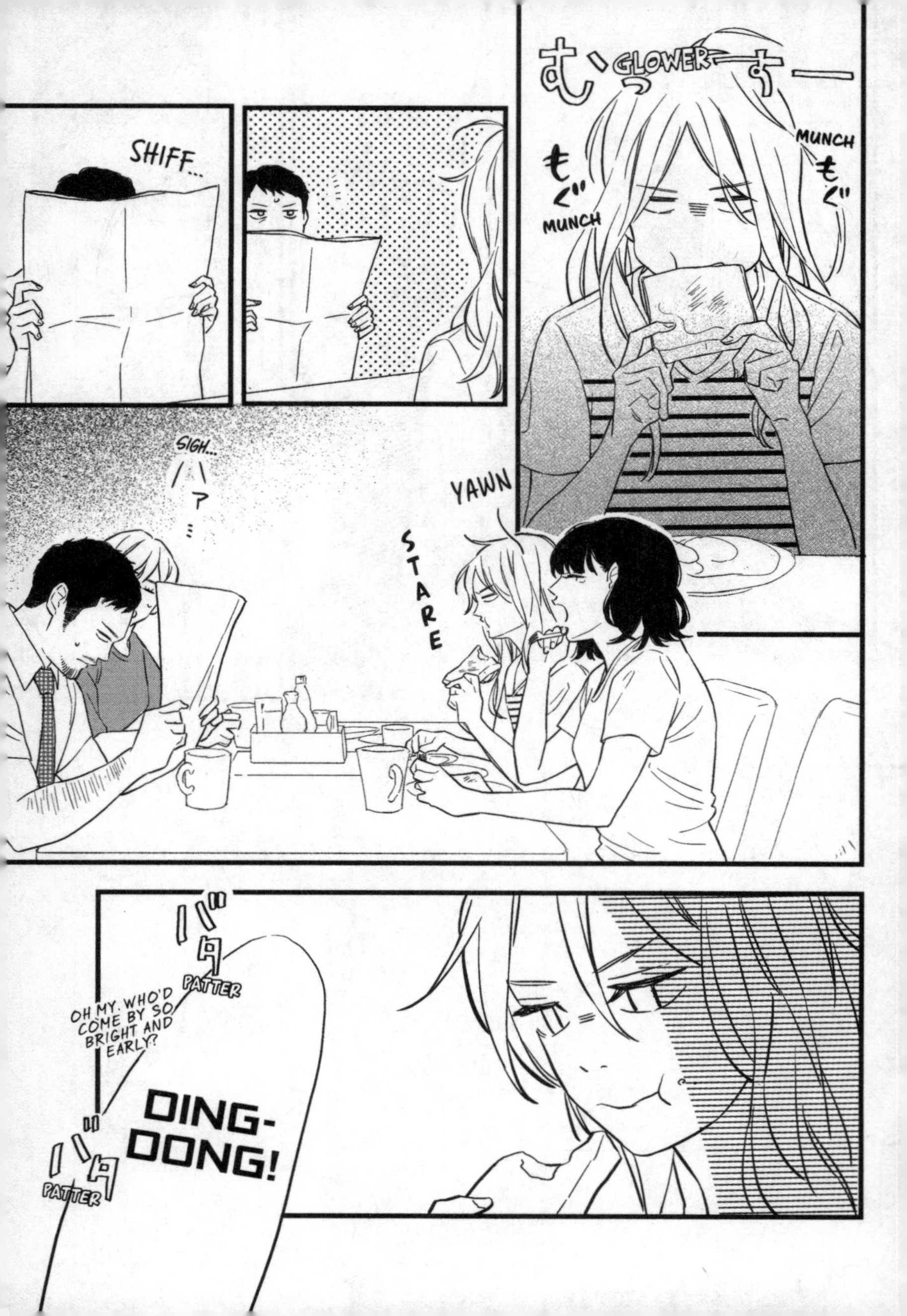

むっすー
GLOWER
MUNCH
もぐ
MUNCH
もぐ
SHIFF...
YAWN
STARE
SIGH...
ハァ…
バタ
PATTER
OH MY. WHO'D COME BY SO BRIGHT AND EARLY?
DING-DONG!
バタ
PATTER

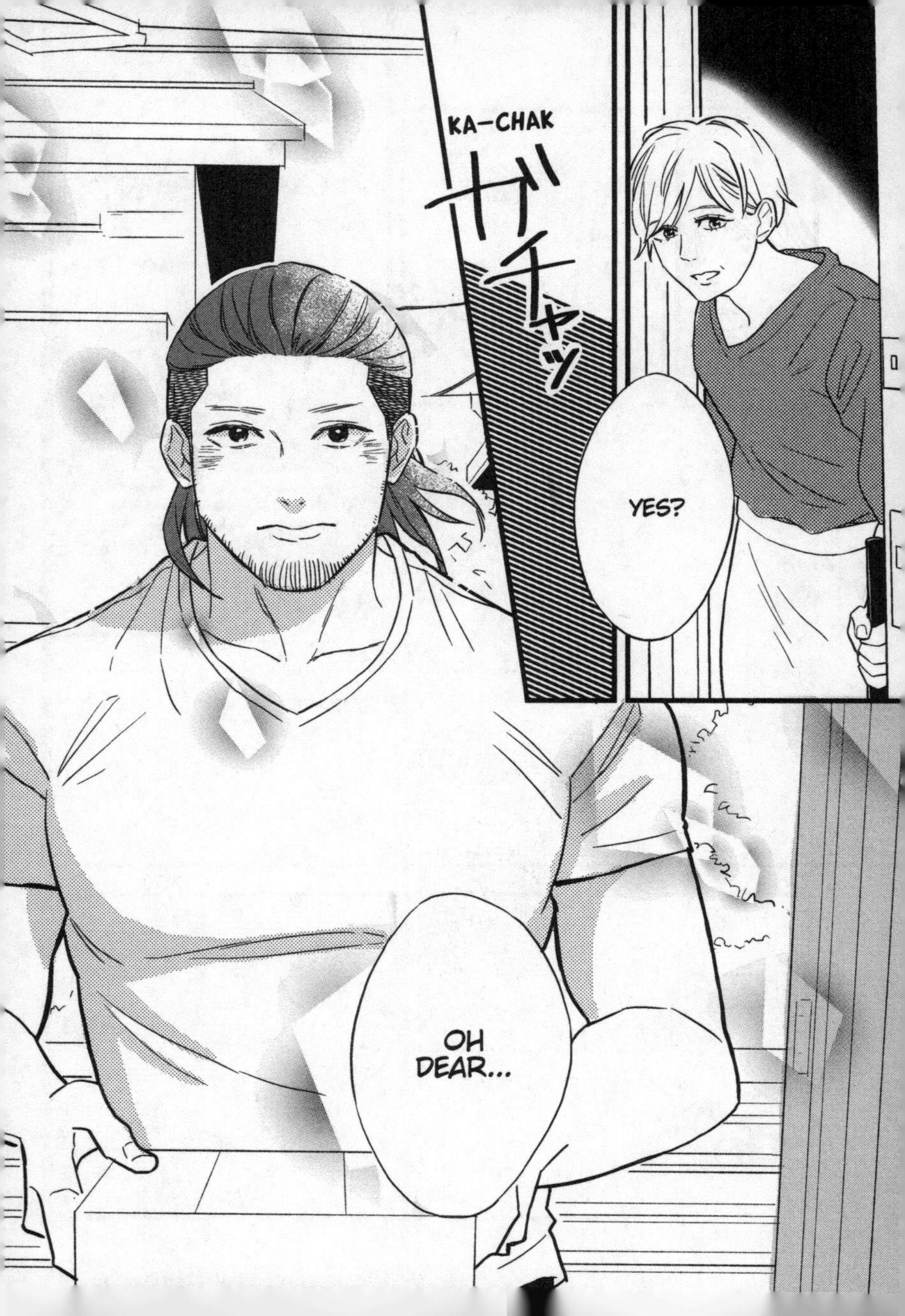
KA-CHAK
ガチャッ
YES?
OH DEAR...

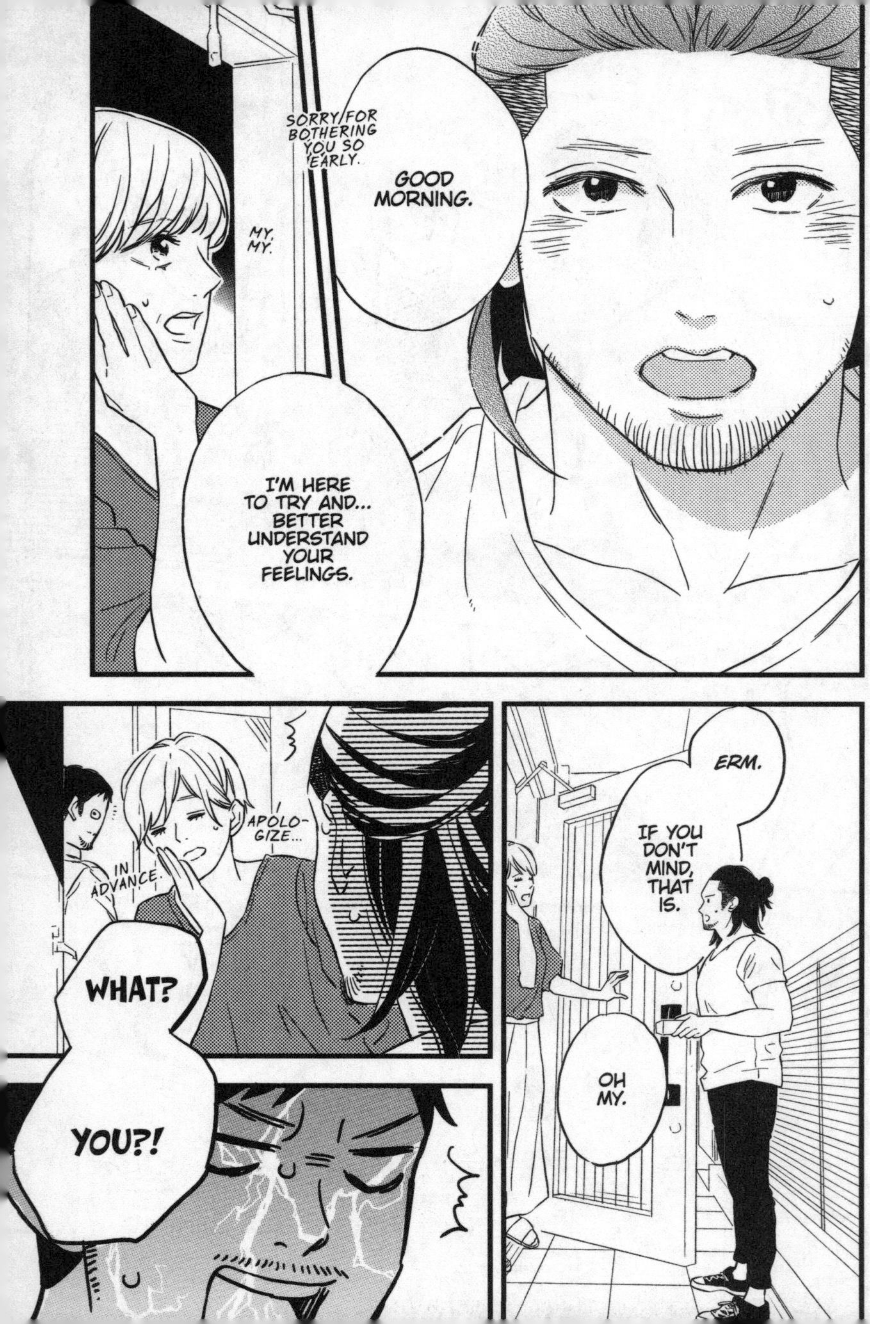
GOOD MORNING.
SORRY FOR BOTHERING YOU SO EARLY.
MY, MY.
I'M HERE TO TRY AND... BETTER UNDERSTAND YOUR FEELINGS.
ERM.
IF YOU DON'T MIND, THAT IS.
OH MY.
I APOLOGIZE...
IN ADVANCE.
WHAT?
YOU?!

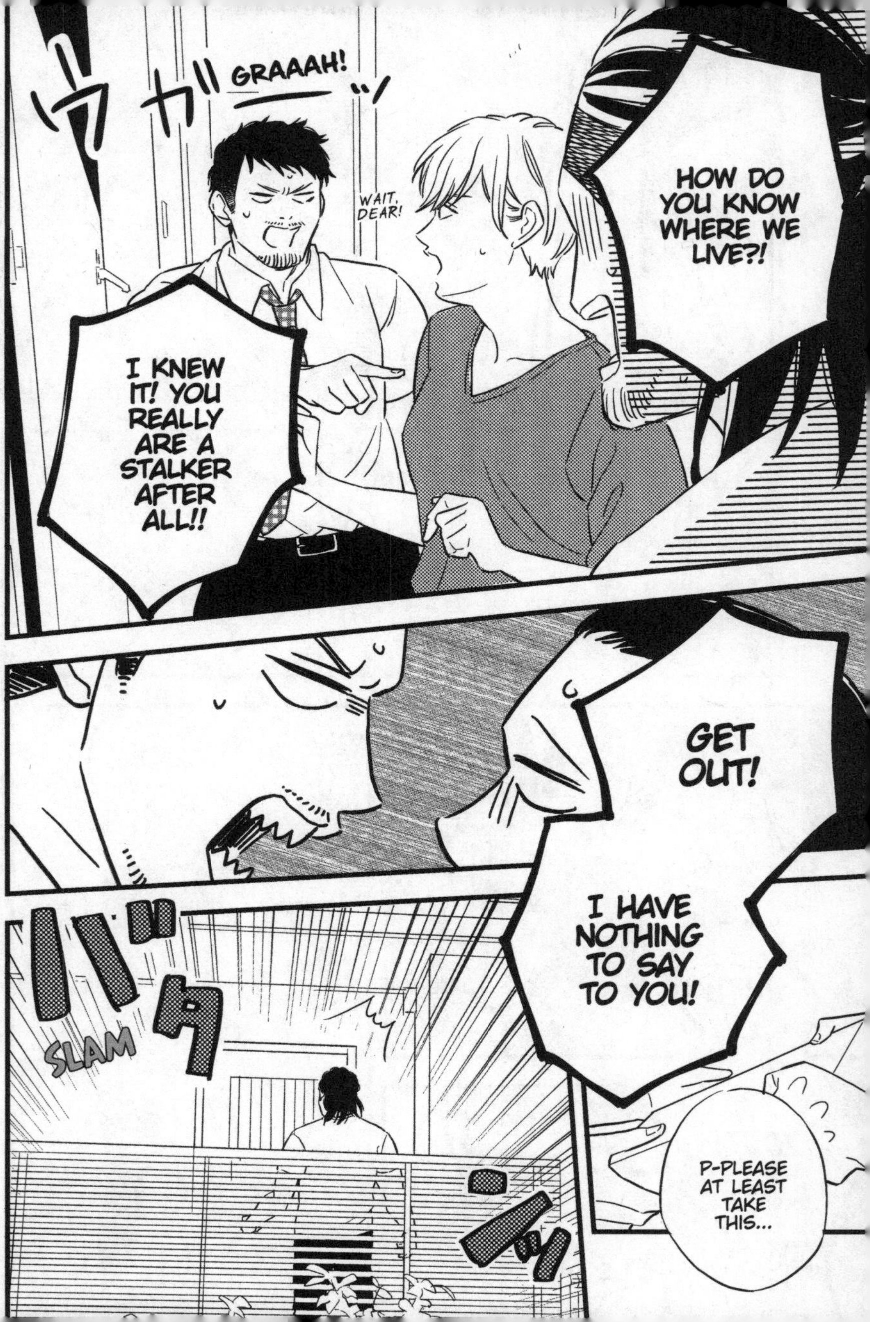
HOW DO YOU KNOW WHERE WE LIVE?!
GRAAAH!
WAIT, DEAR!
I KNEW IT! YOU REALLY ARE A STALKER AFTER ALL!!
GET OUT!
I HAVE NOTHING TO SAY TO YOU!
P-PLEASE AT LEAST TAKE THIS...
SLAM

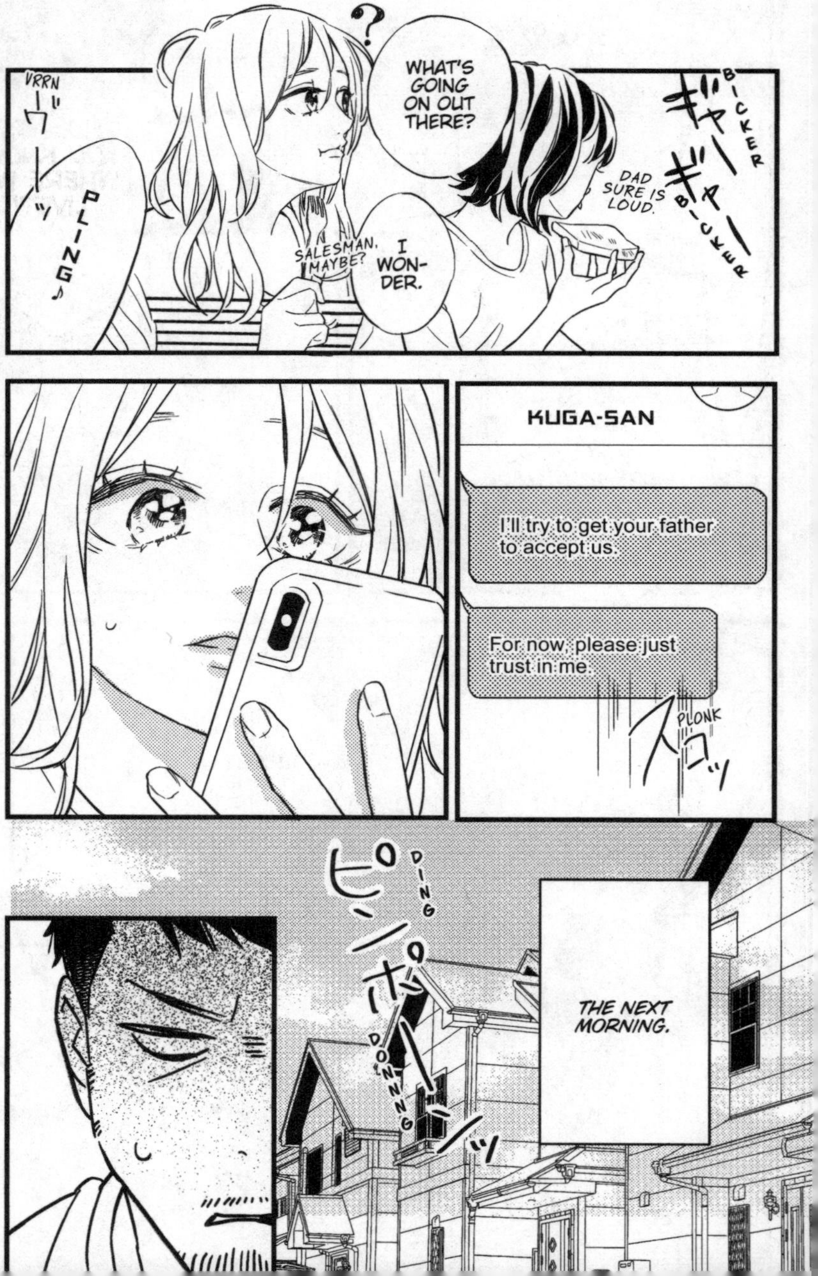
ギャーギャー
BICKER
BICKER
WHAT'S GOING ON OUT THERE?
DAD SURE IS LOUD.
I WONDER.
SALESMAN, MAYBE?
ヴーーッ
VRRN
PLING♪
KUGA-SAN
I'll try to get your father to accept us.
For now, please just trust in me.
スコッ
PLONK
THE NEXT MORNING.
ピンポーンッ
DING
DONNNG

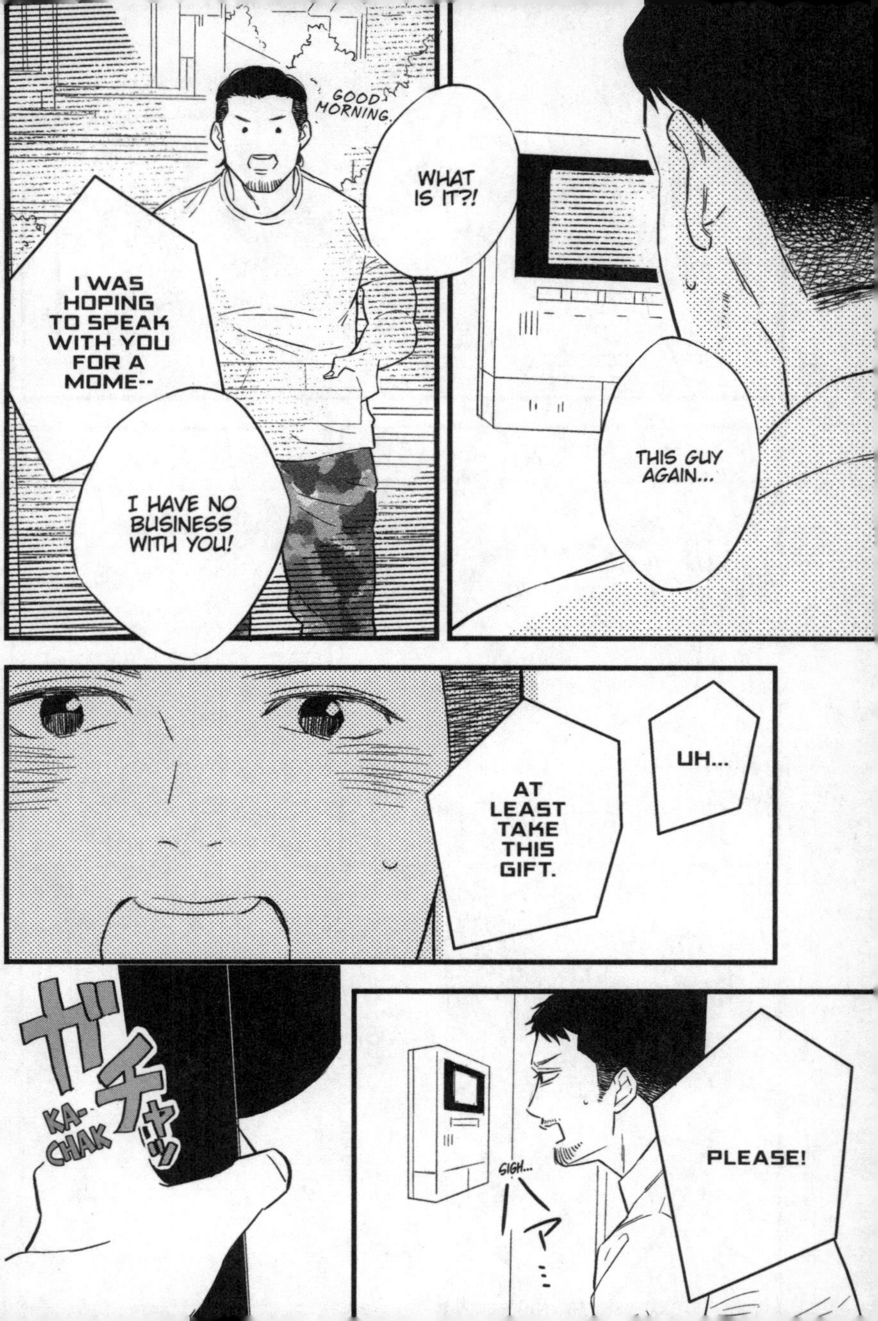
THIS GUY AGAIN...
GOOD MORNING.
WHAT IS IT?!
I WAS HOPING TO SPEAK WITH YOU FOR A MOME--
I HAVE NO BUSINESS WITH YOU!
UH...
AT LEAST TAKE THIS GIFT.
PLEASE!
SIGH...
ハァ…
ガチャッ
KA-CHAK

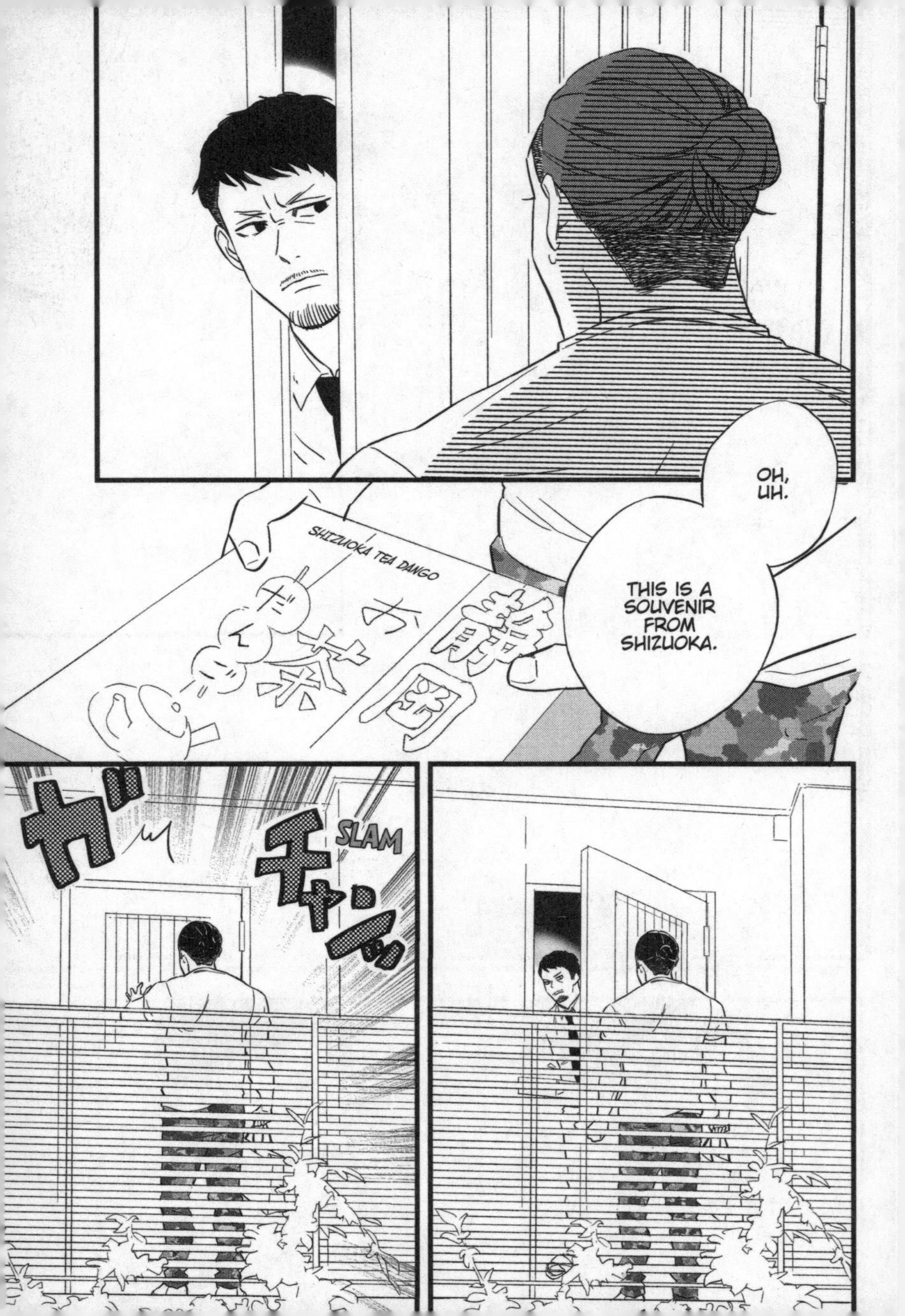

OH, UH.
THIS IS A SOUVENIR FROM SHIZUOKA.
SHIZUOKA TEA DANGO
静岡
お茶
ガチャン
SLAM

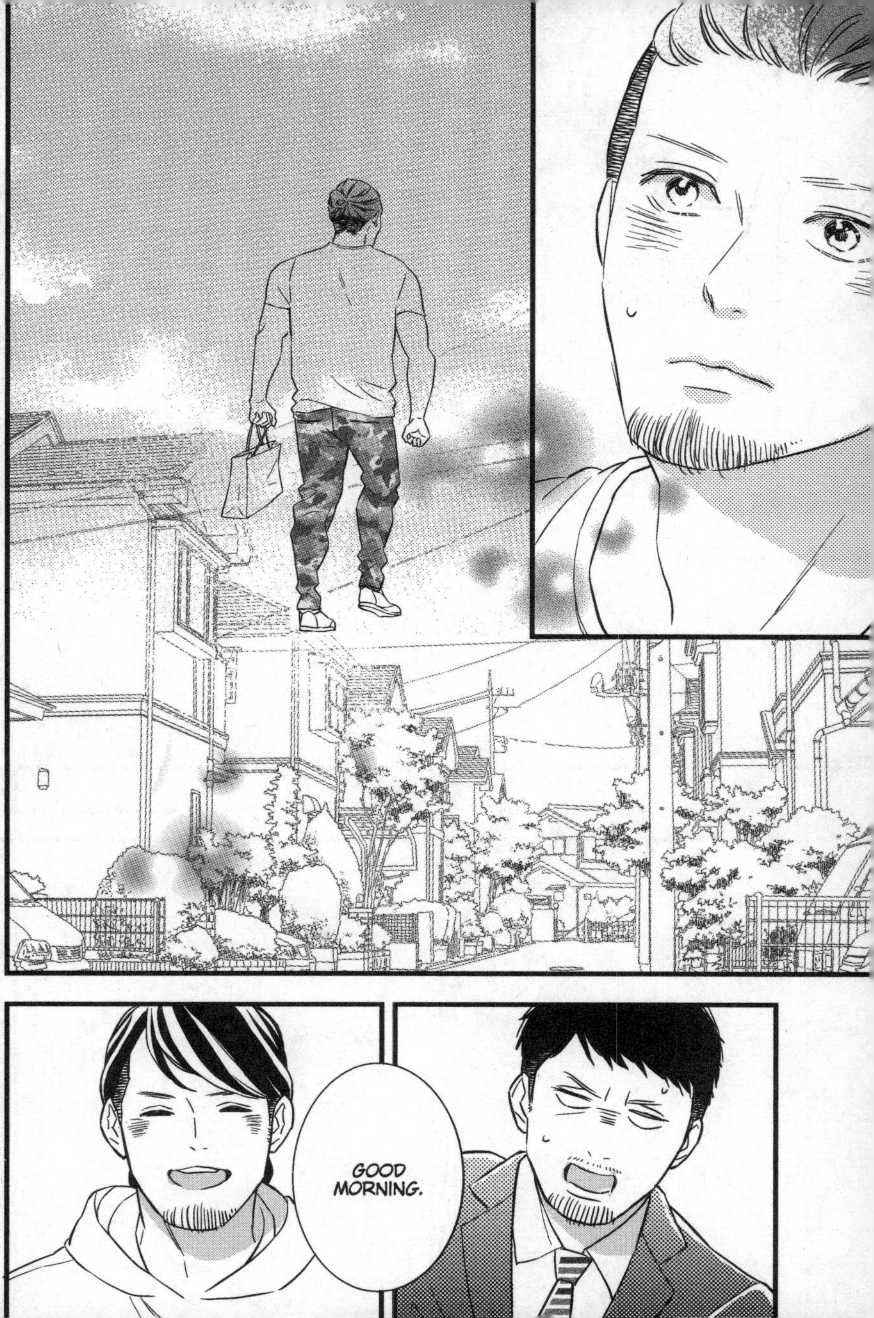
GOOD MORNING.

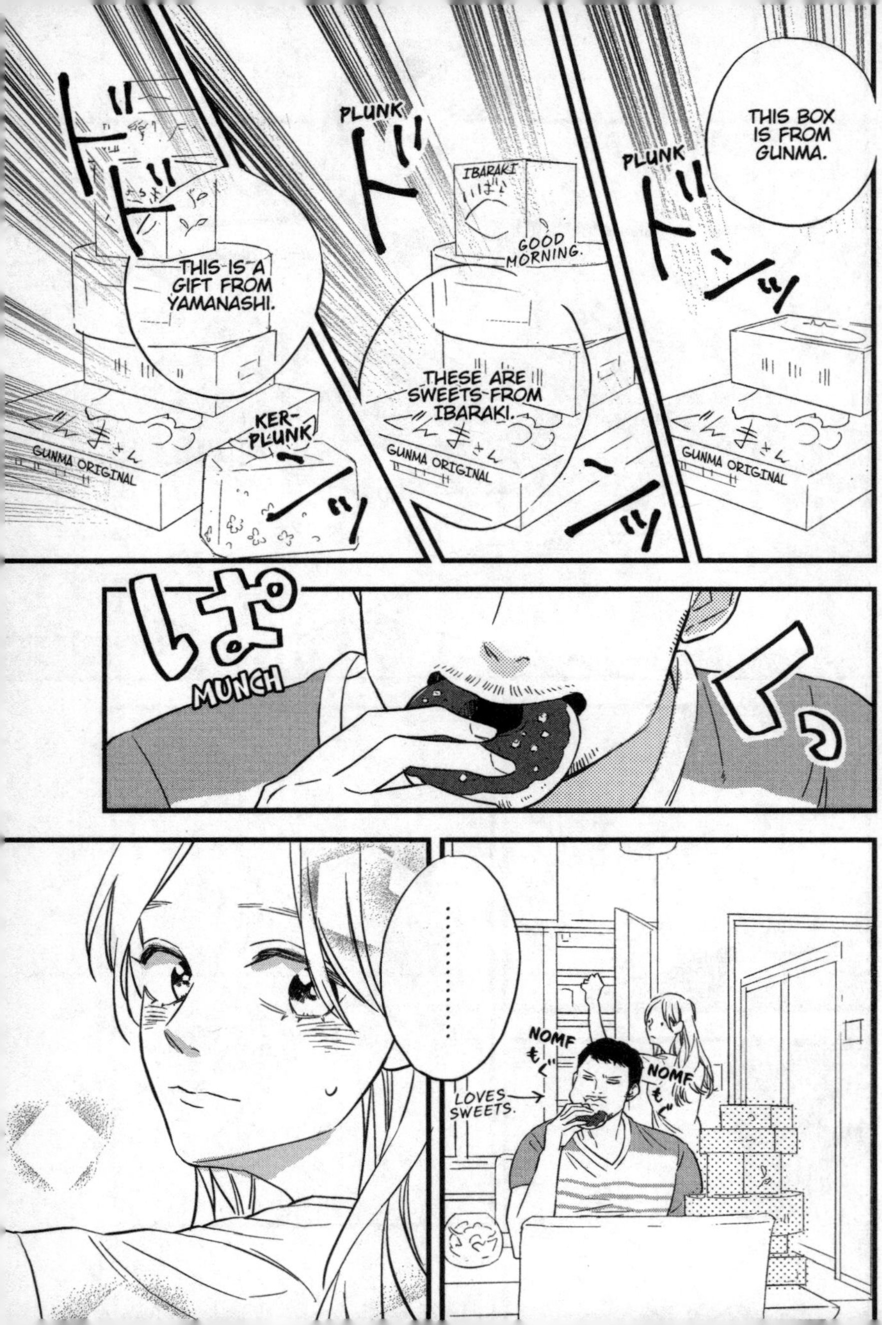
PLUNK
THIS BOX IS FROM GUNMA.
GUNMA ORIGINAL
PLUNK
IBARAKI
GOOD MORNING.
THESE ARE SWEETS FROM IBARAKI.
GUNMA ORIGINAL
THIS IS A GIFT FROM YAMANASHI.
KER-PLUNK
GUNMA ORIGINAL
MUNCH
NOMF
NOMF
LOVES SWEETS.
......

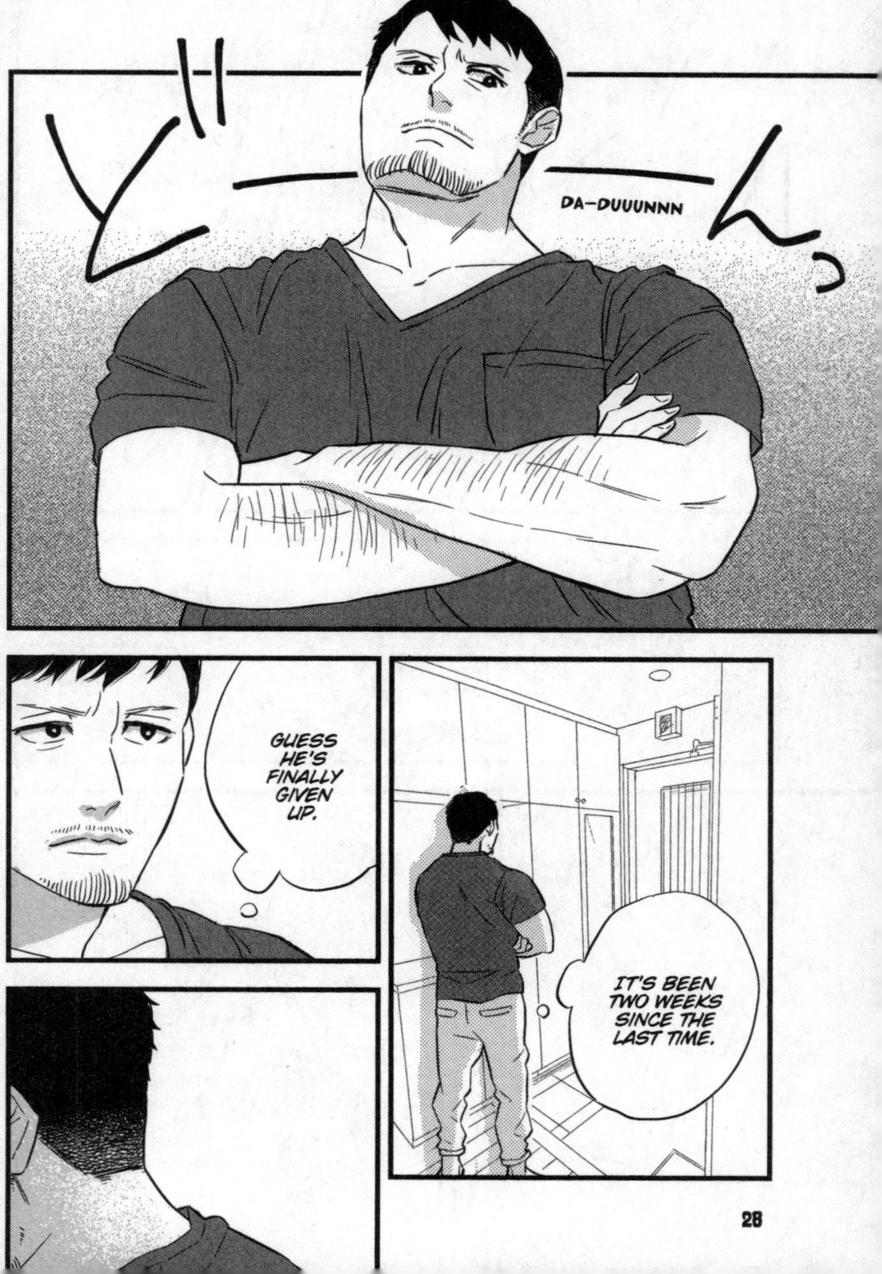
ゾーーーんっ
DA-DUUUNNN
IT'S BEEN TWO WEEKS SINCE THE LAST TIME.
GUESS HE'S FINALLY GIVEN UP.

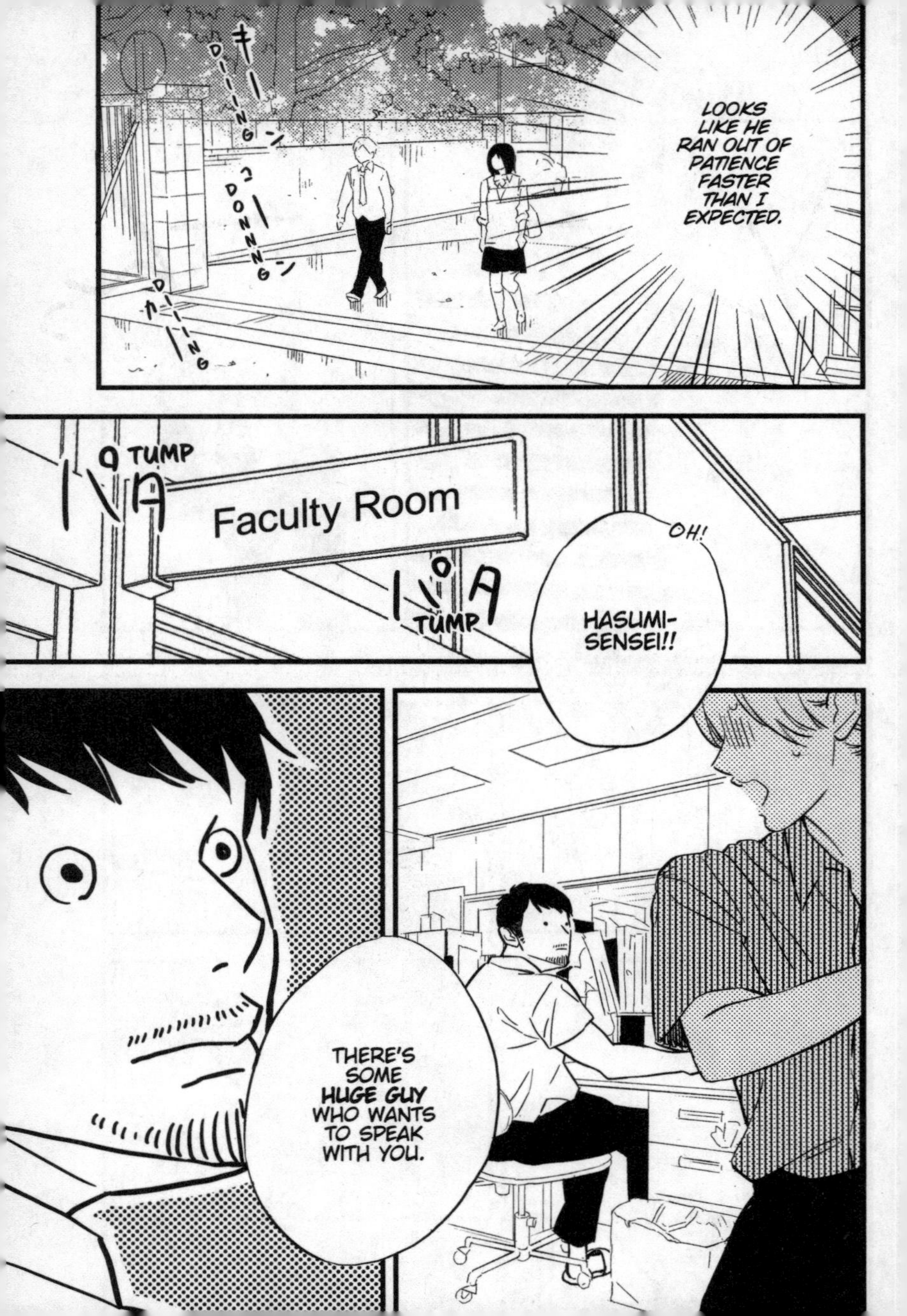
LOOKS LIKE HE RAN OUT OF PATIENCE FASTER THAN I EXPECTED.
DIIIING
DONNNG
DIIIING
OH!
HASUMI-SENSEI!!
TUMP
Faculty Room
TUMP
THERE'S SOME HUGE GUY WHO WANTS TO SPEAK WITH YOU.

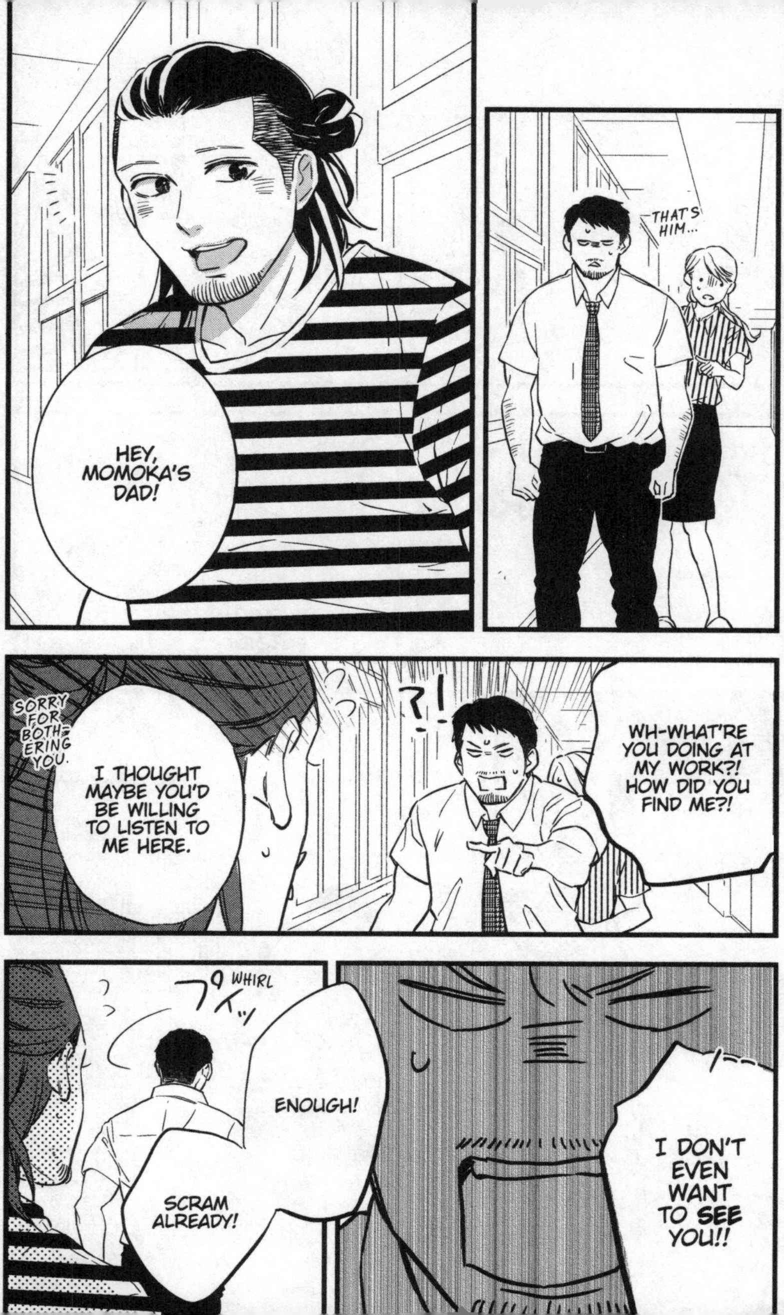
—THAT'S HIM...
HEY, MOMOKA'S DAD!
WH-WHAT'RE YOU DOING AT MY WORK?! HOW DID YOU FIND ME?!
?!
SORRY FOR BOTH-ERING YOU.
I THOUGHT MAYBE YOU'D BE WILLING TO LISTEN TO ME HERE.
—
I DON'T EVEN WANT TO SEE YOU!!
フイッ WHIRL
ENOUGH!
SCRAM ALREADY!

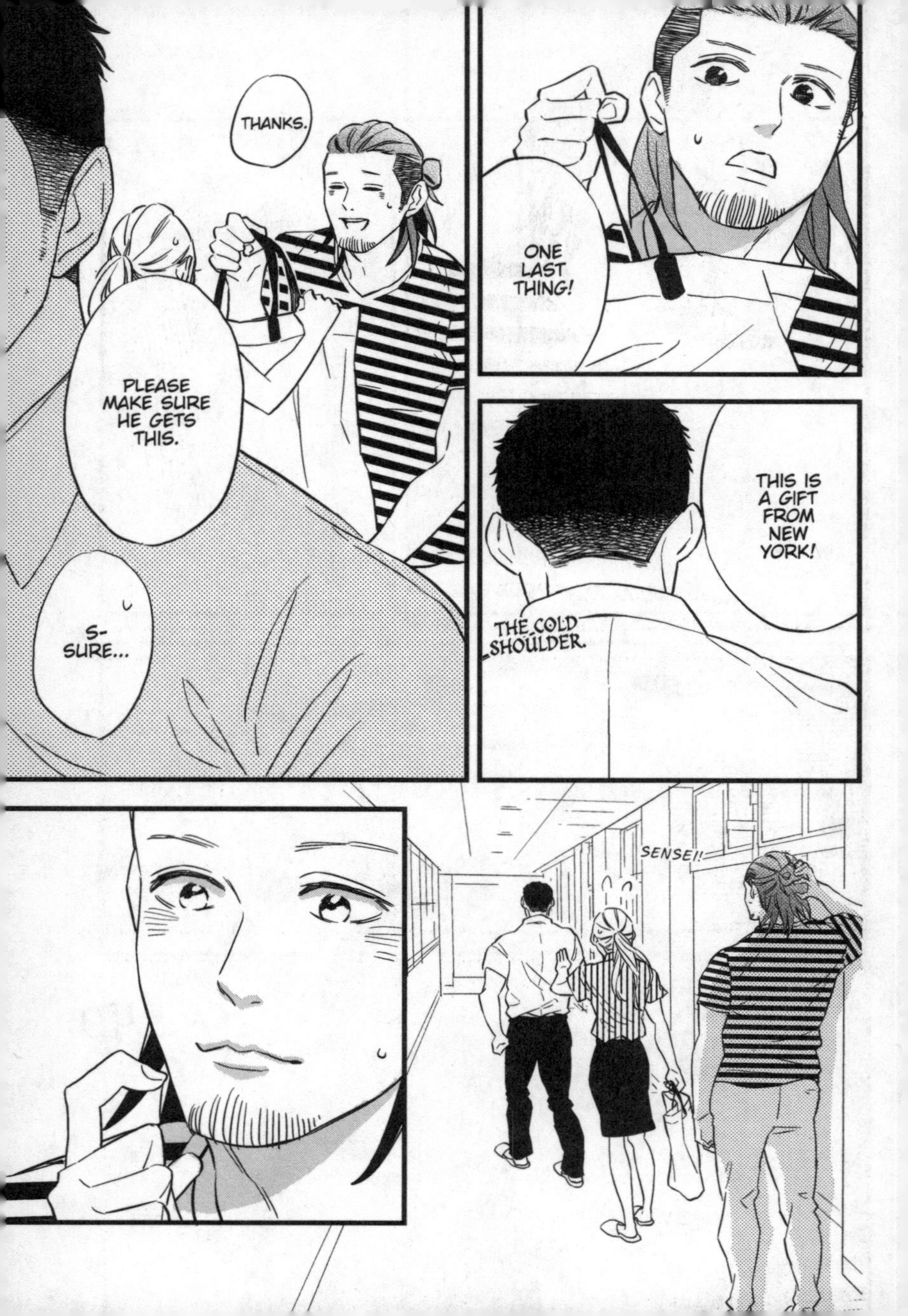
ONE LAST THING!
THIS IS A GIFT FROM NEW YORK!
THE COLD SHOULDER.
THANKS.
PLEASE MAKE SURE HE GETS THIS.
S-SURE...
SENSE!!

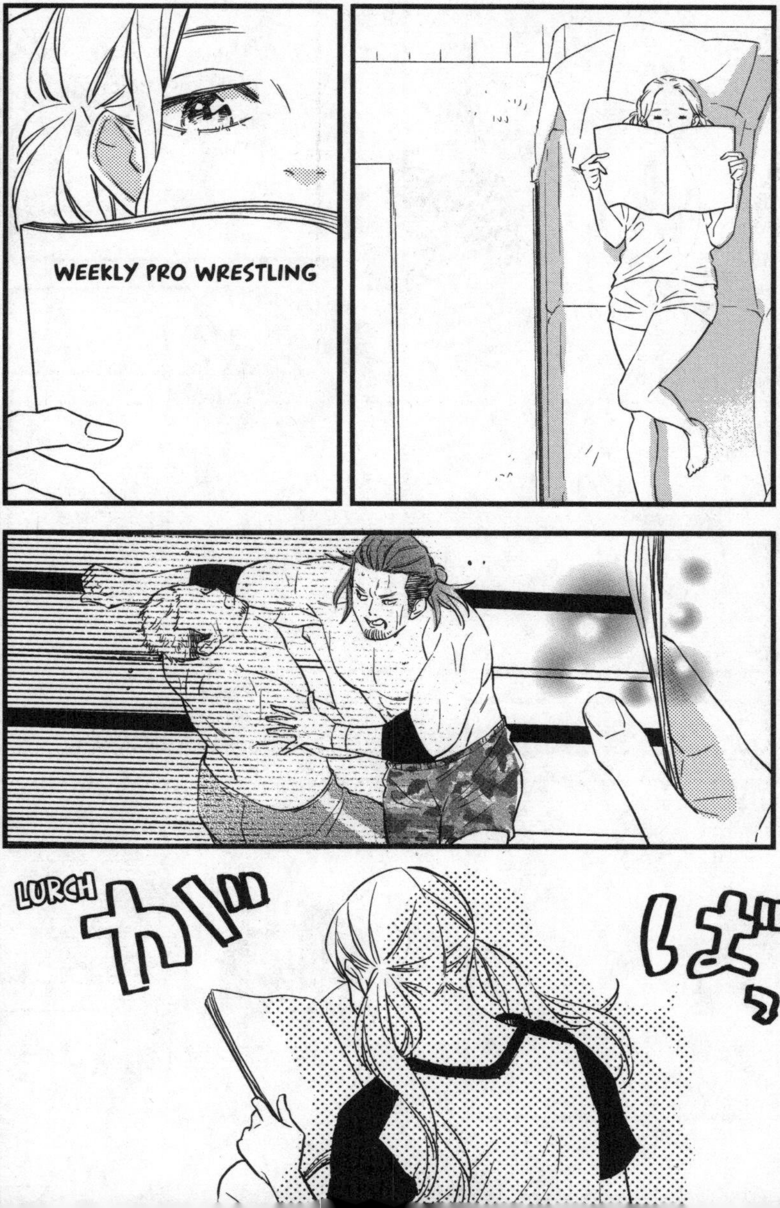
WEEKLY PRO WRESTLING
LURCH

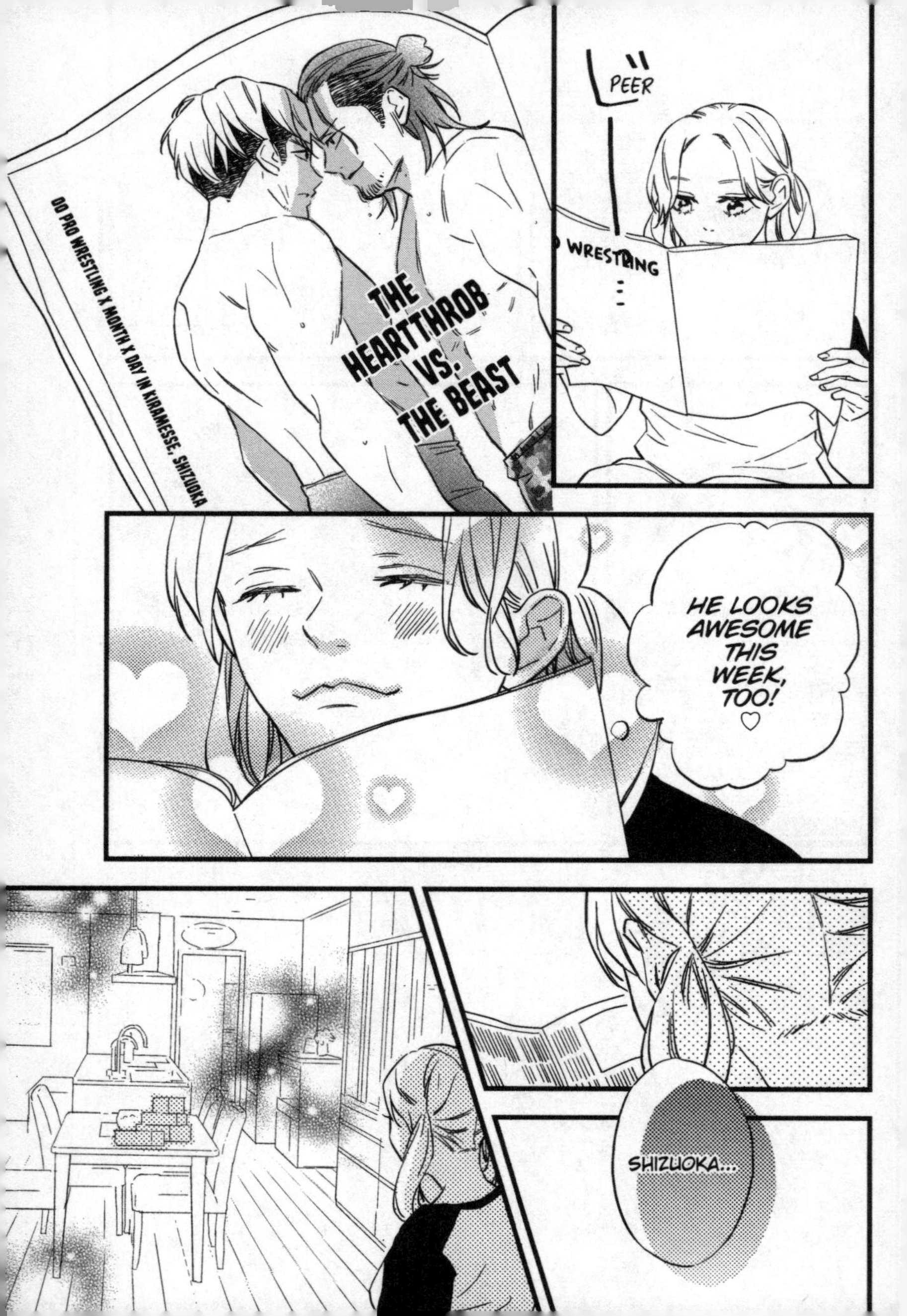
PEER
WRESTLING
THE HEARTTHROB VS. THE BEAST
OO PRO WRESTLING X MONTH X DAY IN KIRAMESSE, SHIZUOKA
HE LOOKS AWESOME THIS WEEK, TOO! ♡
SHIZUOKA...

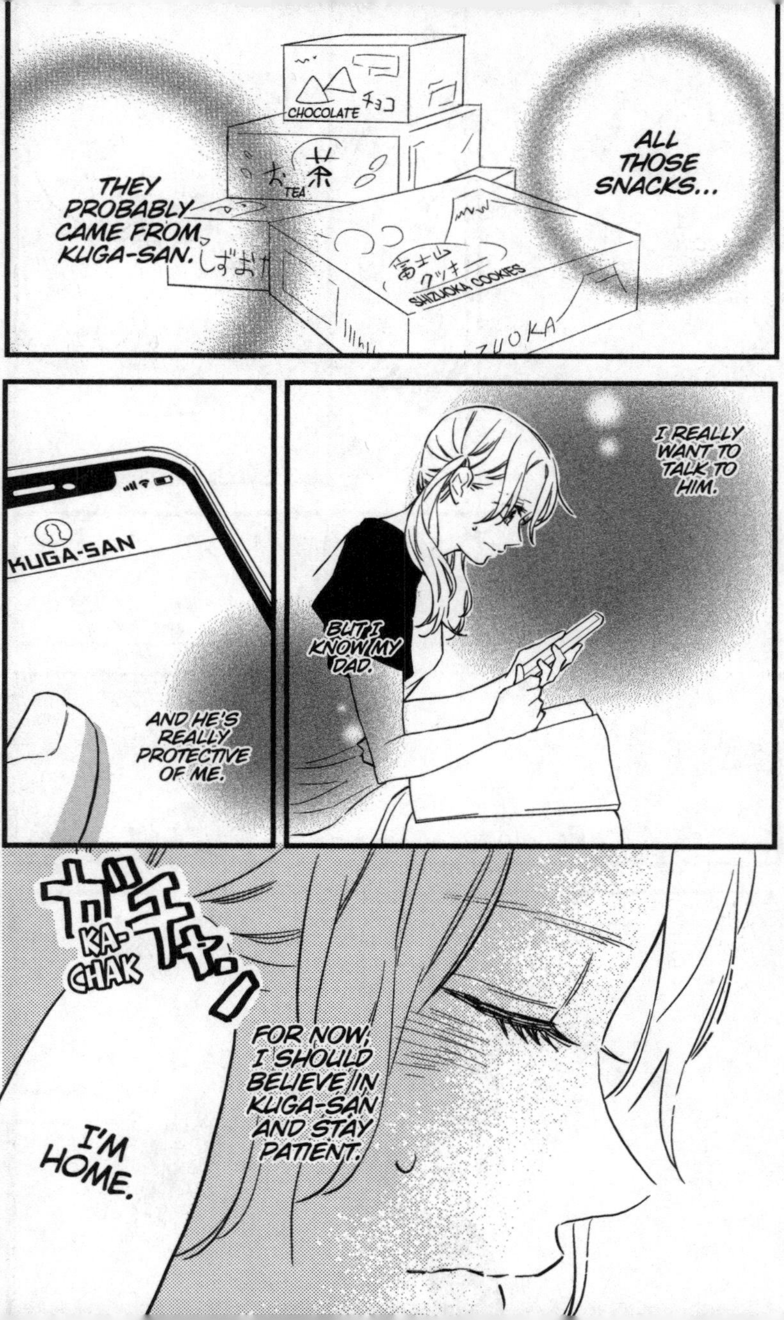
ALL THOSE SNACKS...
THEY PROBABLY CAME FROM KUGA-SAN.
チョコ
CHOCOLATE
お茶
TEA
しずおか
富士山クッキー
SHIZUOKA COOKIES
I REALLY WANT TO TALK TO HIM.
BUT I KNOW MY DAD.
KUGA-SAN
AND HE'S REALLY PROTECTIVE OF ME.
ガチャ
KA-CHAK
FOR NOW, I SHOULD BELIEVE IN KUGA-SAN AND STAY PATIENT.
I'M HOME.

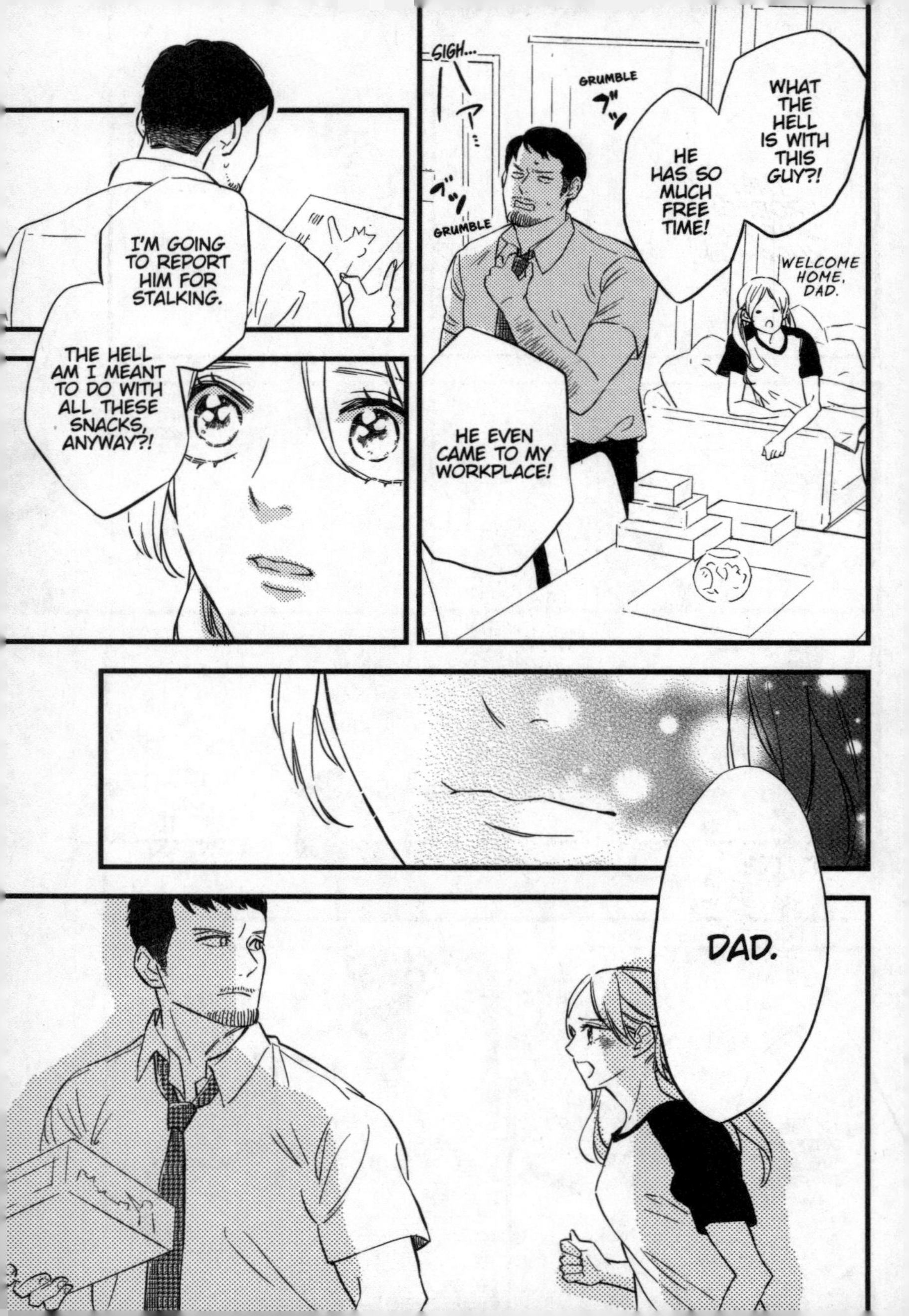
WHAT THE HELL IS WITH THIS GUY?!
HE HAS SO MUCH FREE TIME!
GRUMBLE
SIGH...
WELCOME HOME, DAD.
GRUMBLE
HE EVEN CAME TO MY WORKPLACE!
I'M GOING TO REPORT HIM FOR STALKING.
THE HELL AM I MEANT TO DO WITH ALL THESE SNACKS, ANYWAY?!
DAD.

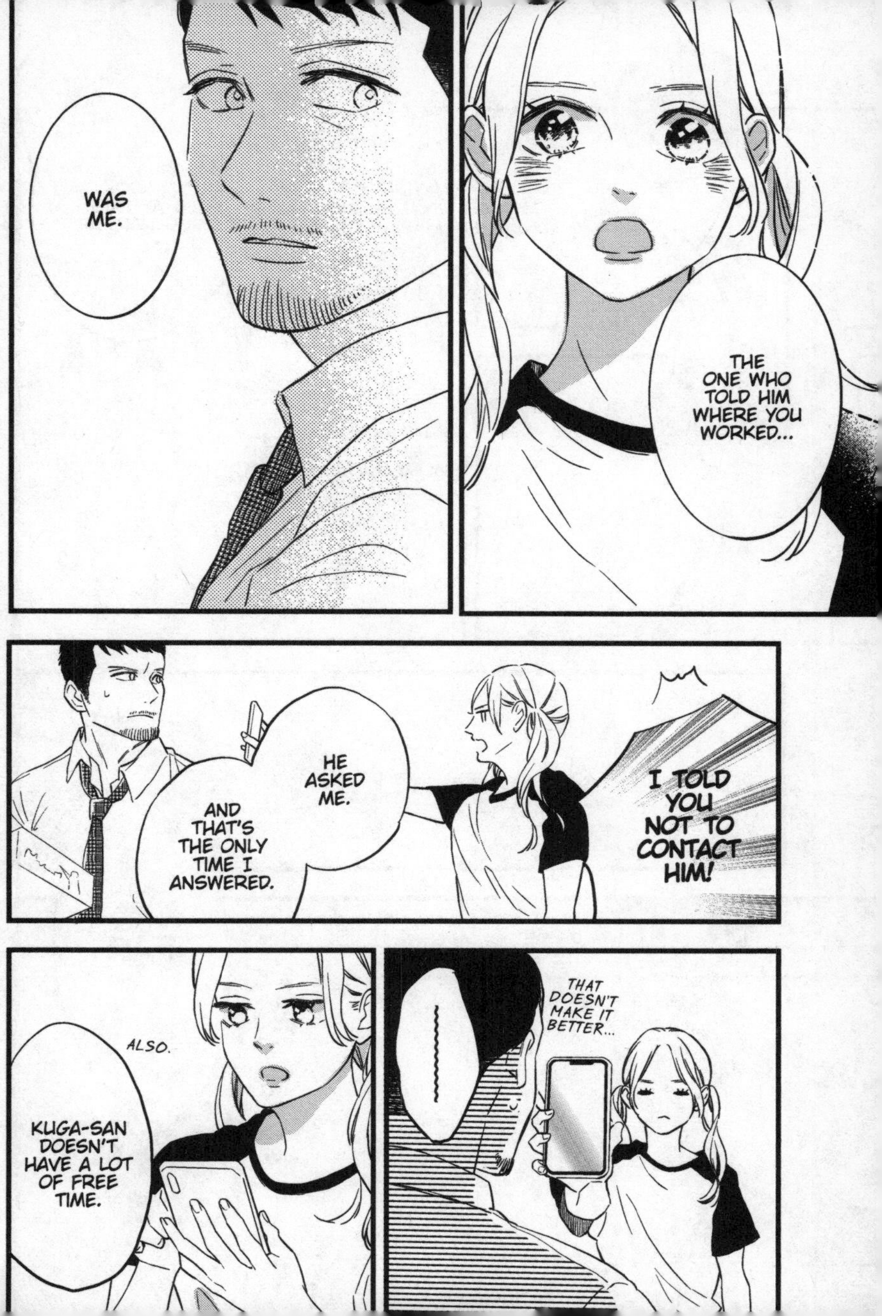
THE ONE WHO TOLD HIM WHERE YOU WORKED...
WAS ME.
I TOLD YOU NOT TO CONTACT HIM!
HE ASKED ME.
AND THAT'S THE ONLY TIME I ANSWERED.
THAT DOESN'T MAKE IT BETTER...
ALSO.
KUGA-SAN DOESN'T HAVE A LOT OF FREE TIME.

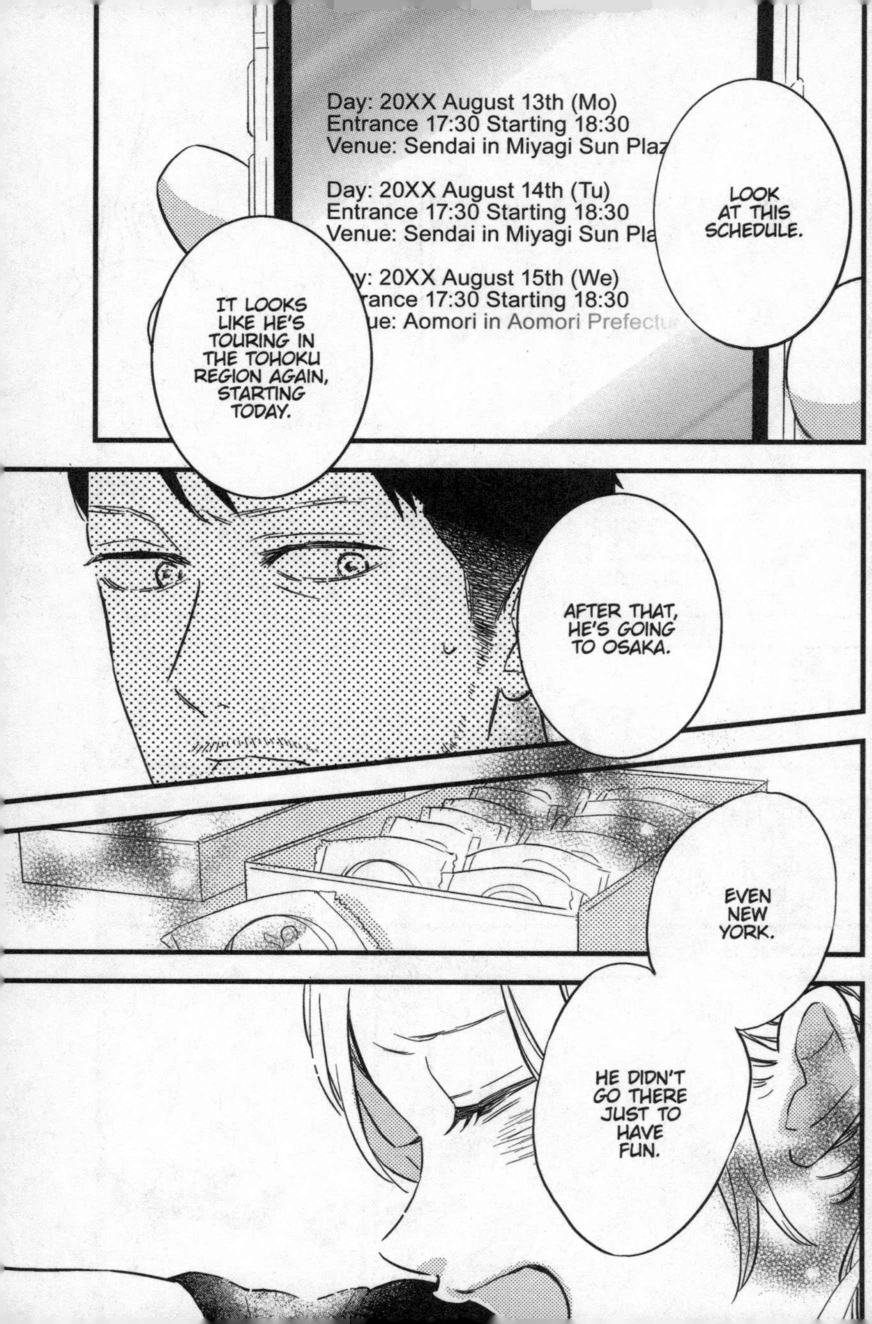
LOOK AT THIS SCHEDULE.
Day: 20XX August 13th (Mo)
Entrance 17:30 Starting 18:30
Venue: Sendai in Miyagi Sun Plaz
Day: 20XX August 14th (Tu)
Entrance 17:30 Starting 18:30
Venue: Sendai in Miyagi Sun Pla
y: 20XX August 15th (We)
rance 17:30 Starting 18:30
ue: Aomori in Aomori Prefectu
IT LOOKS LIKE HE'S TOURING IN THE TOHOKU REGION AGAIN, STARTING TODAY.
AFTER THAT, HE'S GOING TO OSAKA.
EVEN NEW YORK.
HE DIDN'T GO THERE JUST TO HAVE FUN.

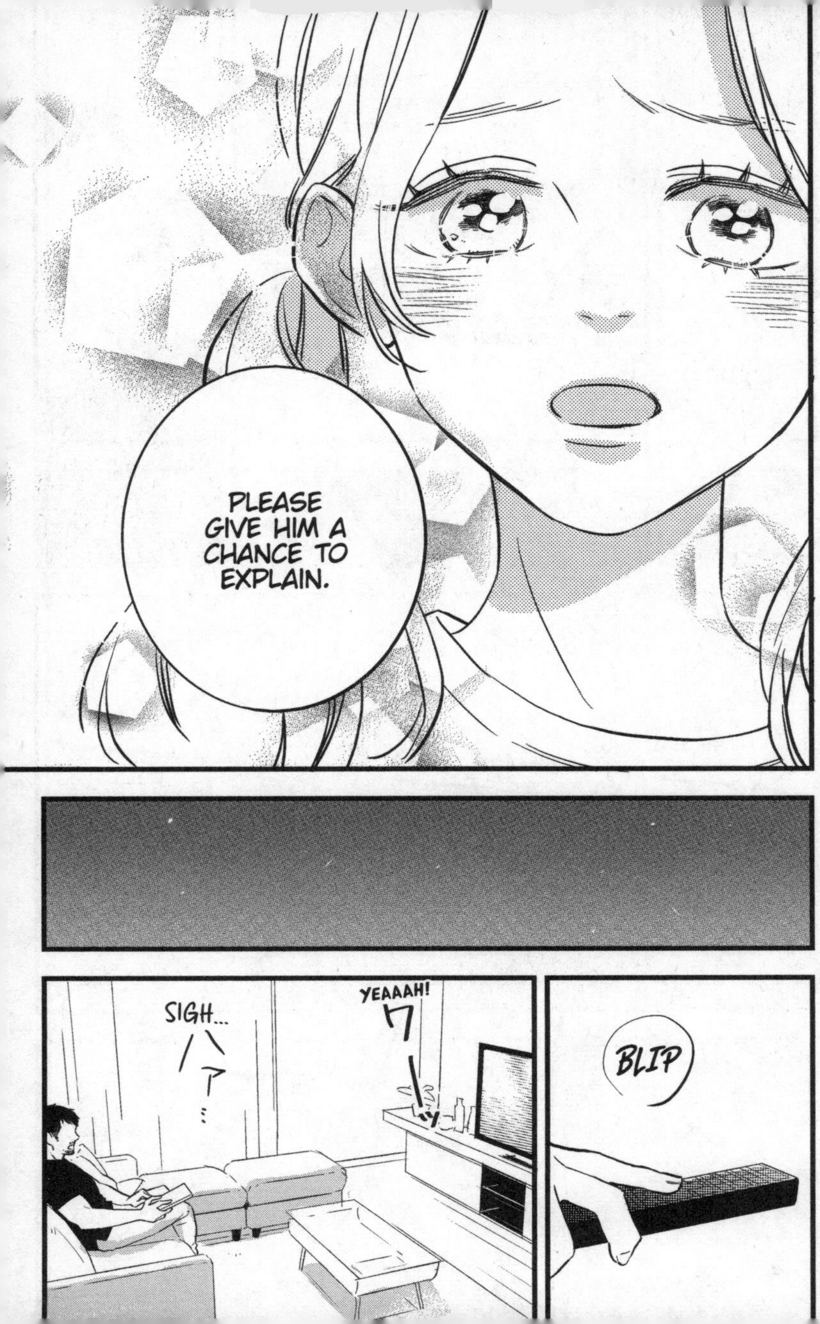
PLEASE GIVE HIM A CHANCE TO EXPLAIN.
BLIP
YEAAAH!
ワー
SIGH...
ハア…

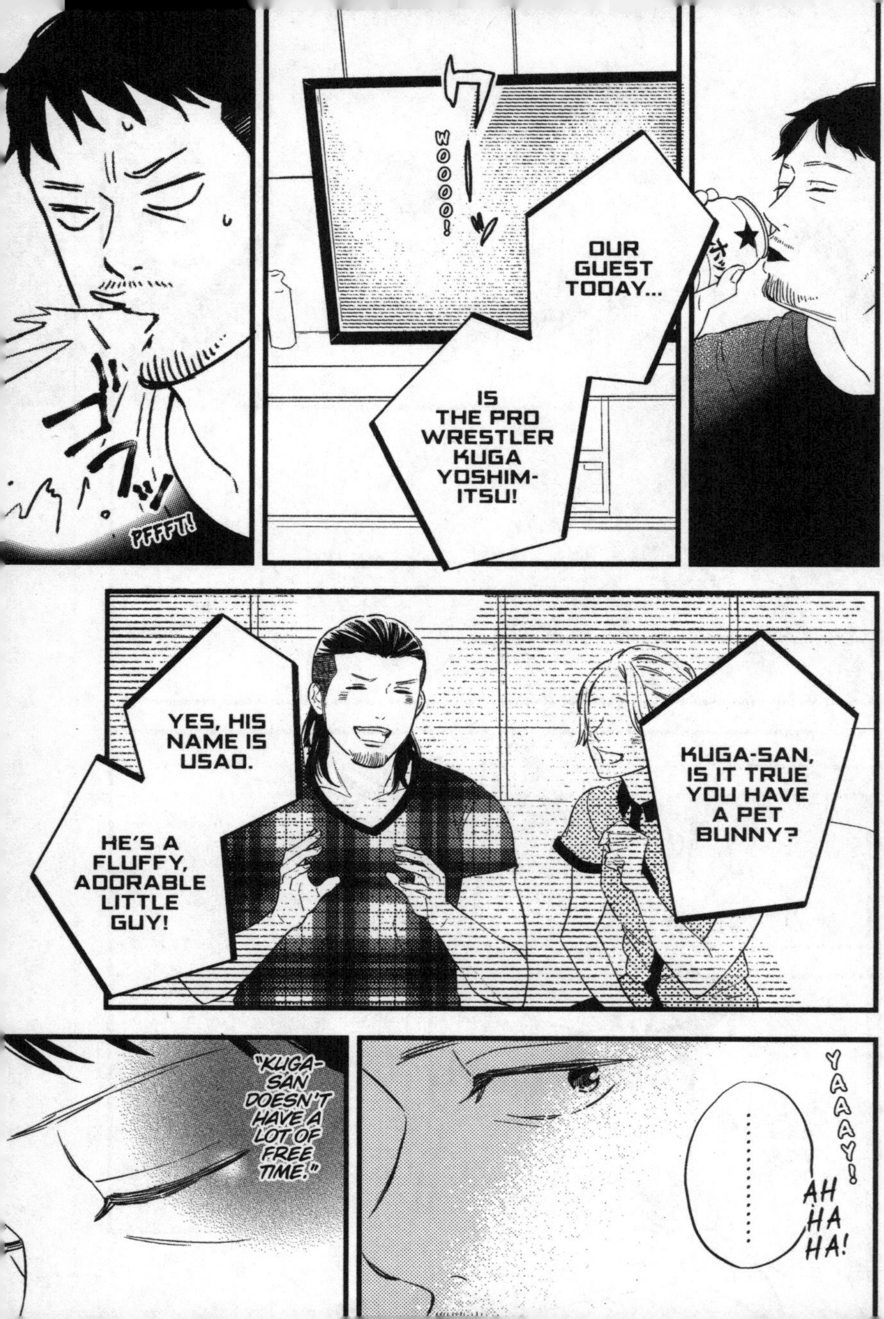
WOOOOO!
OUR GUEST TODAY...
IS THE PRO WRESTLER KUGA YOSHIM-ITSU!
PFFFT!
KUGA-SAN, IS IT TRUE YOU HAVE A PET BUNNY?
YES, HIS NAME IS USAO.
HE'S A FLUFFY, ADORABLE LITTLE GUY!
YAAAAY!
AH HA HA!
......
"KUGA-SAN DOESN'T HAVE A LOT OF FREE TIME."

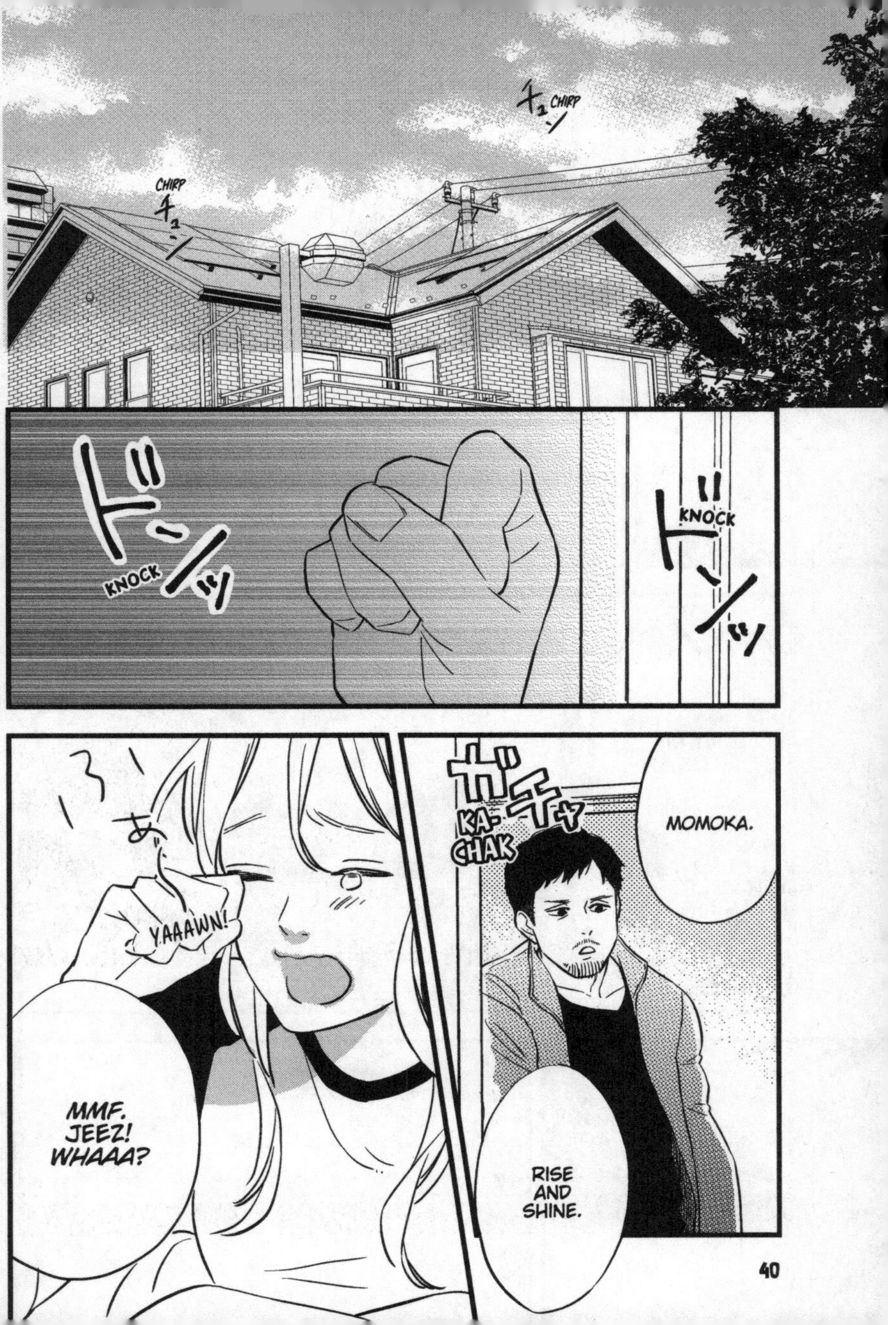
CHIRP
CHIRP
KNOCK
KNOCK
KA-CHAK
MOMOKA.
RISE AND SHINE.
YAAAWN!
MMF. JEEZ! WHAAA?

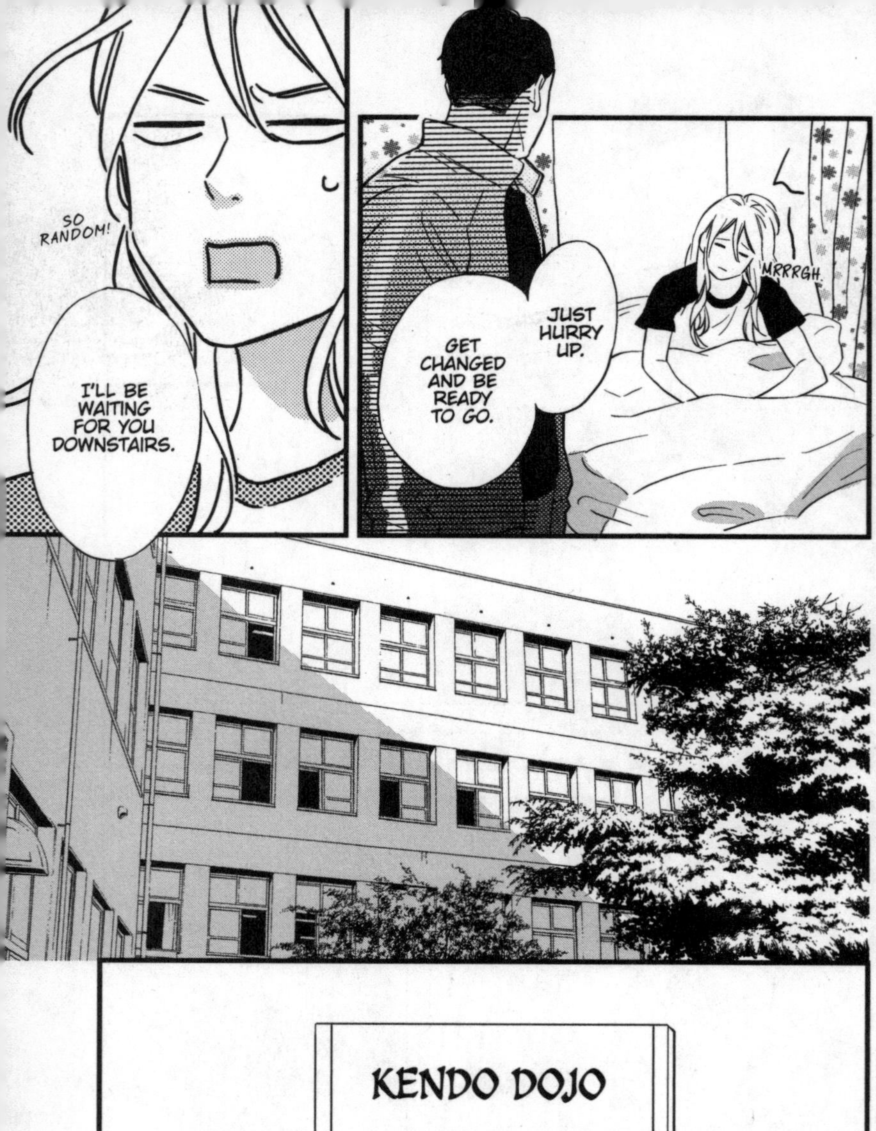
MRRRGH.
JUST HURRY UP.
GET CHANGED AND BE READY TO GO.
SO RANDOM!
I'LL BE WAITING FOR YOU DOWNSTAIRS.
KENDO DOJO

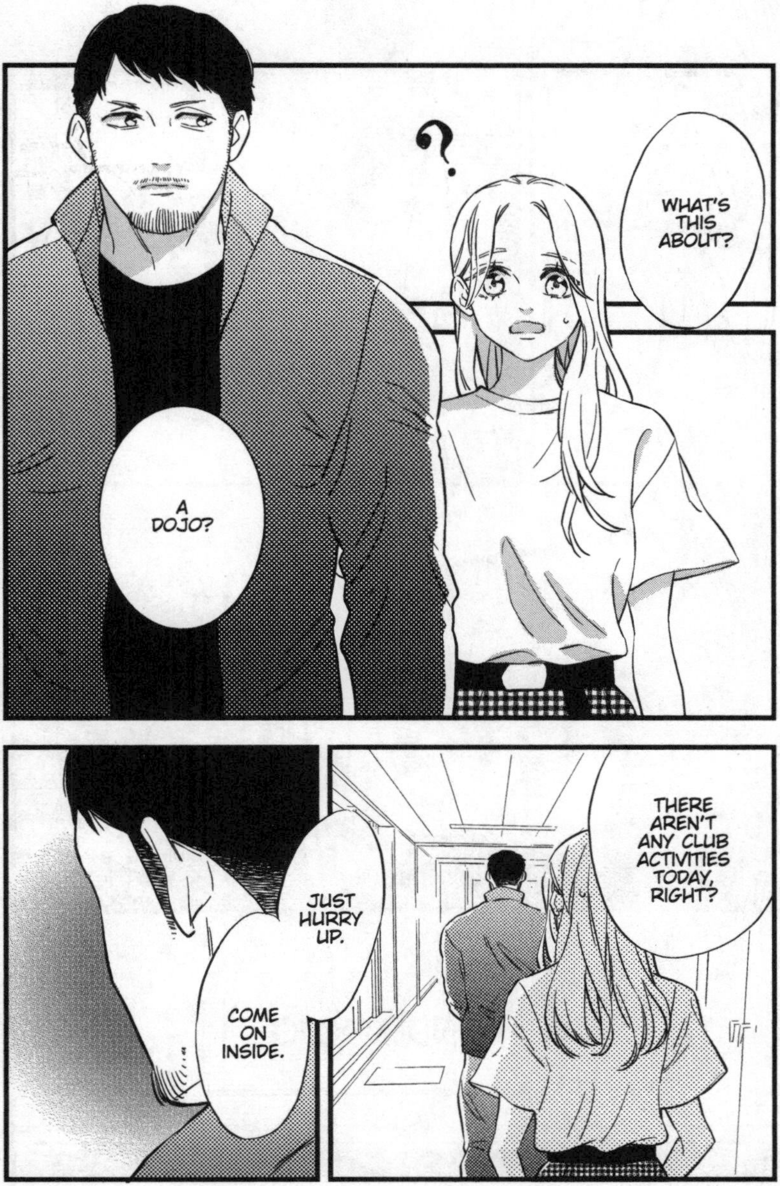
WHAT'S THIS ABOUT?
A DOJO?
THERE AREN'T ANY CLUB ACTIVITIES TODAY, RIGHT?
JUST HURRY UP.
COME ON INSIDE.

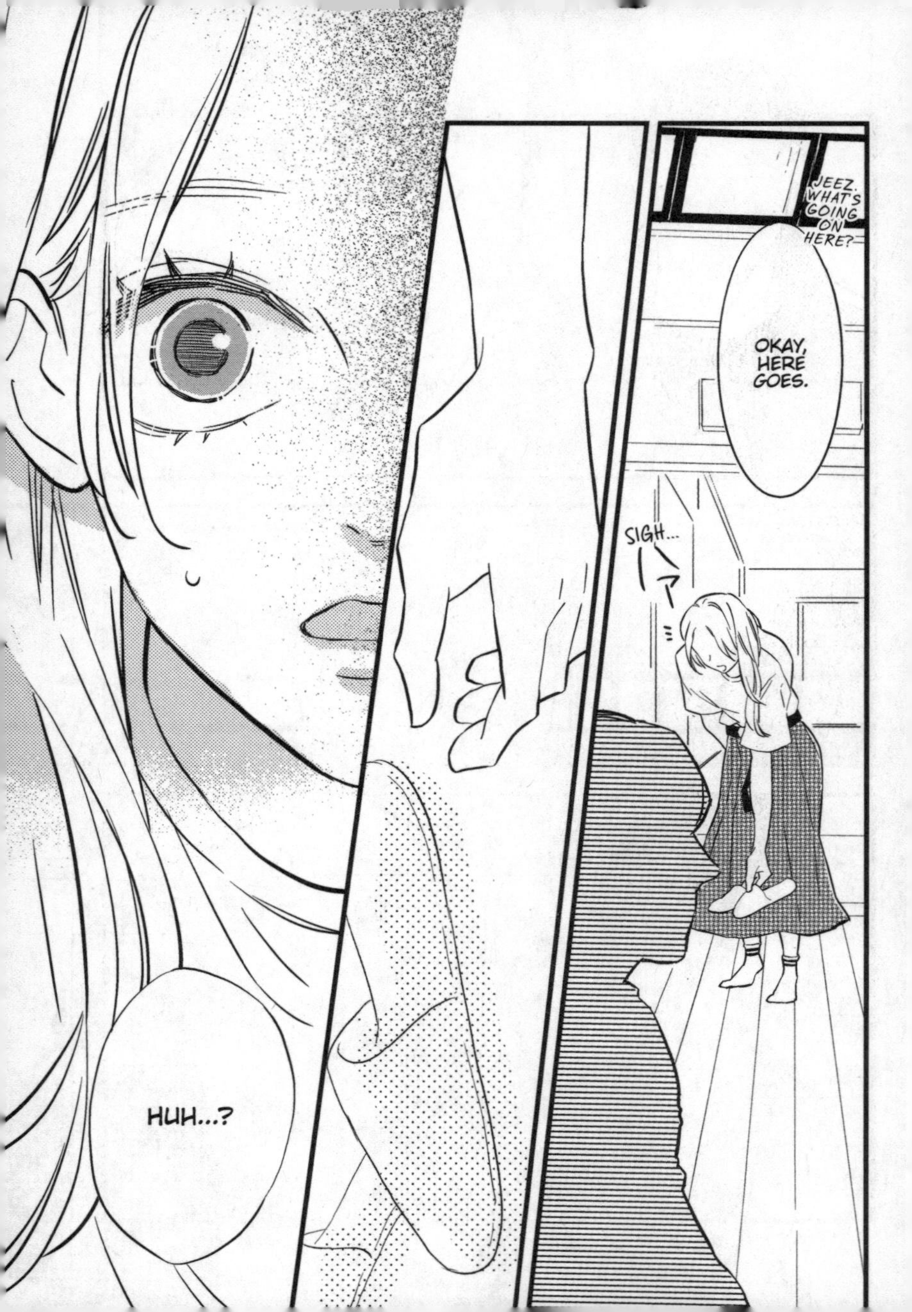
JEEZ. WHAT'S GOING ON HERE?
OKAY, HERE GOES.
SIGH...
ハァ
HUH...?

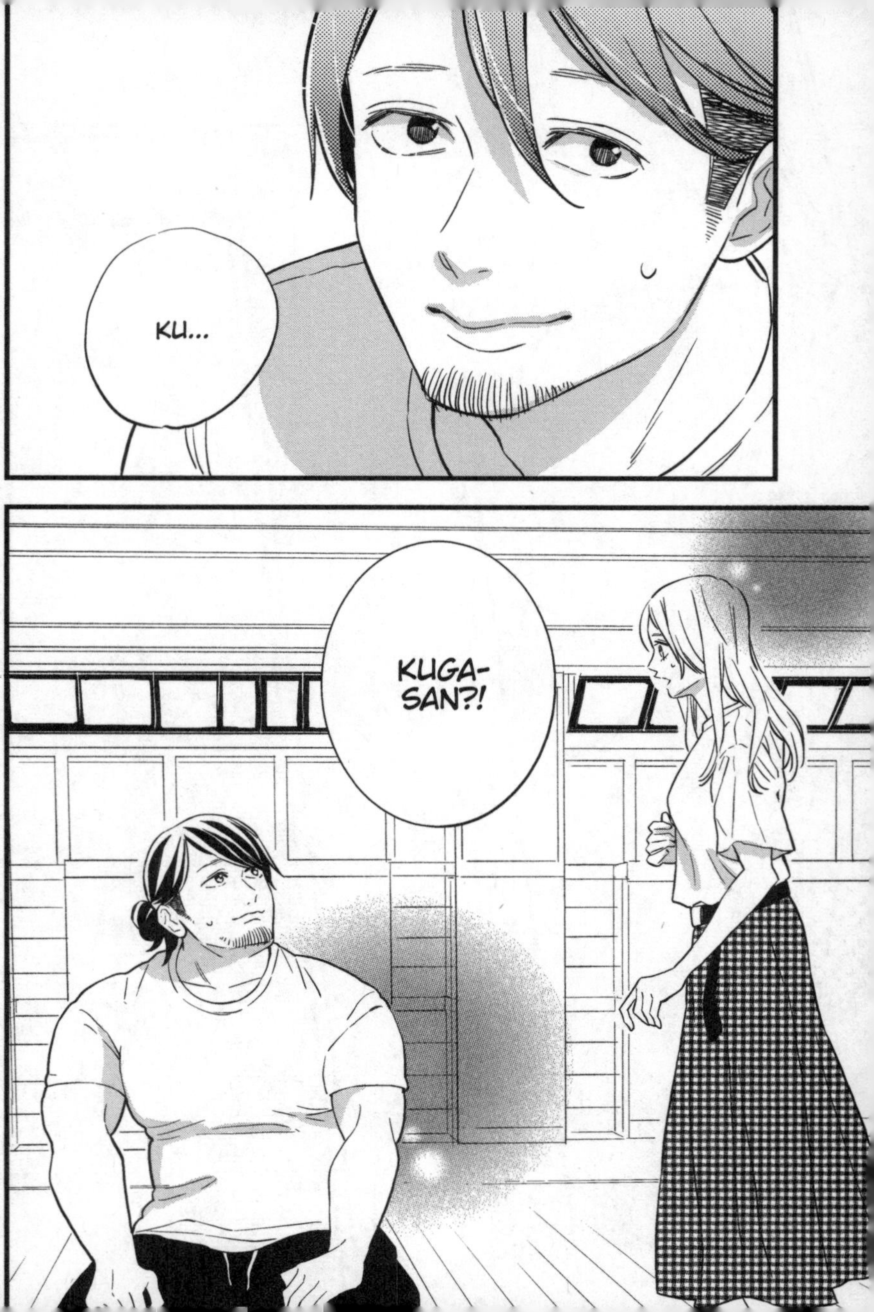
KU...
KUGA-SAN?!

Cutie and the BEAST

Cutie and the BEAST

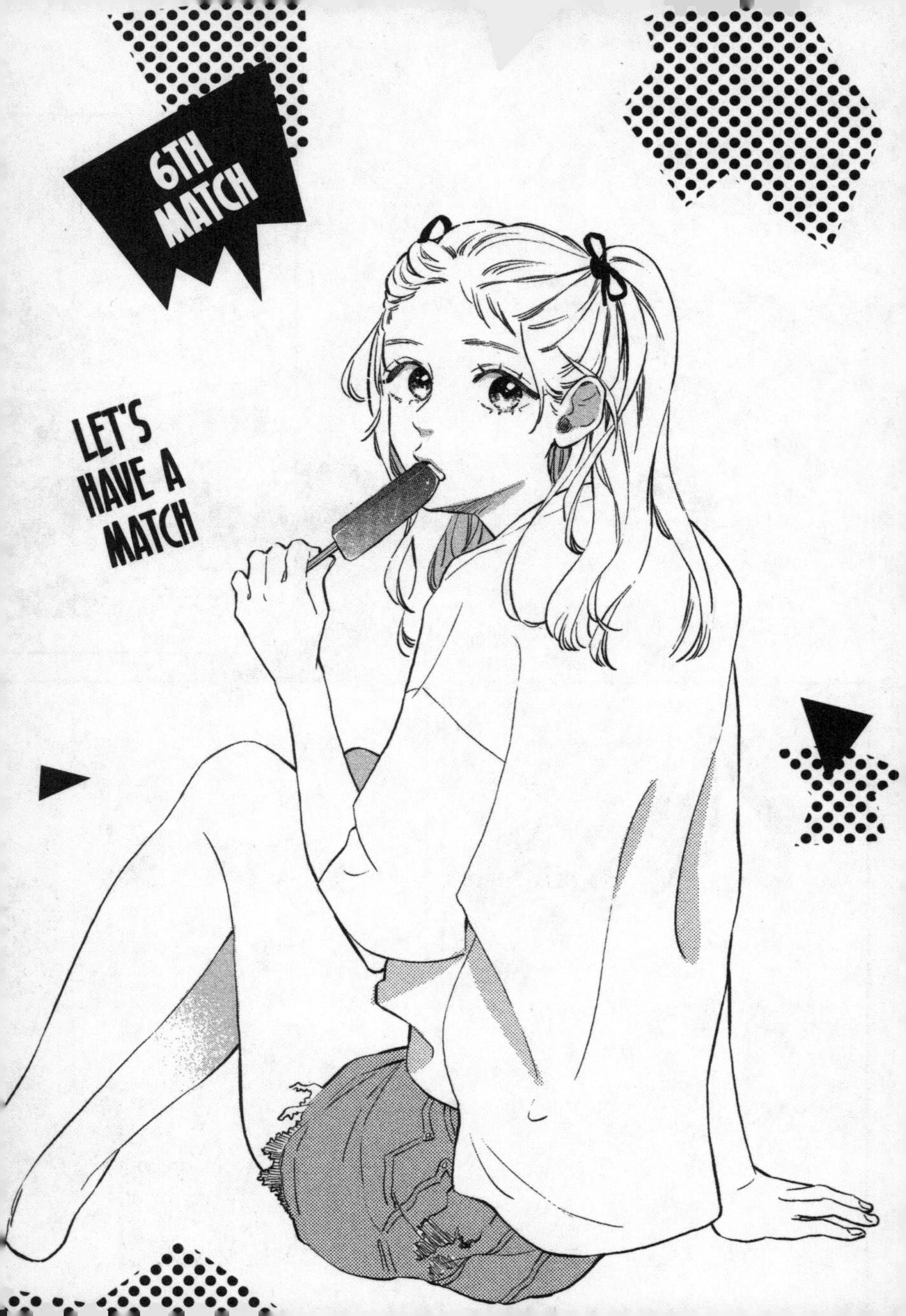
6TH MATCH
LET'S HAVE A MATCH

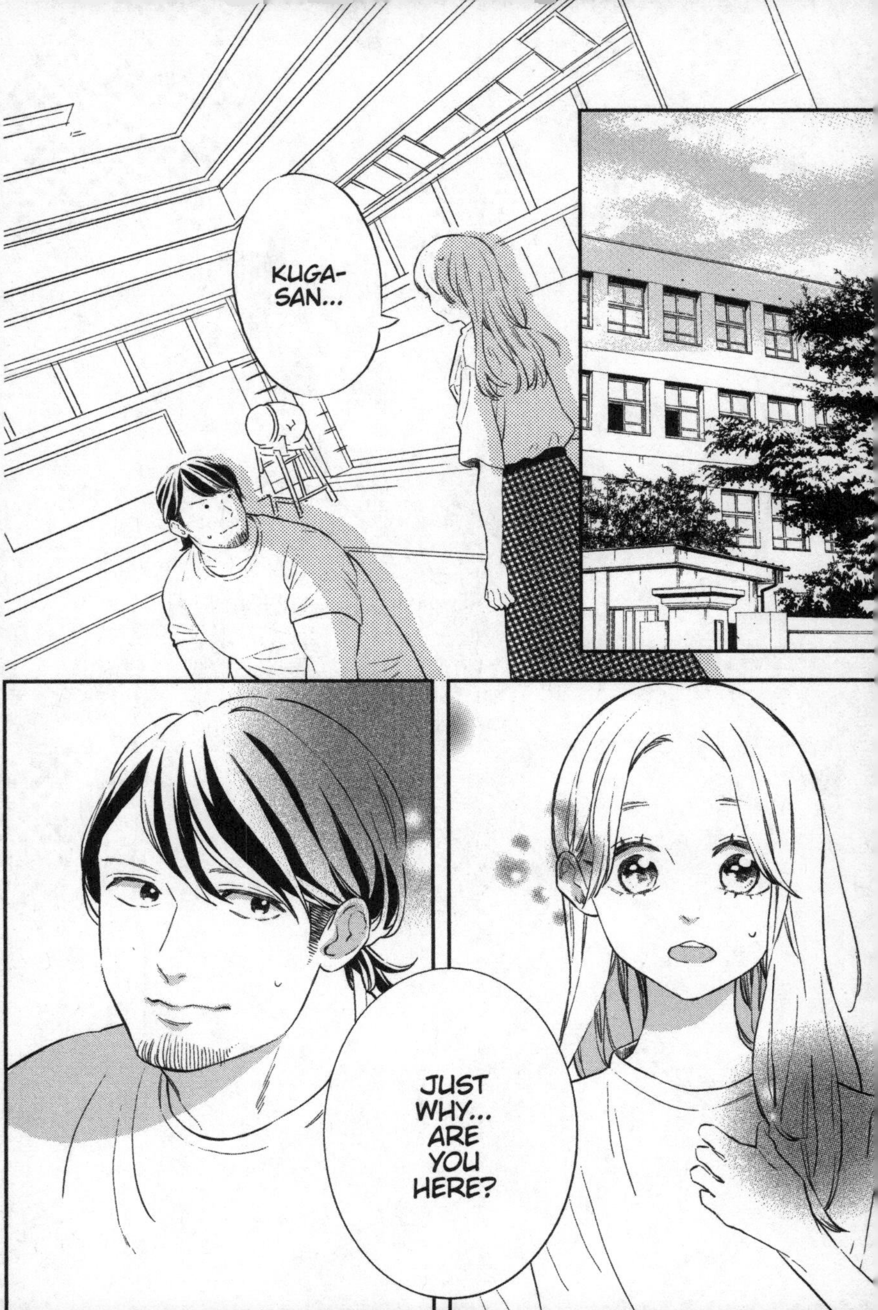
KUGA-SAN...
JUST WHY... ARE YOU HERE?

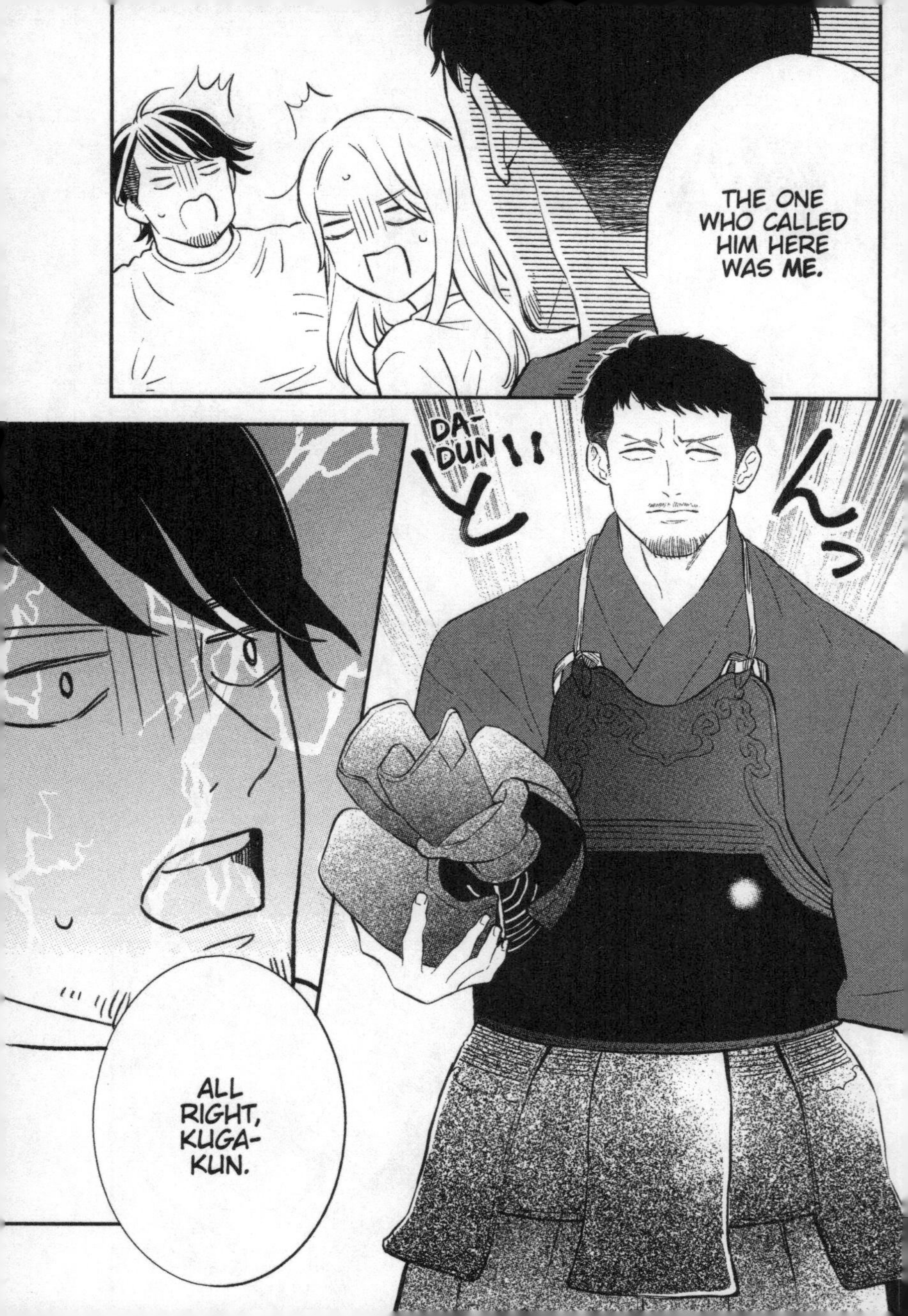
THE ONE WHO CALLED HIM HERE WAS ME.
んっ
DA-DUN
ど
ALL RIGHT, KUGA-KUN.

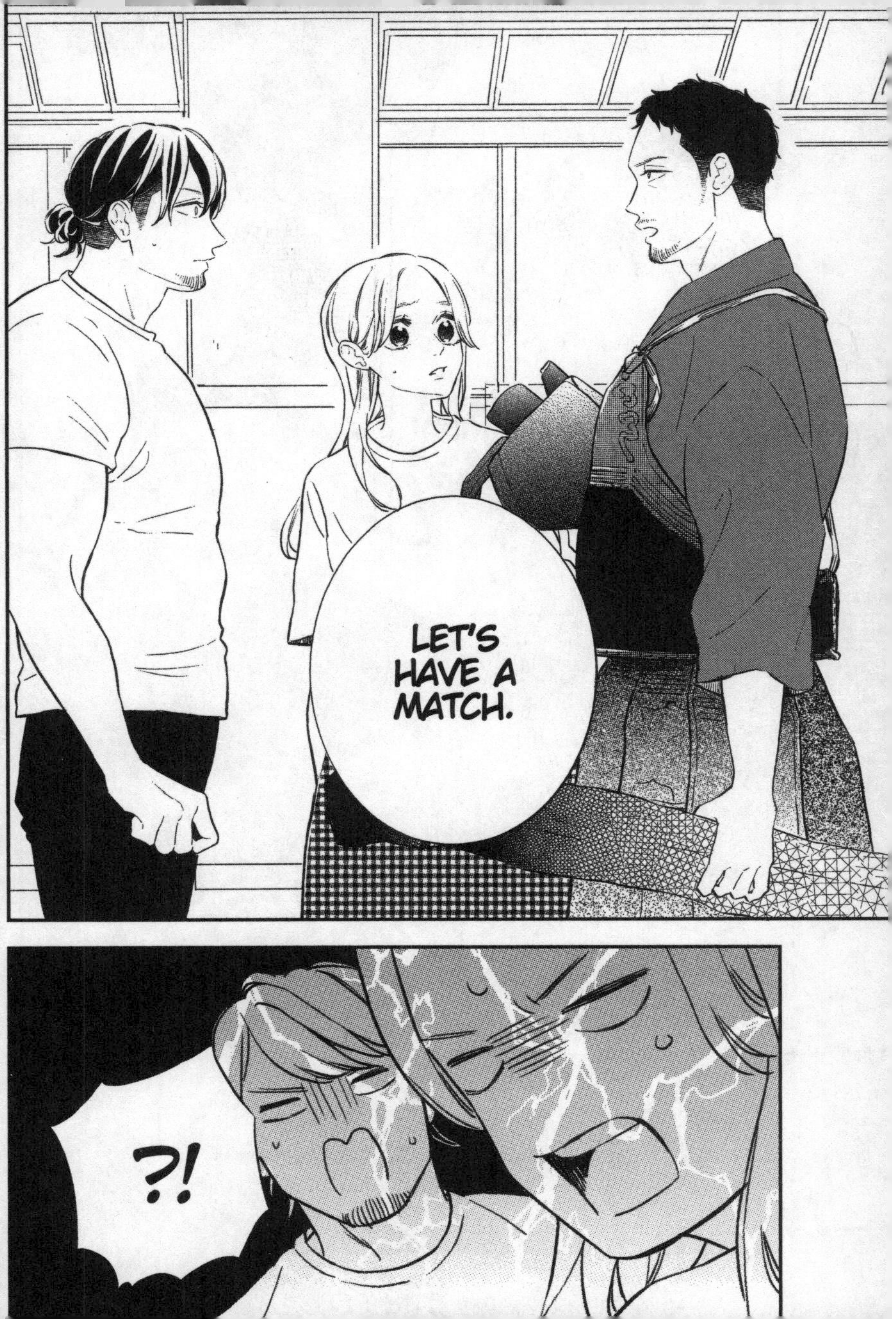
LET'S HAVE A MATCH.
?!

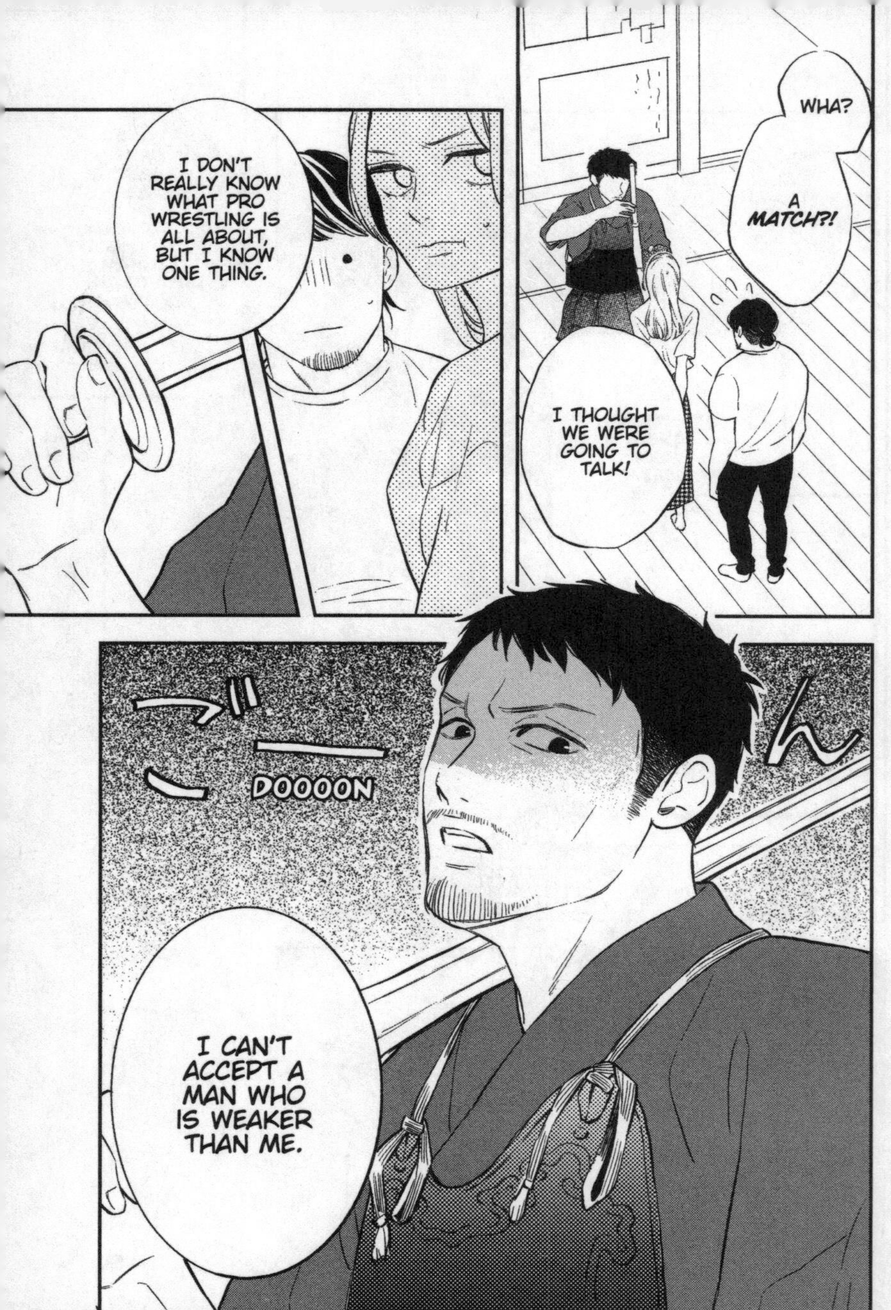
WHA?
A MATCH?!
I THOUGHT WE WERE GOING TO TALK!
I DON'T REALLY KNOW WHAT PRO WRESTLING IS ALL ABOUT, BUT I KNOW ONE THING.
DOOOON
I CAN'T ACCEPT A MAN WHO IS WEAKER THAN ME.

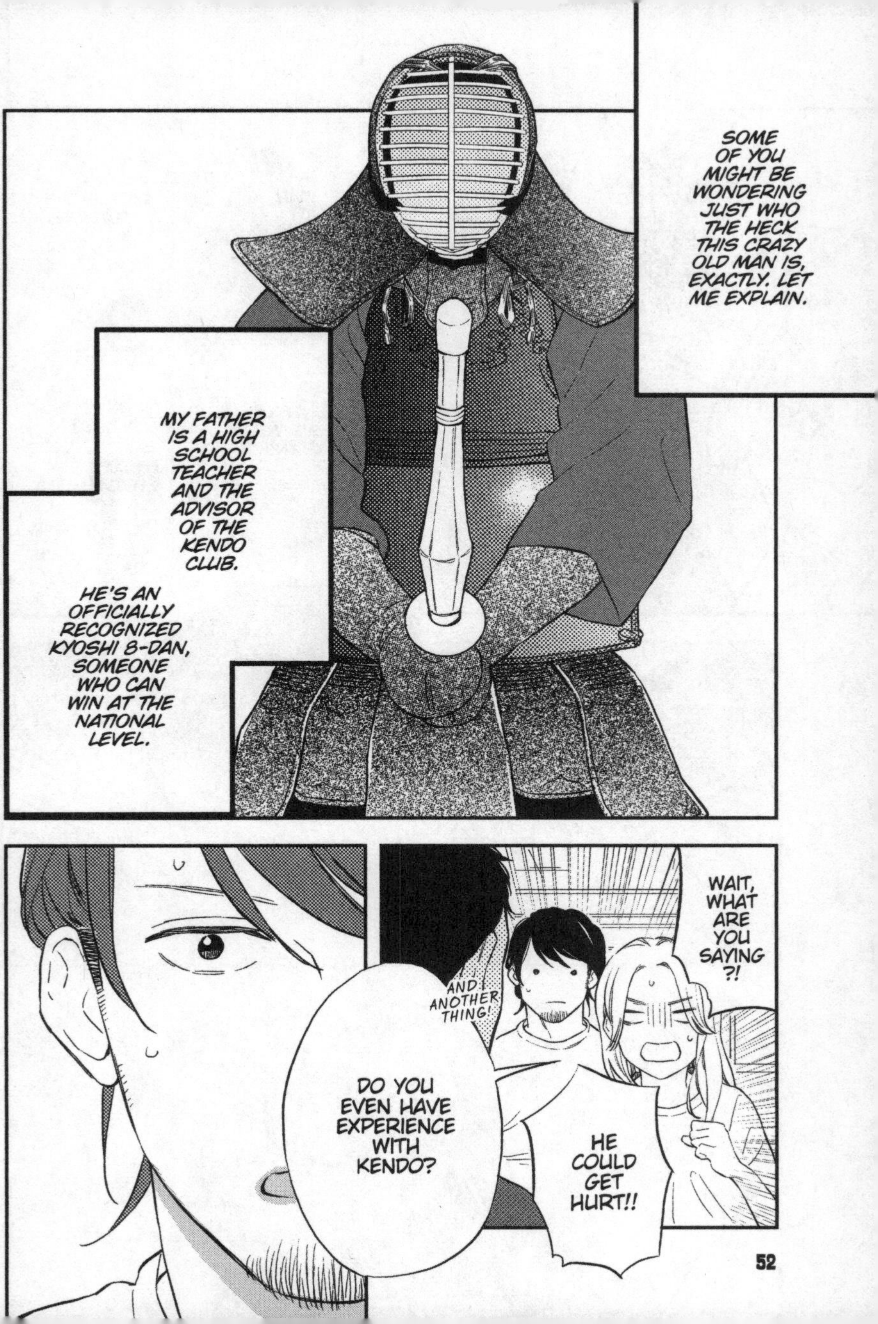
SOME OF YOU MIGHT BE WONDERING JUST WHO THE HECK THIS CRAZY OLD MAN IS, EXACTLY. LET ME EXPLAIN.
MY FATHER IS A HIGH SCHOOL TEACHER AND THE ADVISOR OF THE KENDO CLUB.
HE'S AN OFFICIALLY RECOGNIZED KYOSHI 8-DAN, SOMEONE WHO CAN WIN AT THE NATIONAL LEVEL.
WAIT, WHAT ARE YOU SAYING?!
AND ANOTHER THING!
HE COULD GET HURT!!
DO YOU EVEN HAVE EXPERIENCE WITH KENDO?

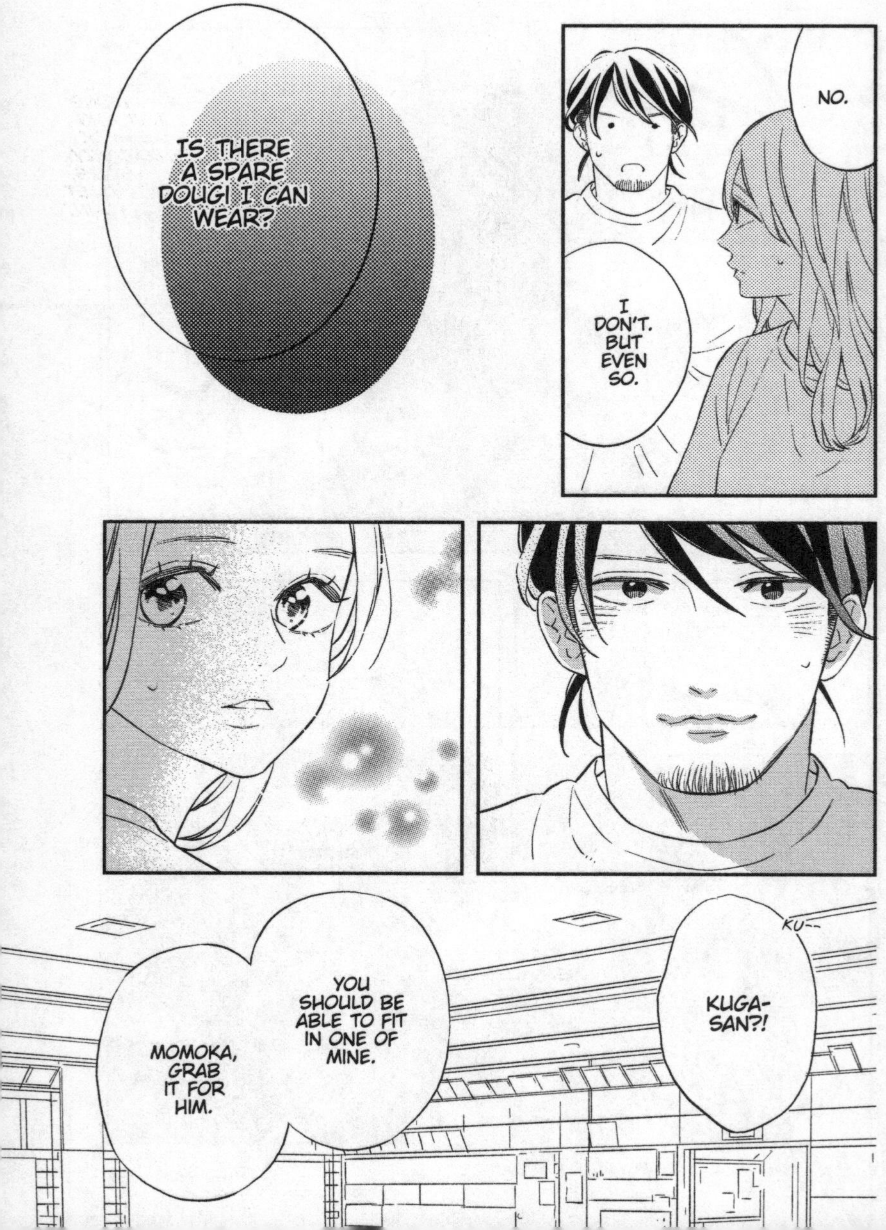
NO.
I DON'T. BUT EVEN SO.
IS THERE A SPARE DOUGI I CAN WEAR?
KU--
KUGA-SAN?!
YOU SHOULD BE ABLE TO FIT IN ONE OF MINE.
MOMOKA, GRAB IT FOR HIM.

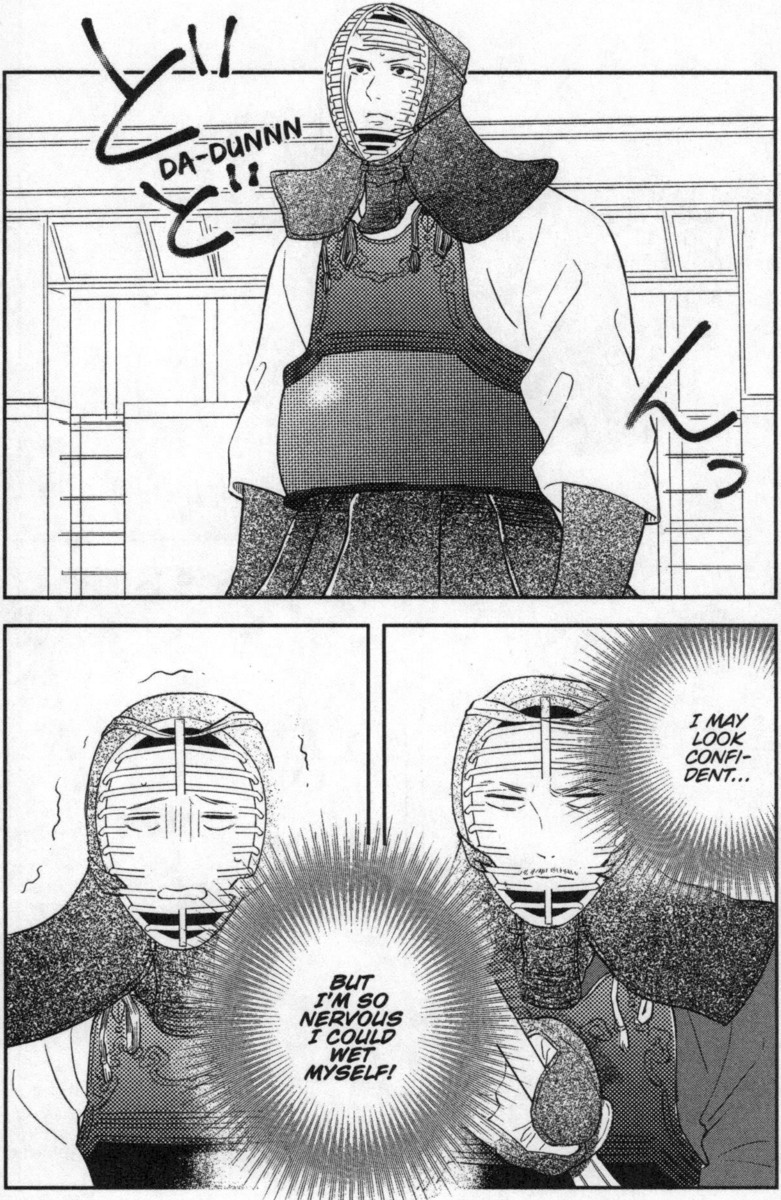
DA-DUNNN
I MAY LOOK CONFIDENT...
BUT I'M SO NERVOUS I COULD WET MYSELF!

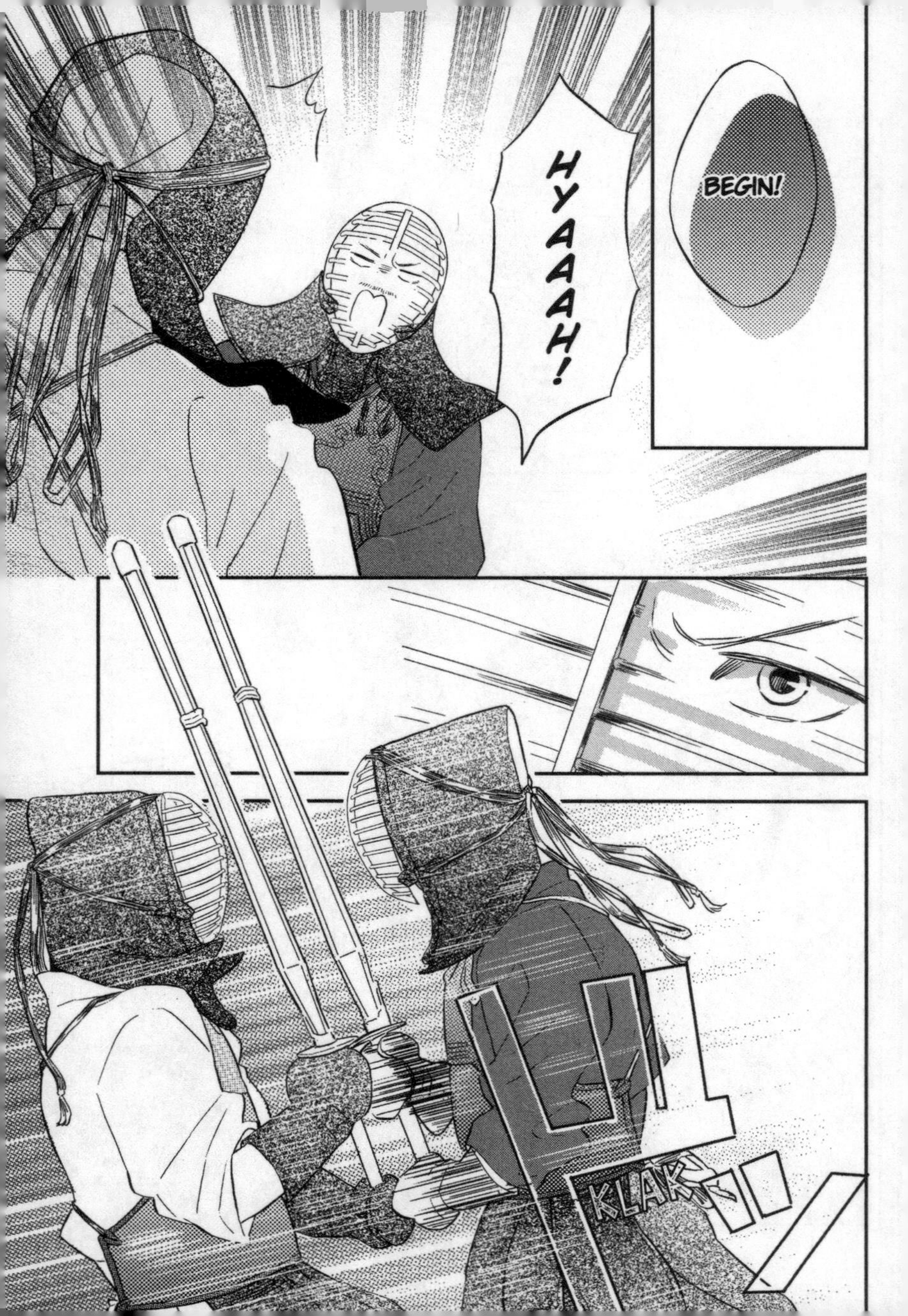
BEGIN!
HYAAAAH!
KLAK

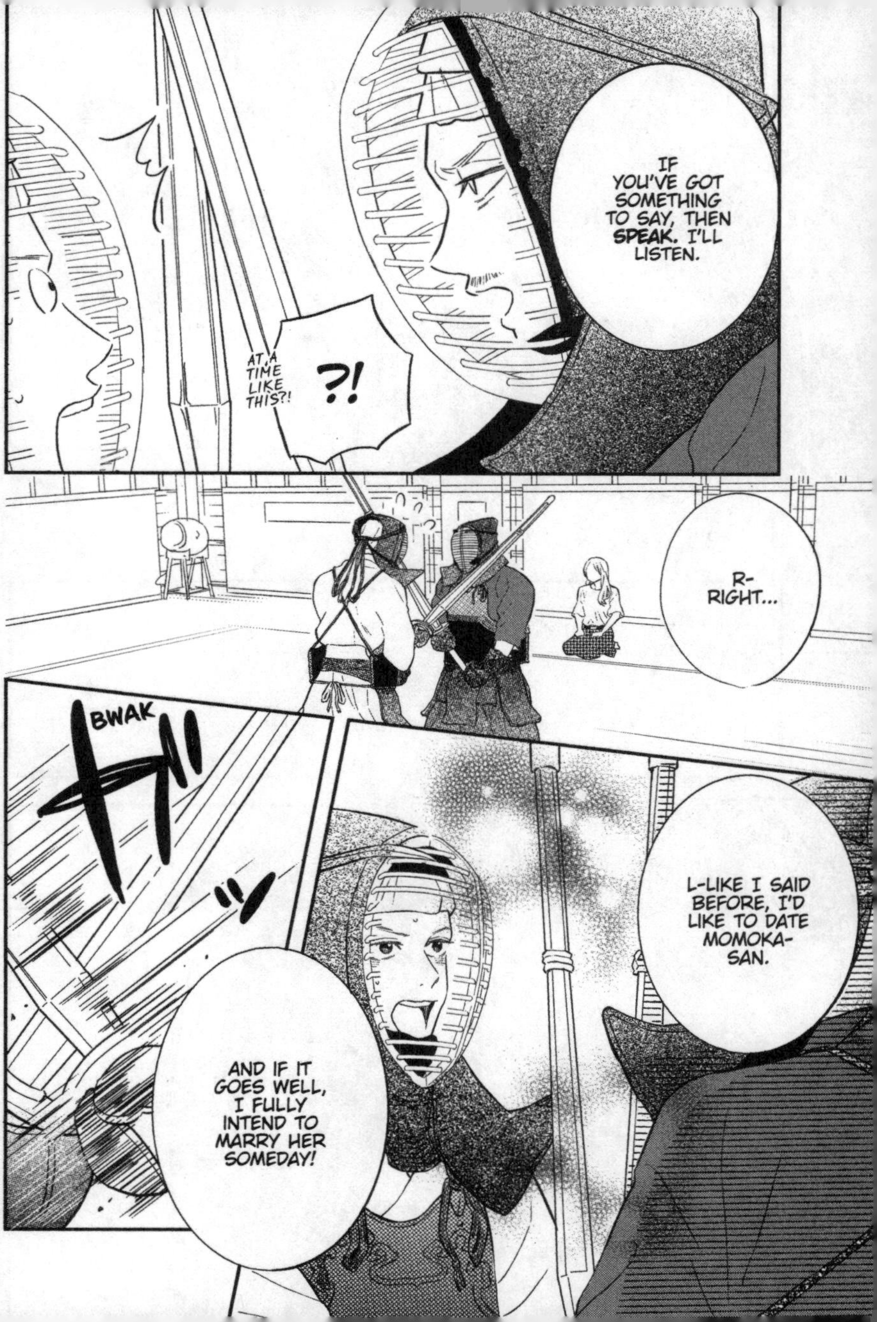
IF YOU'VE GOT SOMETHING TO SAY, THEN SPEAK. I'LL LISTEN.
?!
AT A TIME LIKE THIS?!
R-RIGHT...
L-LIKE I SAID BEFORE, I'D LIKE TO DATE MOMOKA-SAN.
AND IF IT GOES WELL, I FULLY INTEND TO MARRY HER SOMEDAY!
BWAK

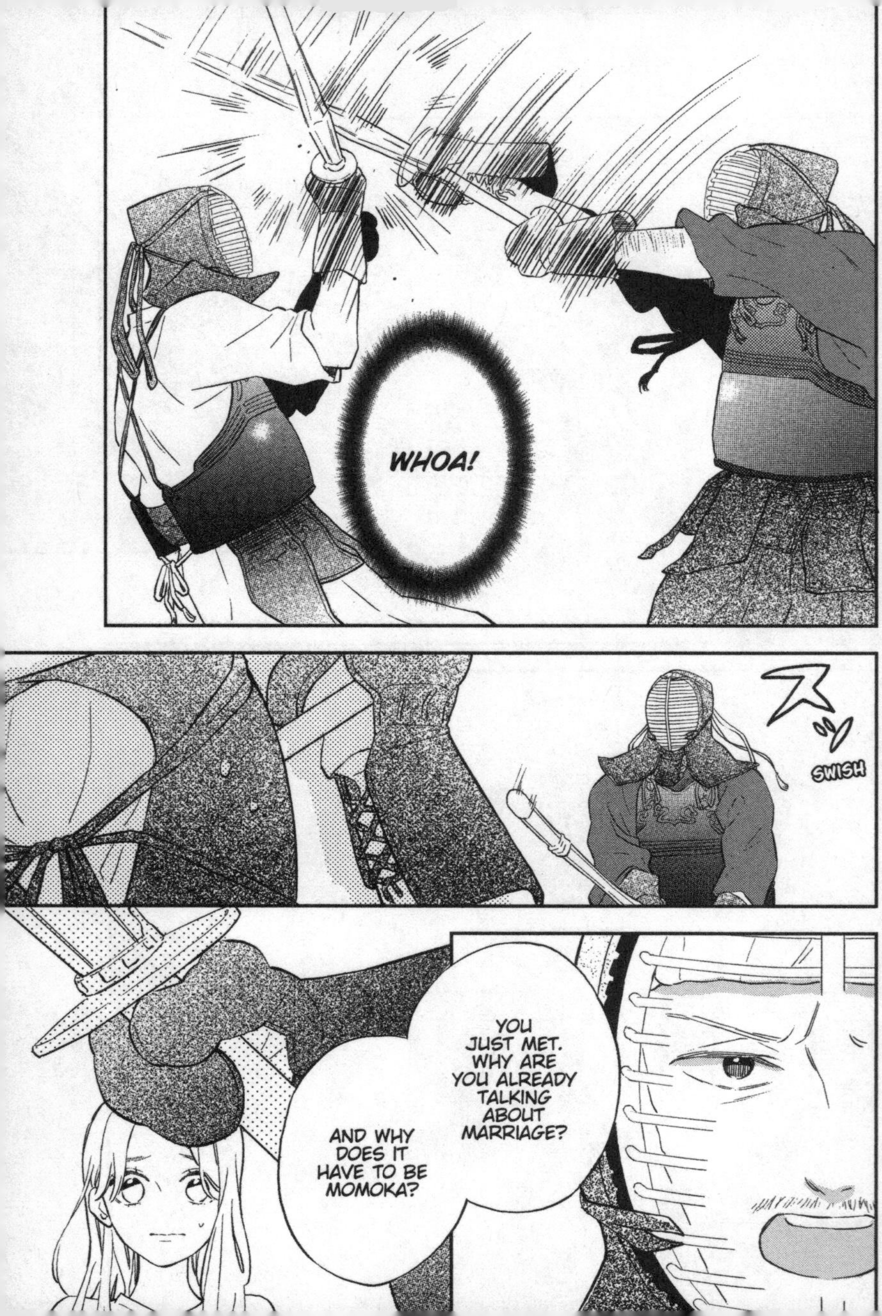
WHOA!
ス
SWISH
YOU JUST MET. WHY ARE YOU ALREADY TALKING ABOUT MARRIAGE?
AND WHY DOES IT HAVE TO BE MOMOKA?

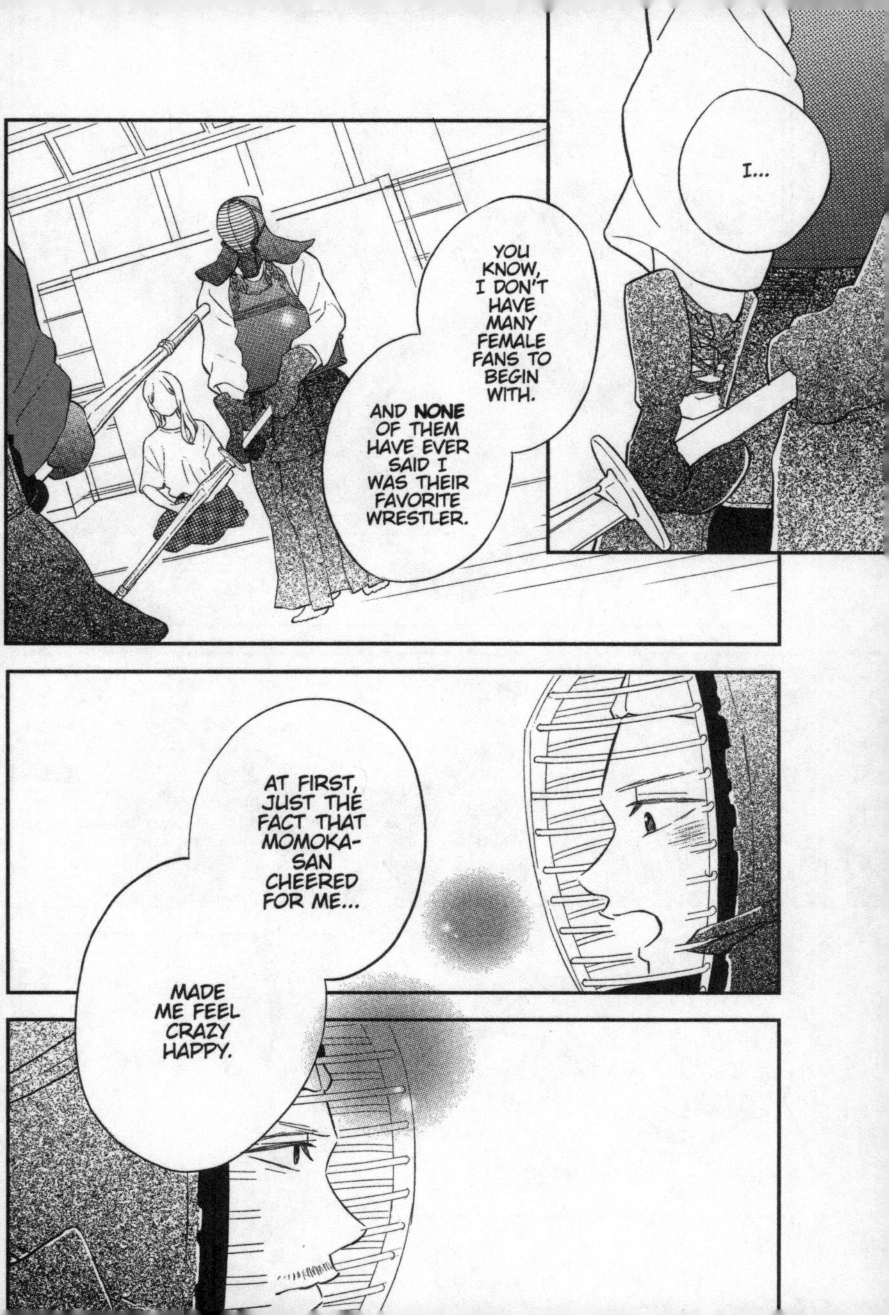
I...
YOU KNOW, I DON'T HAVE MANY FEMALE FANS TO BEGIN WITH.
AND **NONE** OF THEM HAVE EVER SAID I WAS THEIR FAVORITE WRESTLER.
AT FIRST, JUST THE FACT THAT MOMOKA-SAN CHEERED FOR ME...
MADE ME FEEL CRAZY HAPPY.

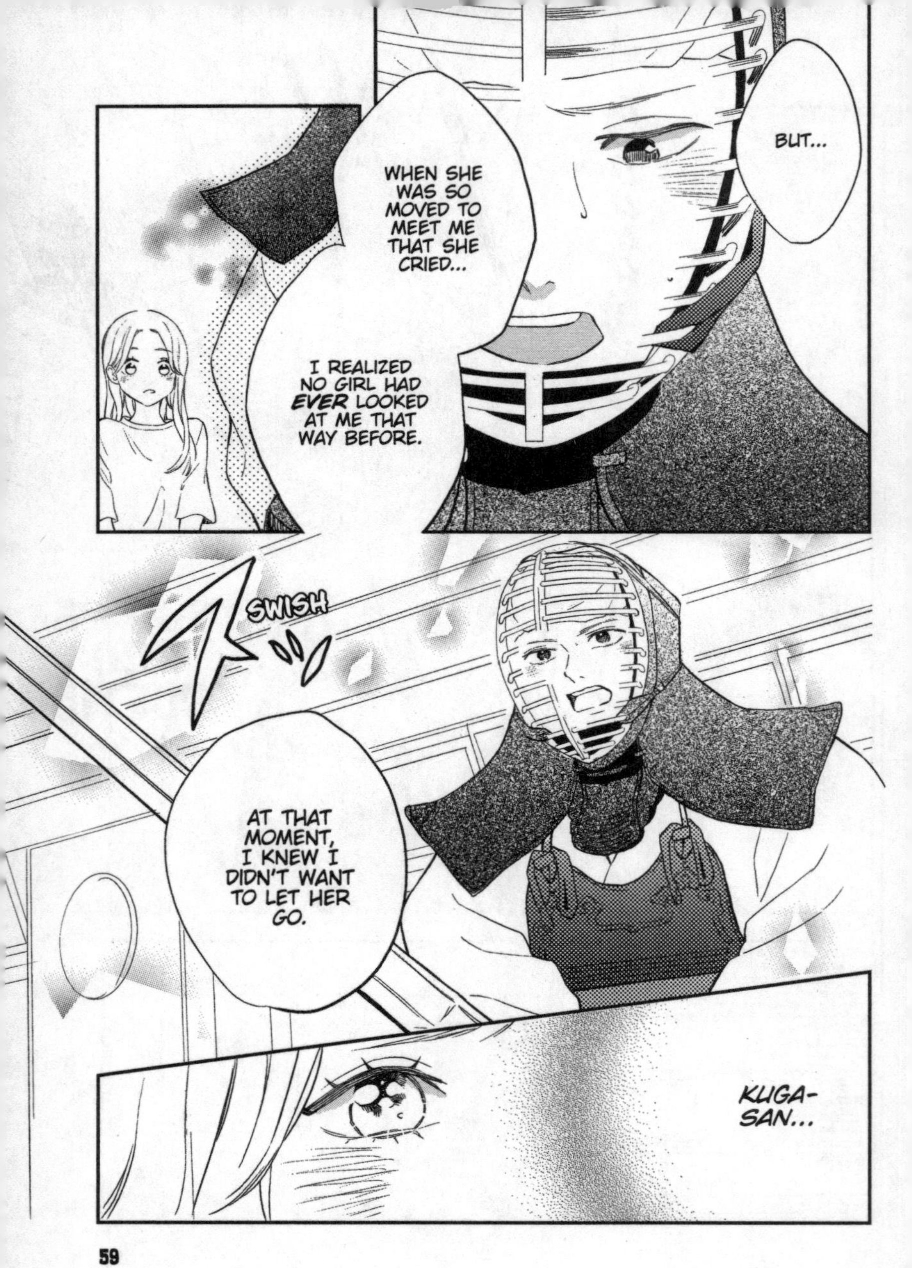
BUT...
WHEN SHE WAS SO MOVED TO MEET ME THAT SHE CRIED...
I REALIZED NO GIRL HAD **EVER** LOOKED AT ME THAT WAY BEFORE.
SWISH
AT THAT MOMENT, I KNEW I DIDN'T WANT TO LET HER GO.
KUGA-SAN...

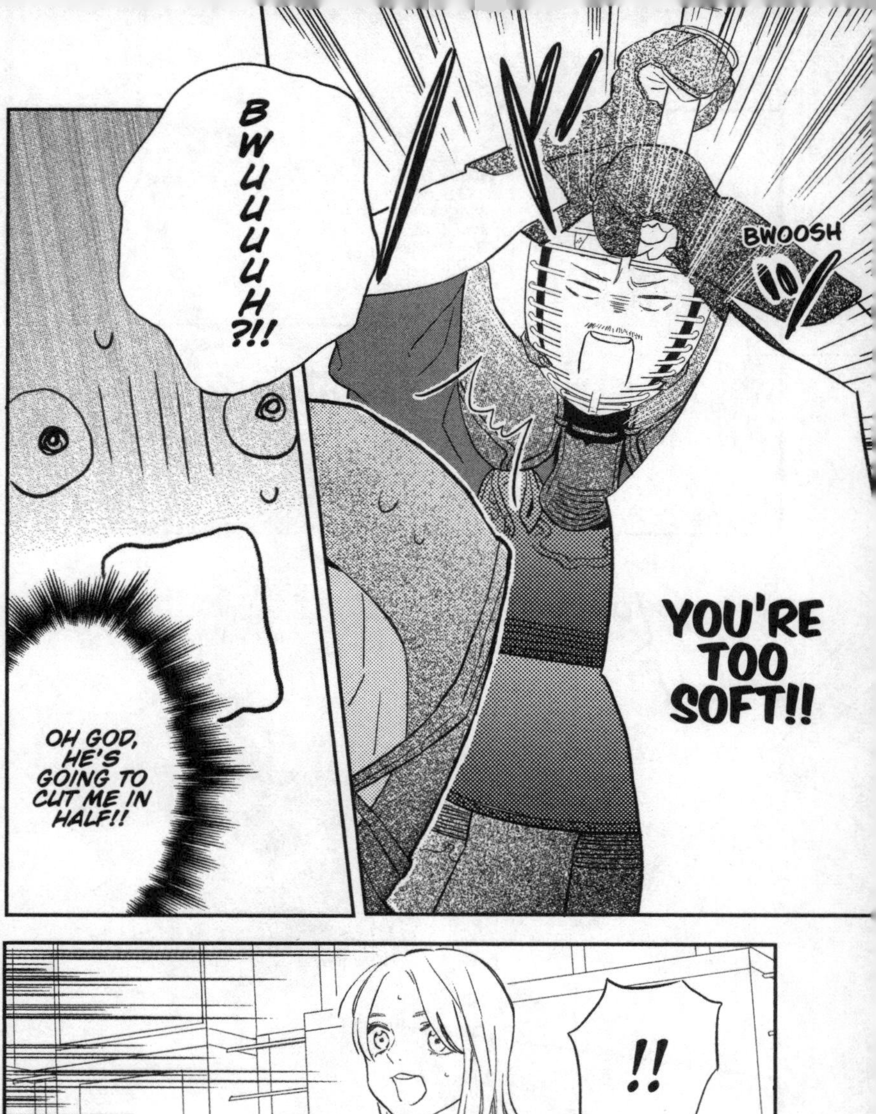
BWOOSH
BWUUUUUH?!!
YOU'RE TOO SOFT!!
OH GOD, HE'S GOING TO CUT ME IN HALF!!
!!

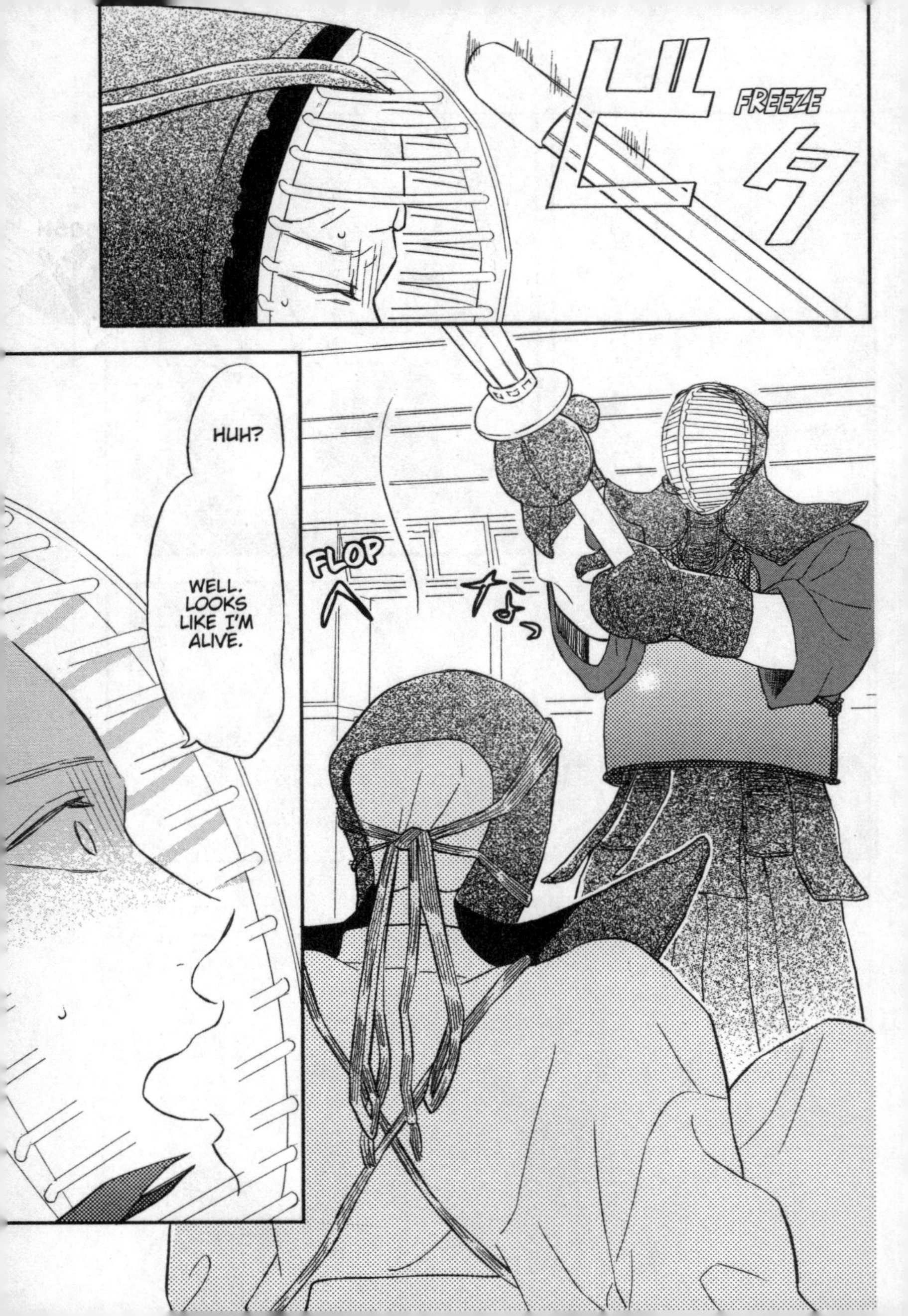
FREEZE
FLOP
HUH?
WELL. LOOKS LIKE I'M ALIVE.

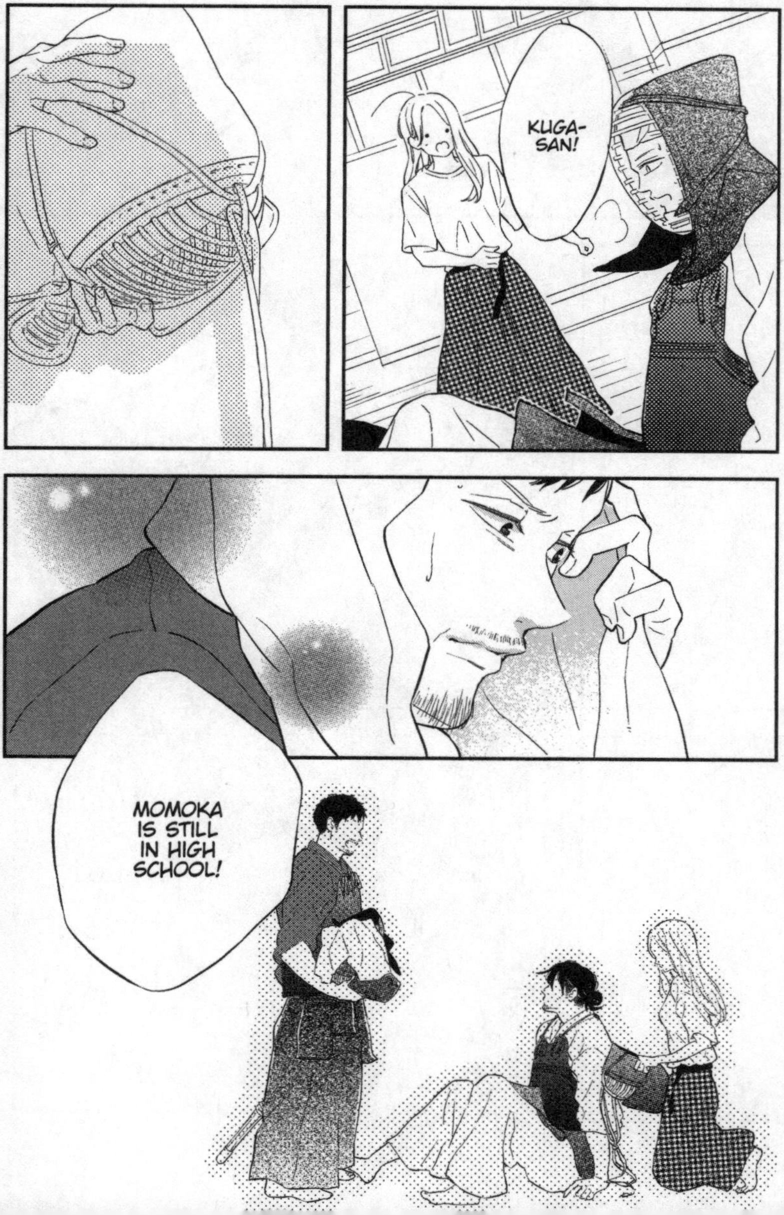
KUGA-SAN!
MOMOKA IS STILL IN HIGH SCHOOL!

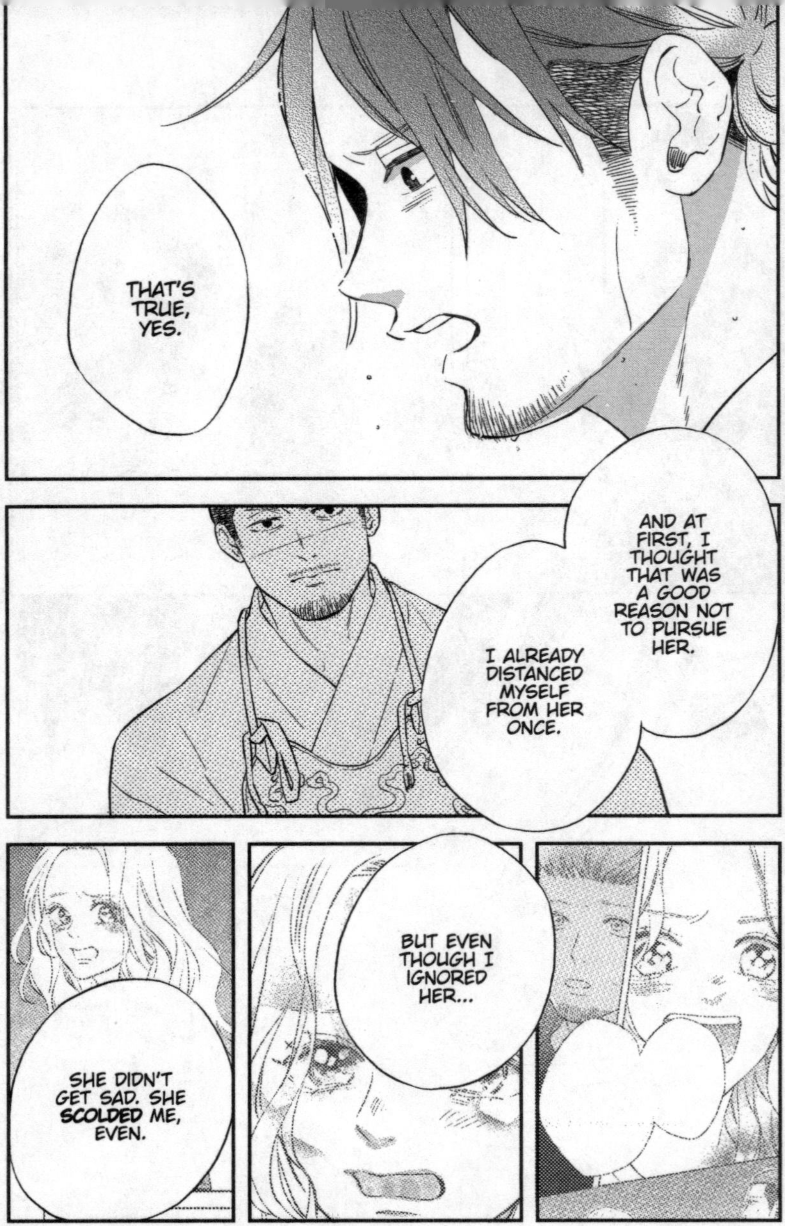
THAT'S TRUE, YES.
I ALREADY DISTANCED MYSELF FROM HER ONCE.
AND AT FIRST, I THOUGHT THAT WAS A GOOD REASON NOT TO PURSUE HER.
BUT EVEN THOUGH I IGNORED HER...
SHE DIDN'T GET SAD. SHE **SCOLDED** ME, EVEN.

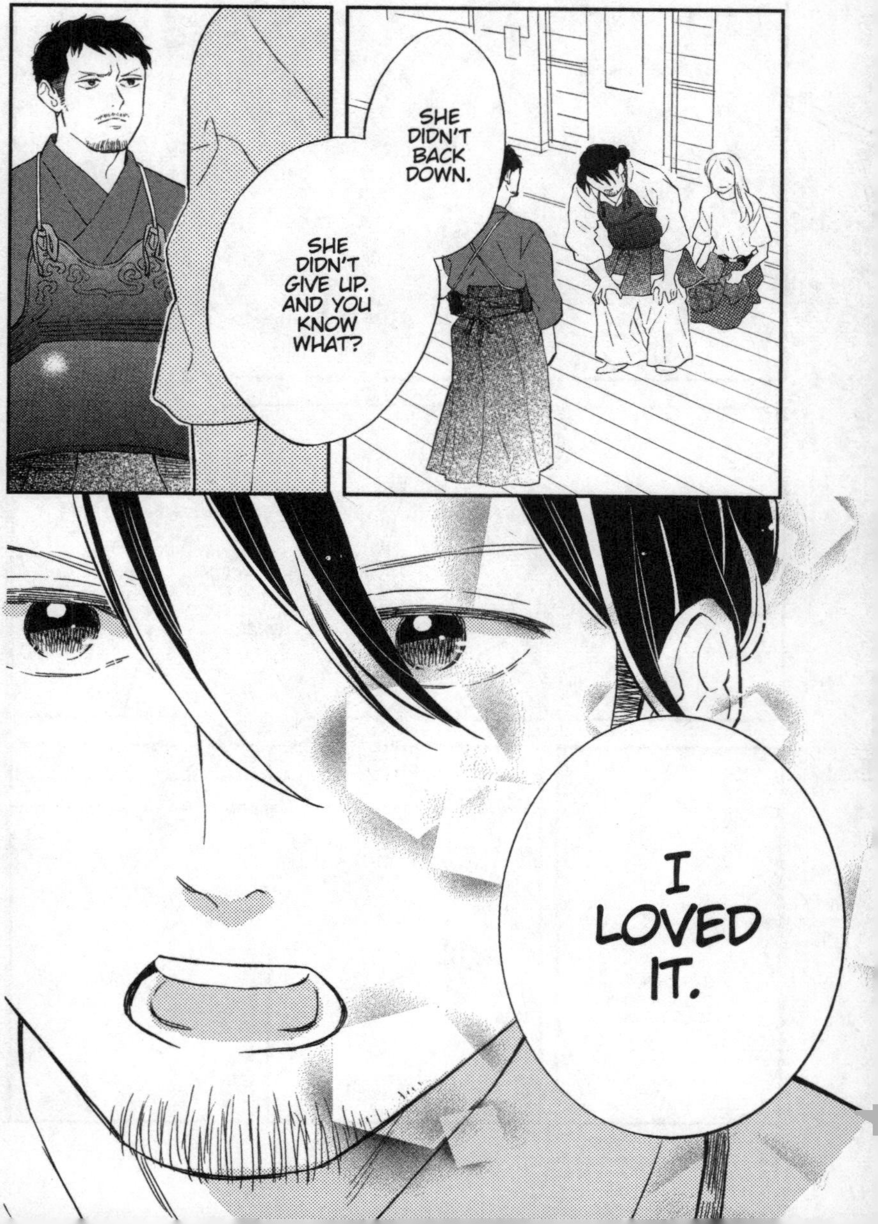
SHE DIDN'T BACK DOWN.
SHE DIDN'T GIVE UP. AND YOU KNOW WHAT?
I LOVED IT.

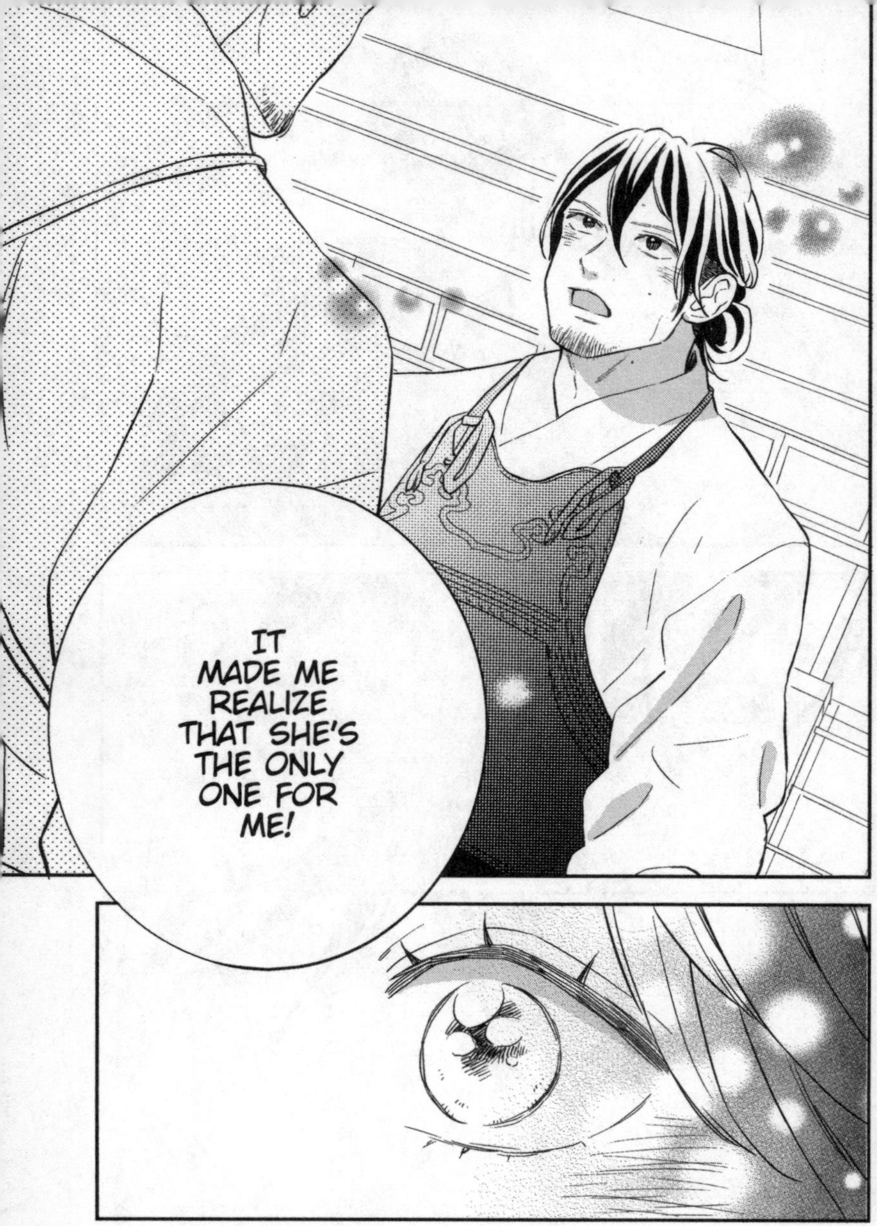
IT MADE ME REALIZE THAT SHE'S THE ONLY ONE FOR ME!

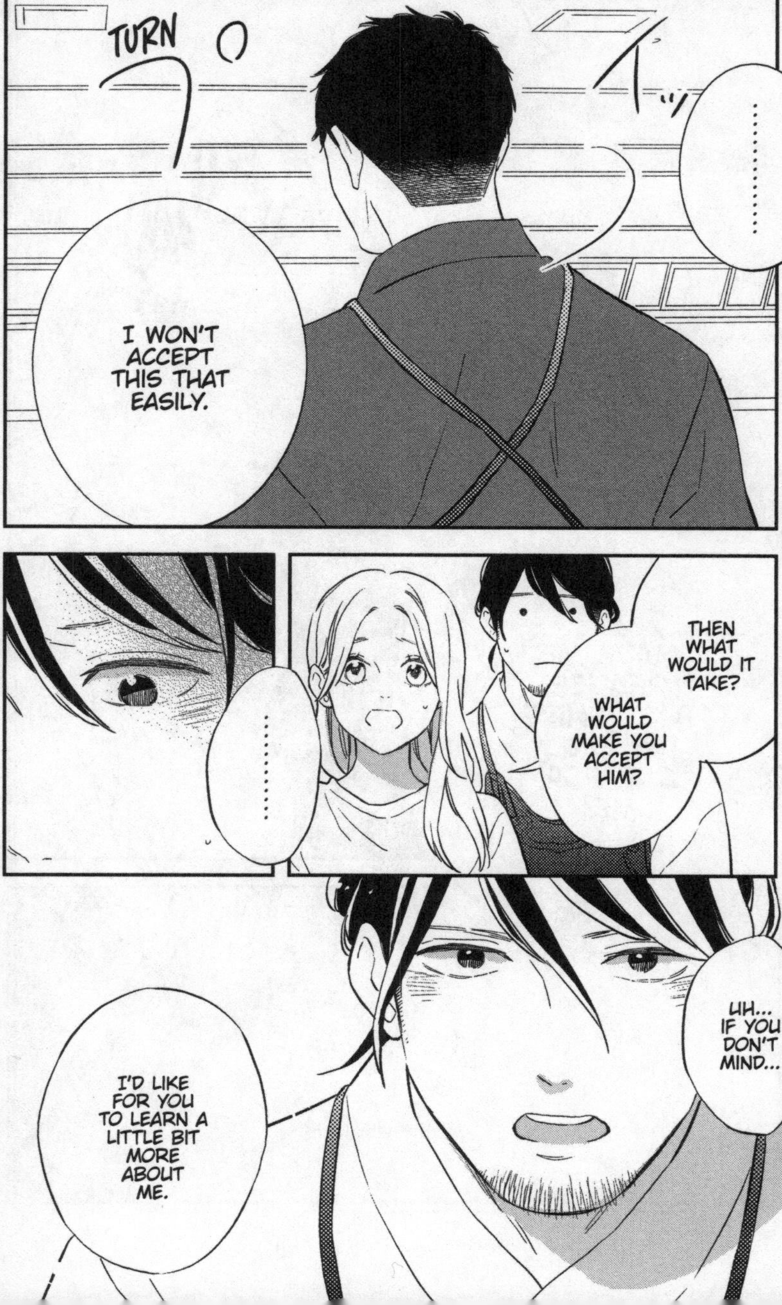
......
TURN
I WON'T ACCEPT THIS THAT EASILY.
THEN WHAT WOULD IT TAKE?
WHAT WOULD MAKE YOU ACCEPT HIM?
......
UH... IF YOU DON'T MIND...
I'D LIKE FOR YOU TO LEARN A LITTLE BIT MORE ABOUT ME.

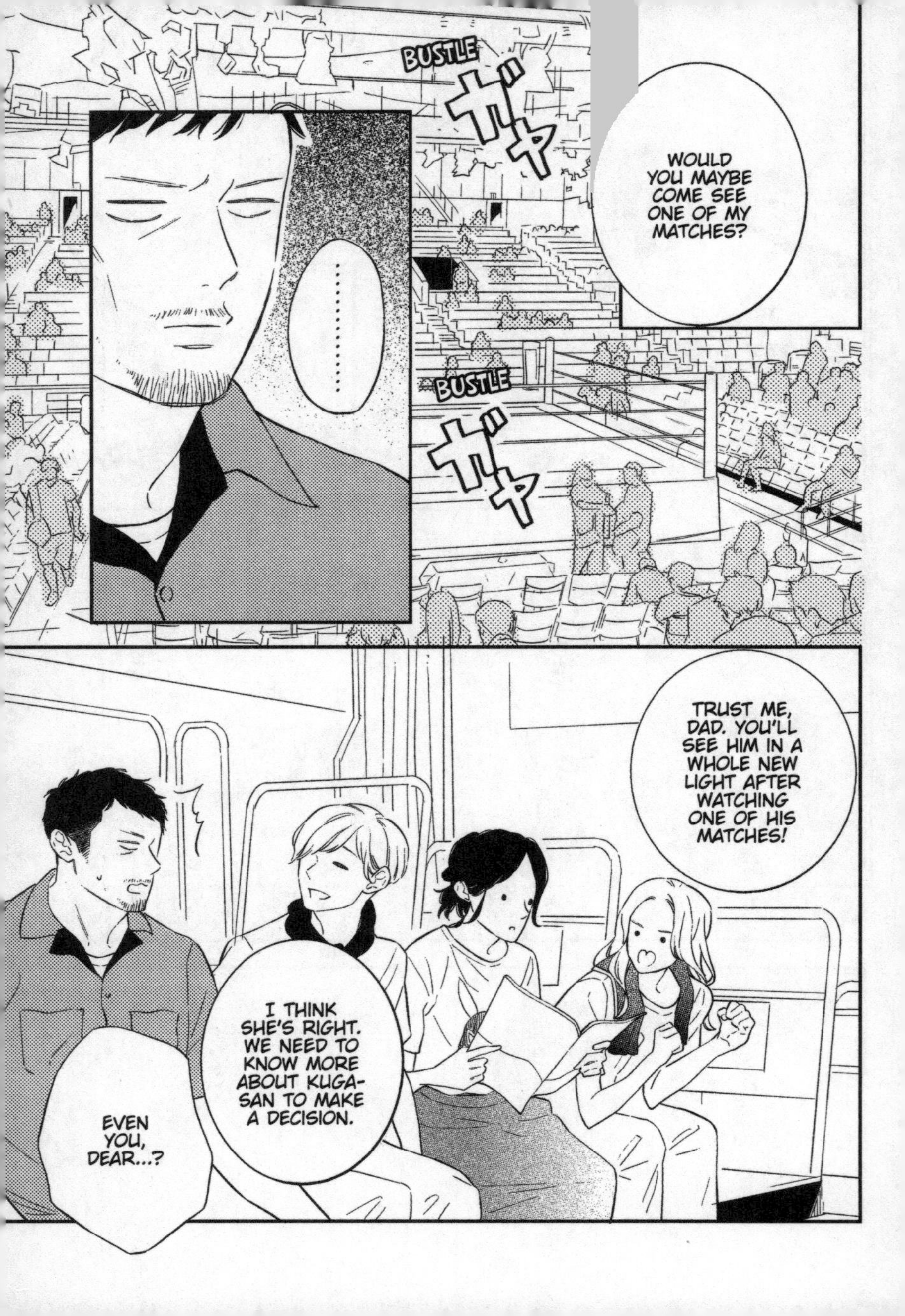
WOULD YOU MAYBE COME SEE ONE OF MY MATCHES?
BUSTLE
ガヤ
BUSTLE
ガヤ
……
TRUST ME, DAD. YOU'LL SEE HIM IN A WHOLE NEW LIGHT AFTER WATCHING ONE OF HIS MATCHES!
I THINK SHE'S RIGHT. WE NEED TO KNOW MORE ABOUT KUGA-SAN TO MAKE A DECISION.
EVEN YOU, DEAR...?

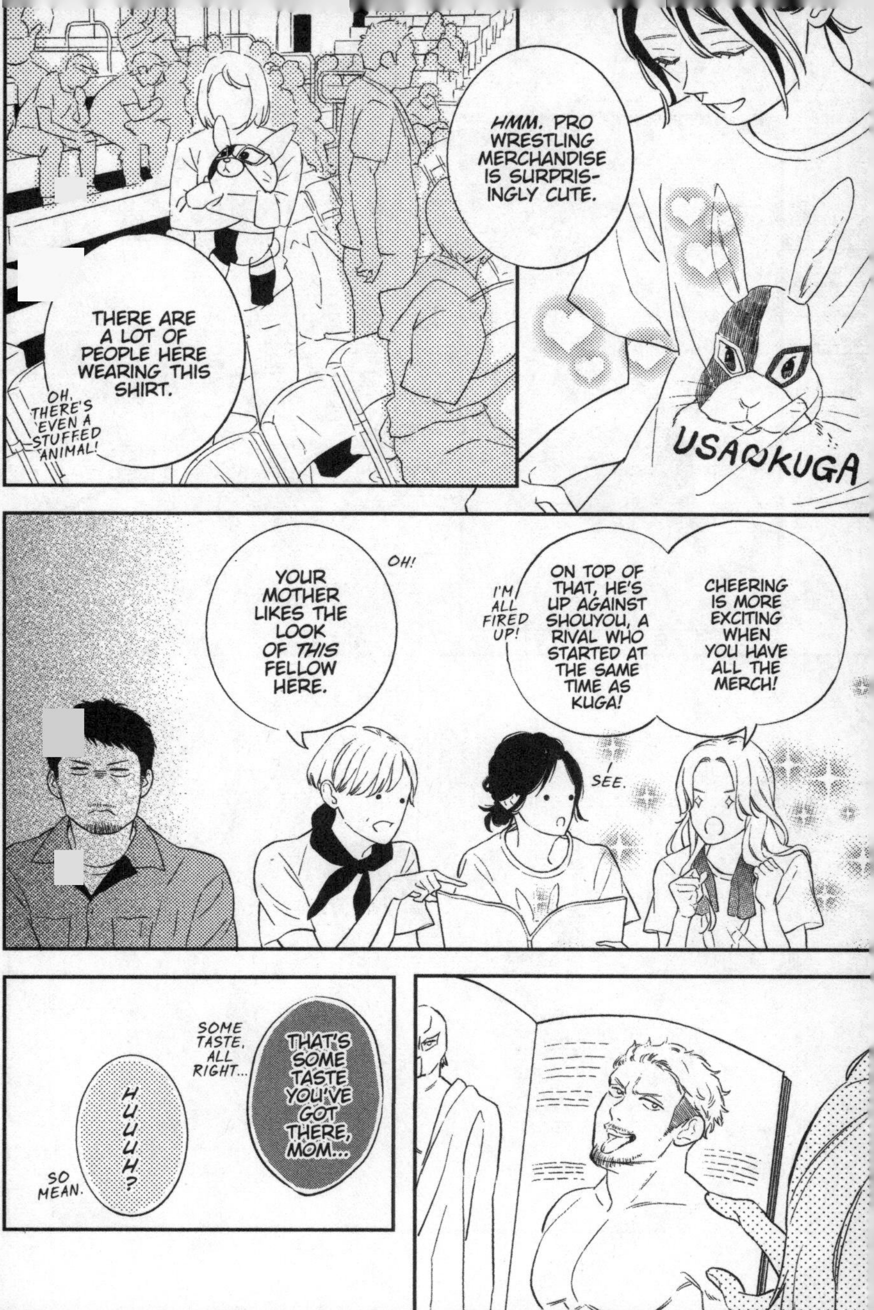
HMM. PRO WRESTLING MERCHANDISE IS SURPRISINGLY CUTE.
USA KUGA
THERE ARE A LOT OF PEOPLE HERE WEARING THIS SHIRT.
OH, THERE'S EVEN A STUFFED ANIMAL!
CHEERING IS MORE EXCITING WHEN YOU HAVE ALL THE MERCH!
ON TOP OF THAT, HE'S UP AGAINST SHOUYOU, A RIVAL WHO STARTED AT THE SAME TIME AS KUGA!
I'M ALL FIRED UP!
I SEE.
OH!
YOUR MOTHER LIKES THE LOOK OF *THIS* FELLOW HERE.
THAT'S SOME TASTE YOU'VE GOT THERE, MOM...
SOME TASTE, ALL RIGHT...
HUUUH?
SO MEAN.

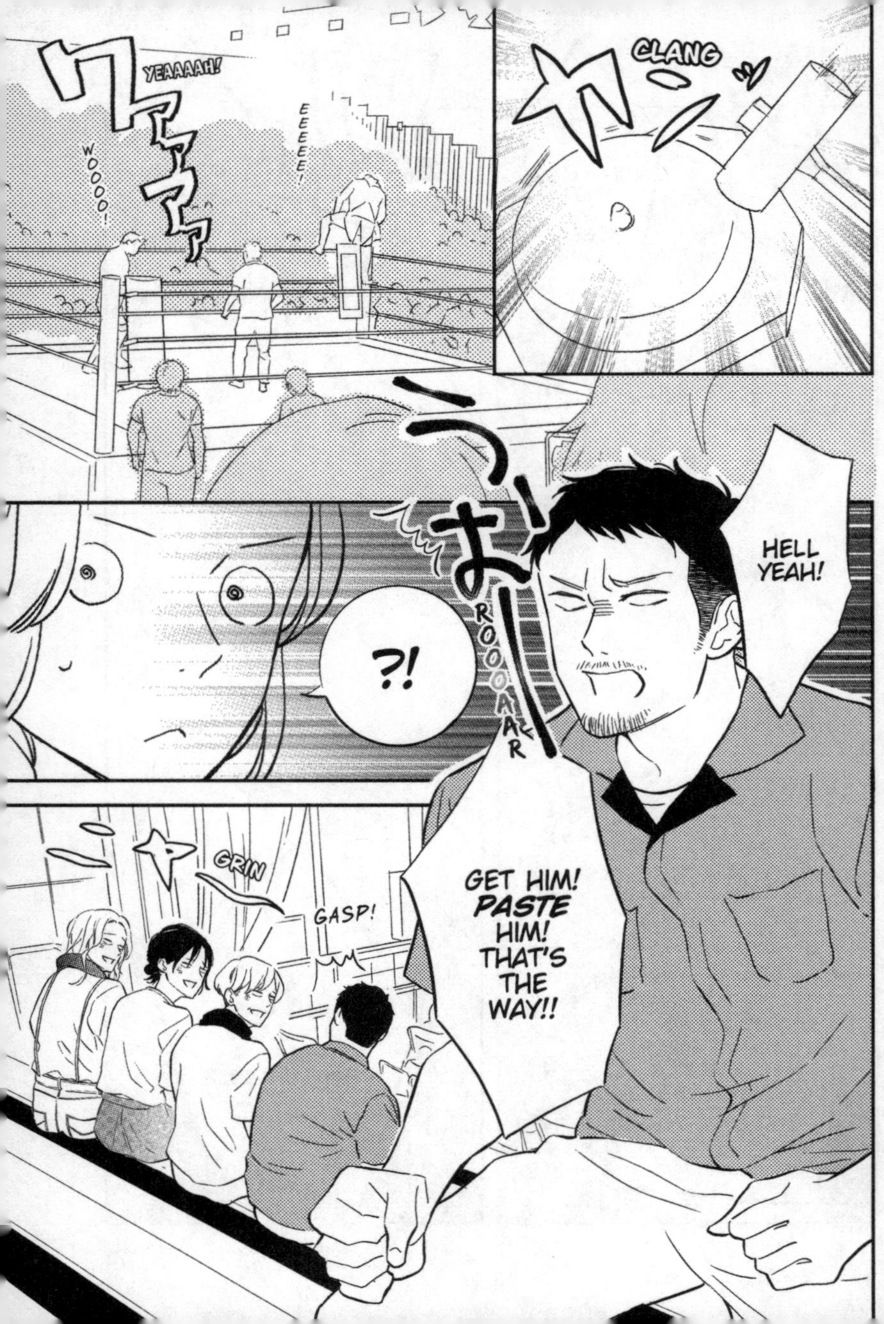
CLANG
YEAAAAH!
EEEEEE!
WOOOOO!
HELL YEAH!
ROOOAAR
?!
GET HIM! *PASTE* HIM! THAT'S THE WAY!!
GRIN
GASP!

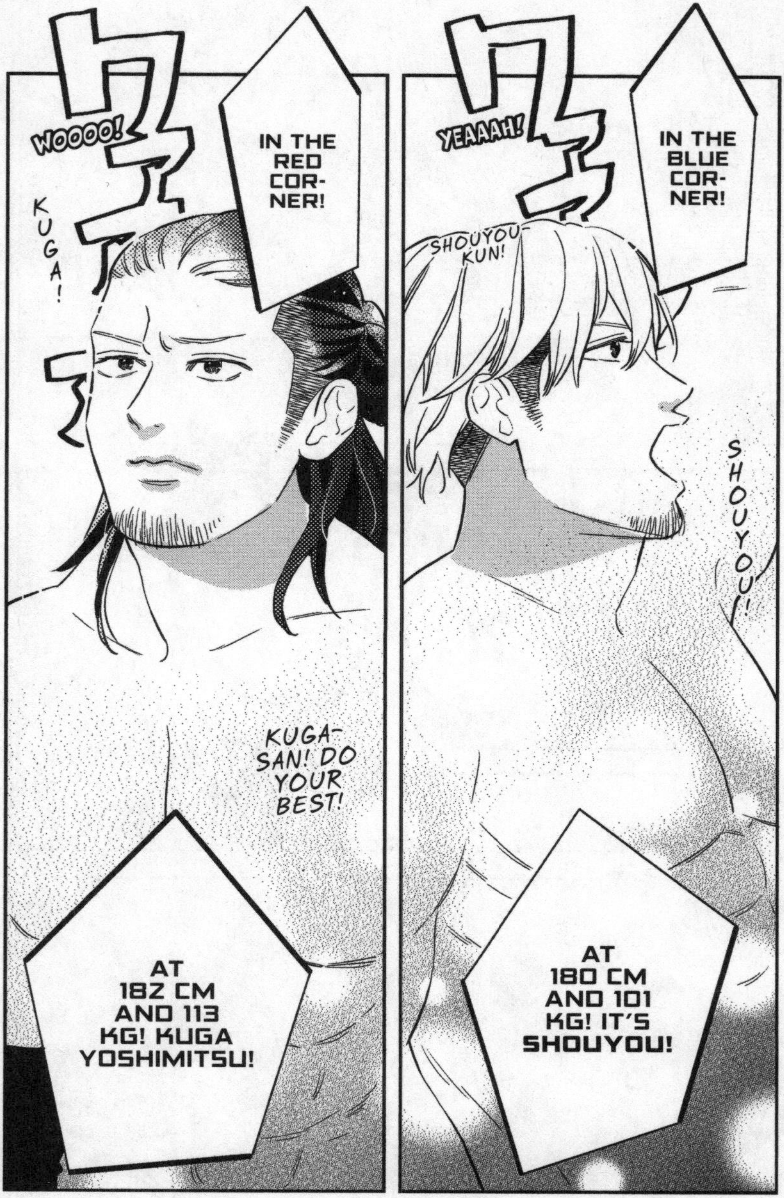
YEAAAH!
IN THE BLUE CORNER!
SHOUYOU-KUN!
SHOUYOU!!
AT 180 CM AND 101 KG! IT'S SHOUYOU!
WOOOO!
IN THE RED CORNER!
KUGA!
KUGA-SAN! DO YOUR BEST!
AT 182 CM AND 113 KG! KUGA YOSHIMITSU!

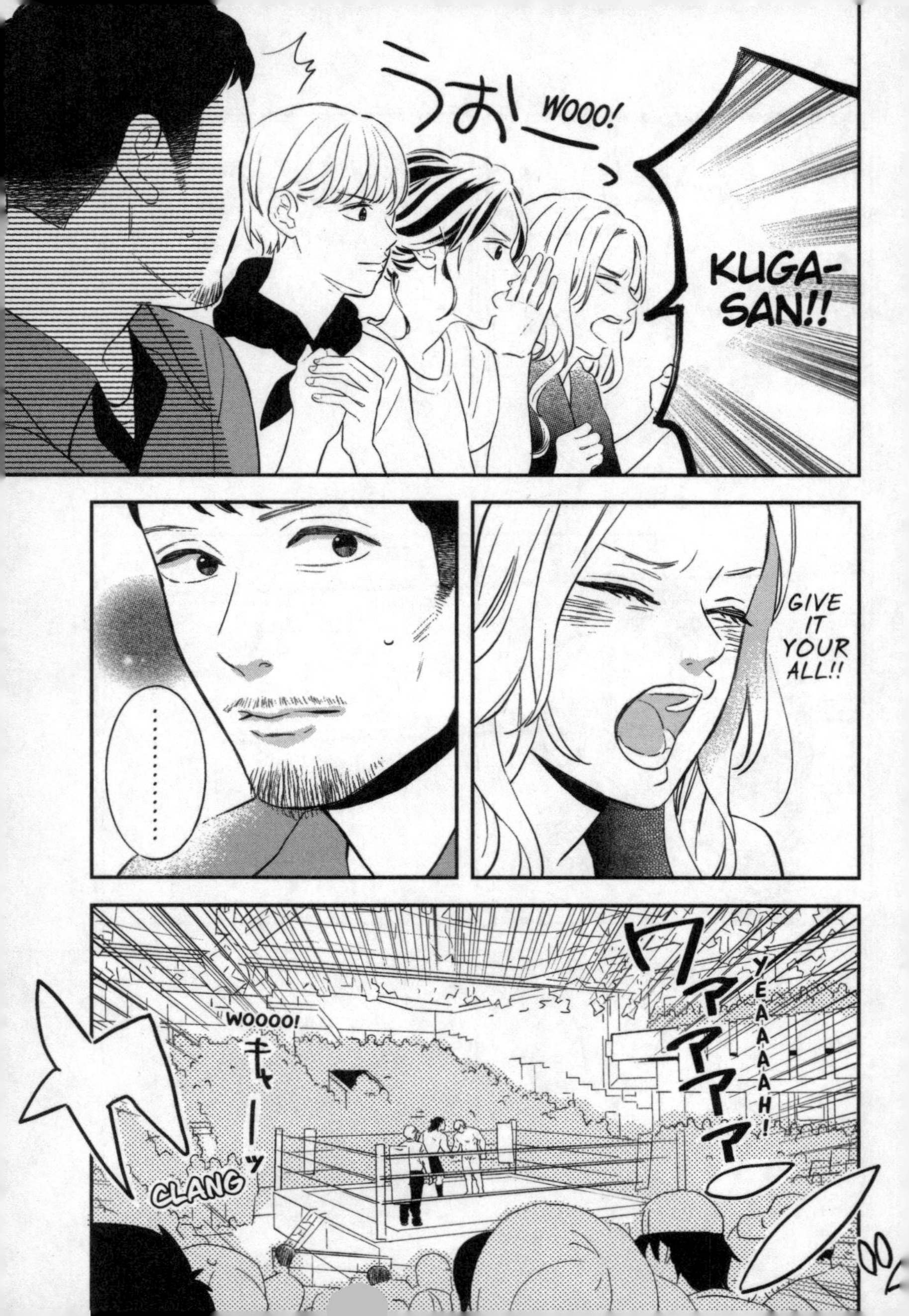
KUGA-SAN!!
うおー
WOOO!
GIVE IT YOUR ALL!!
……
ワアアアアー
YEAAAAAH!
キャーッ
WOOOO!
CLANG

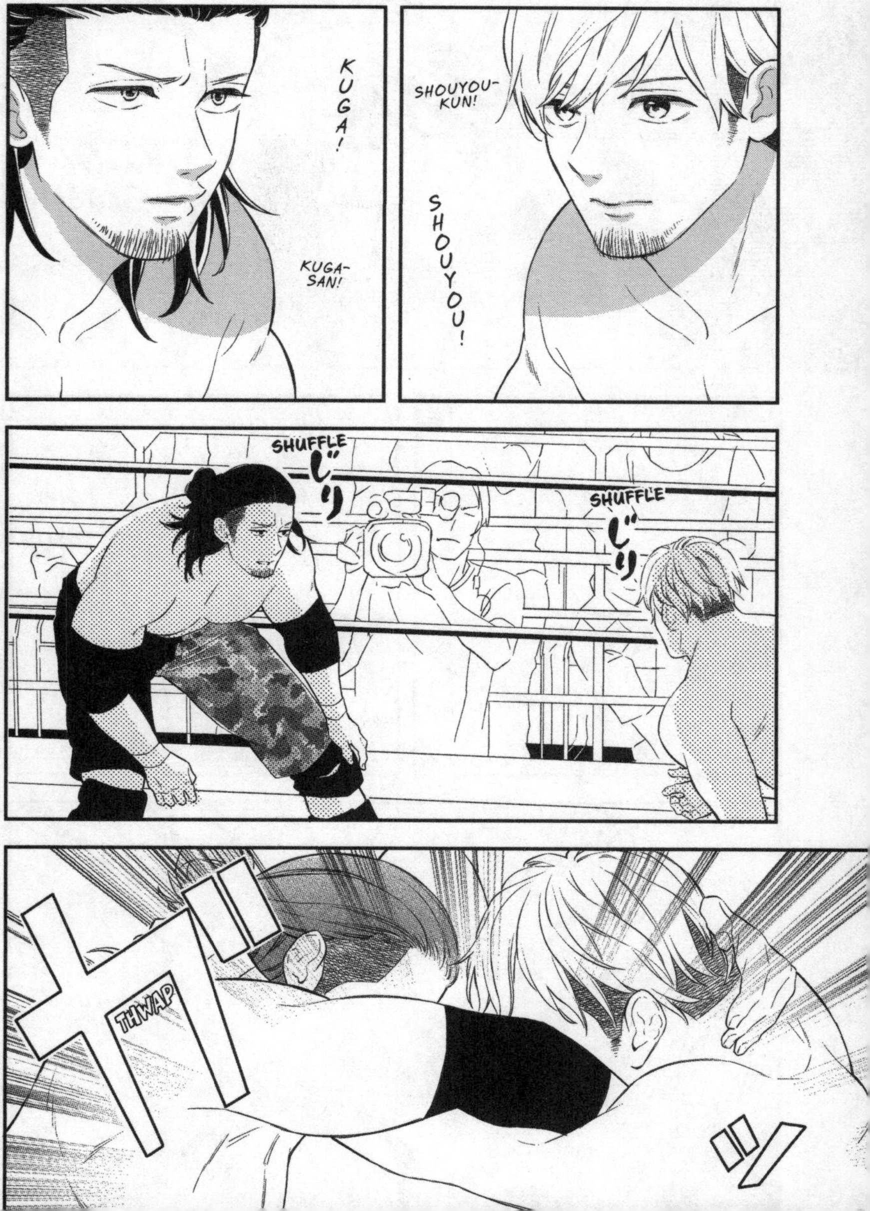
SHOUYOU-KUN!
SHOUYOU!
KUGA!
KUGA-SAN!
SHUFFLE
じり
SHUFFLE
じり
THWAP

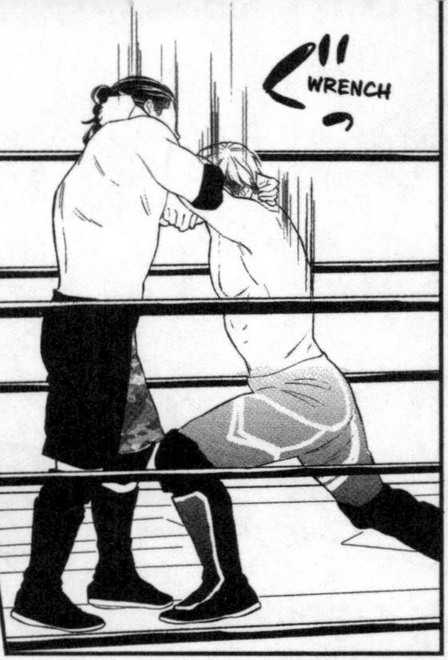
WRENCH
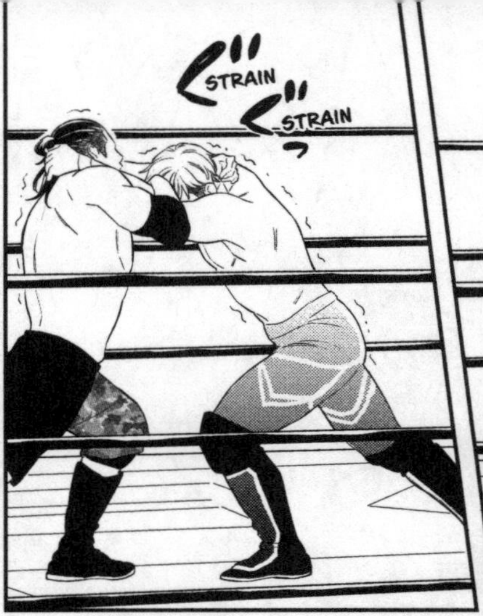
STRAIN
STRAIN
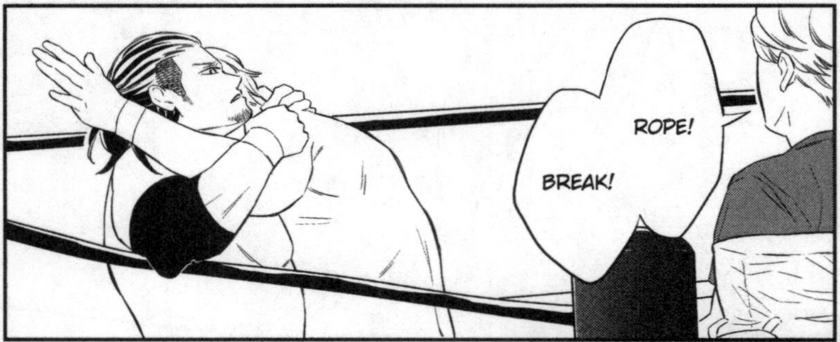
ROPE!
BREAK!
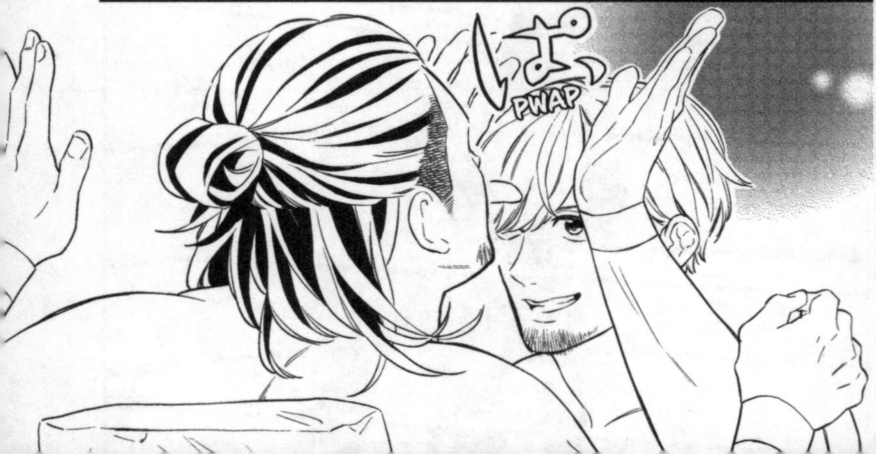
PWAP

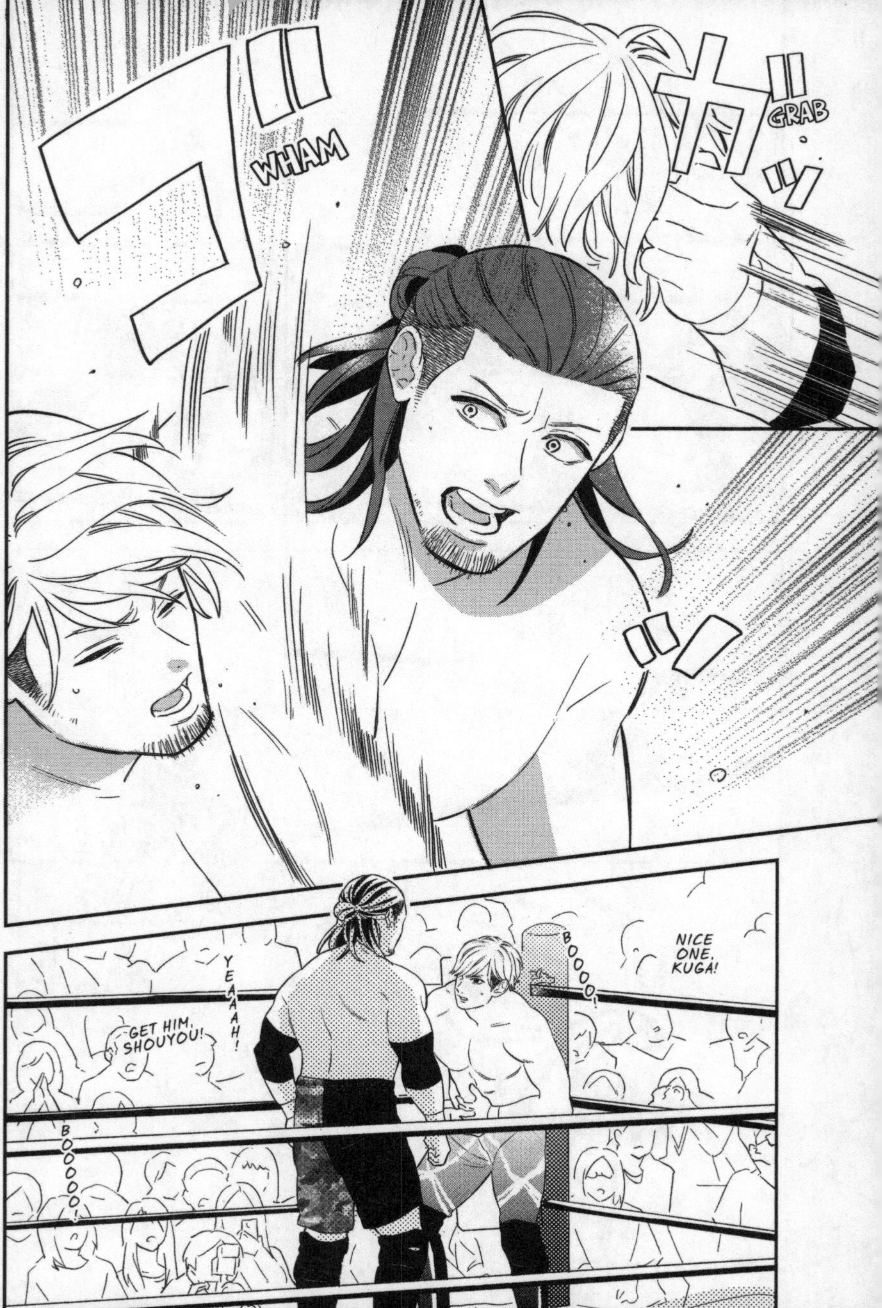
GRAB
WHAM
NICE ONE, KUGA!
BOOOOO!
YEAAAH!
GET HIM, SHOUYOU!
BOOOOOO!

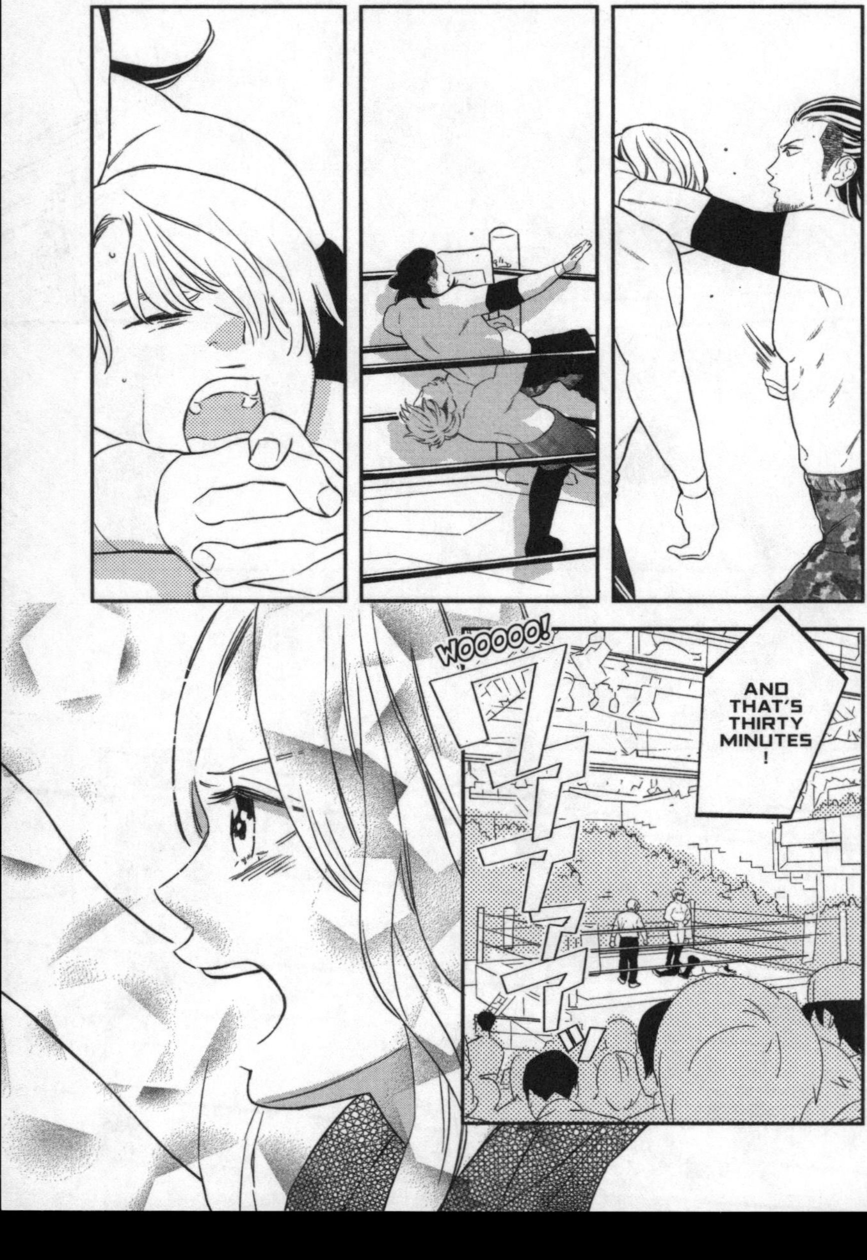
AND THAT'S THIRTY MINUTES!
WOOOOO!

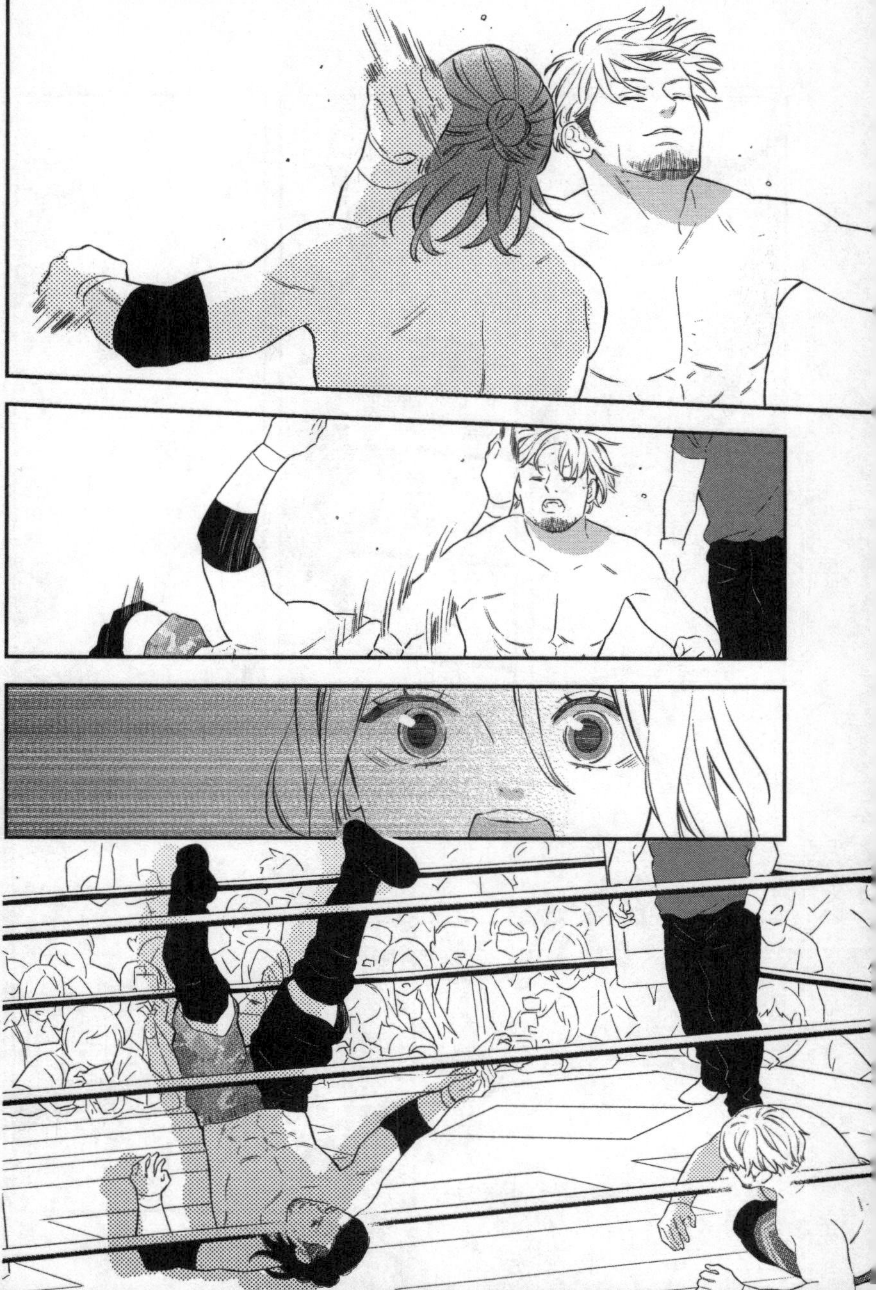

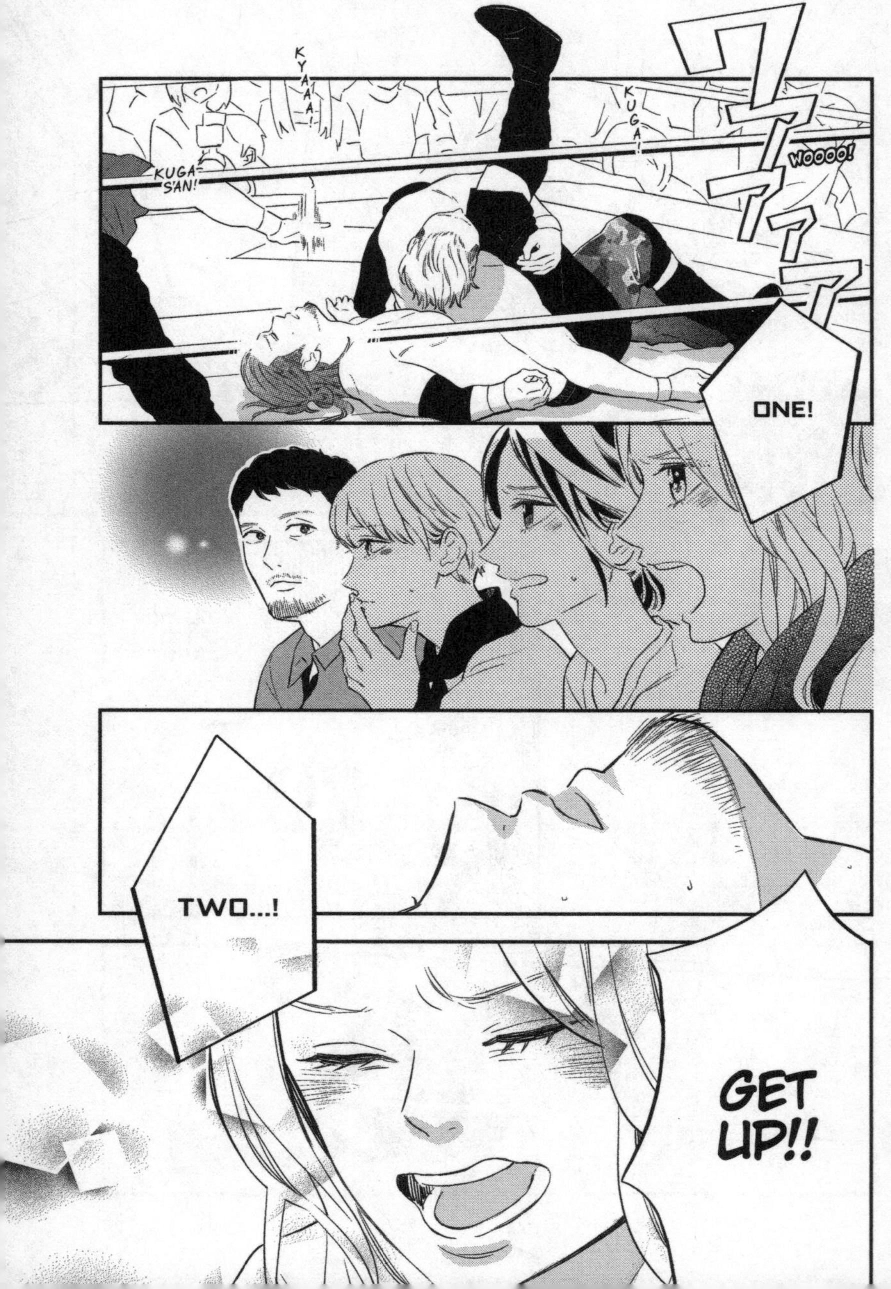

ワアアアア
WOOOO!
KUGA!
KYAAAA!
KUGA-SAN!
ONE!
TWO...!
GET UP!!

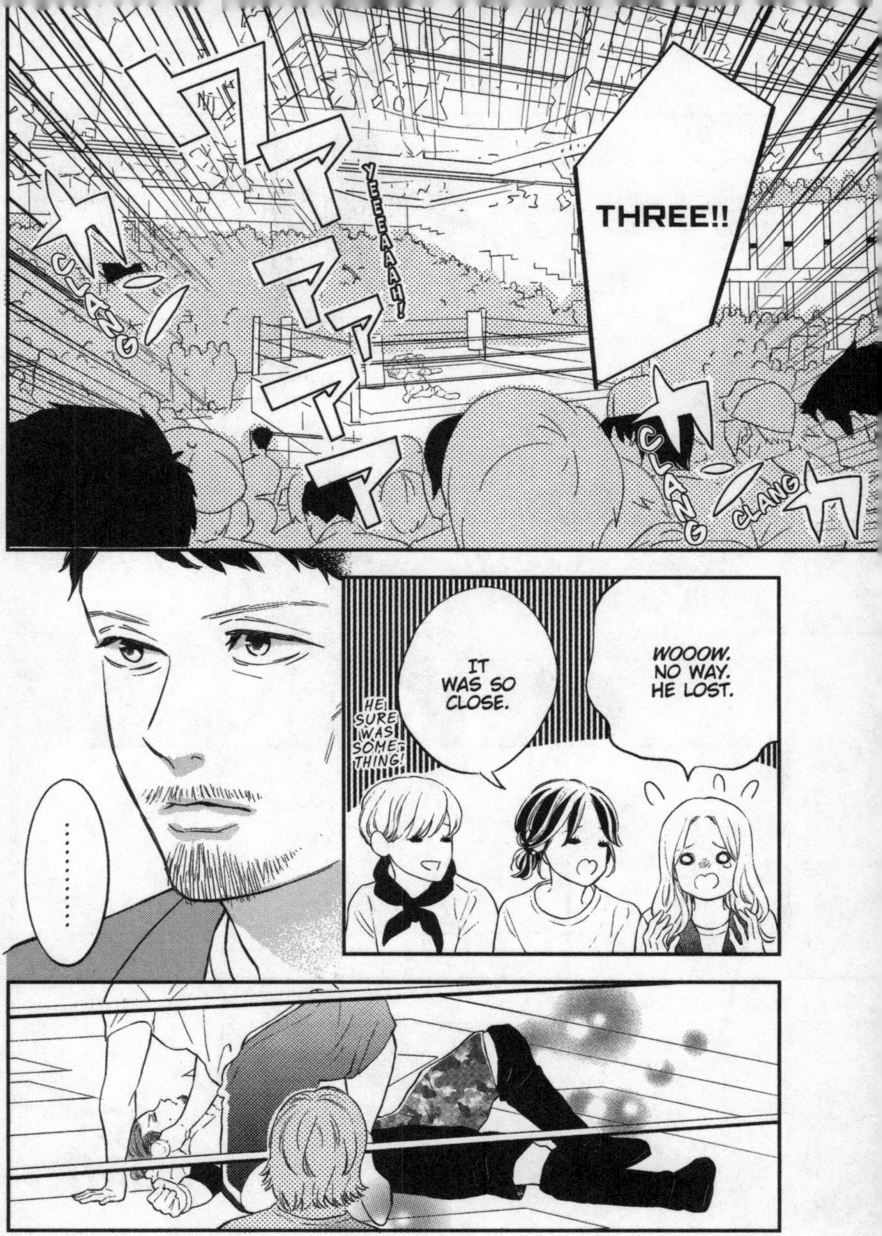
THREE!!
YEEEAAAAH!
CLANG
CLANG
CLANG
WOOOW. NO WAY. HE LOST.
IT WAS SO CLOSE.
HE SURE WAS SOME-THING!
....

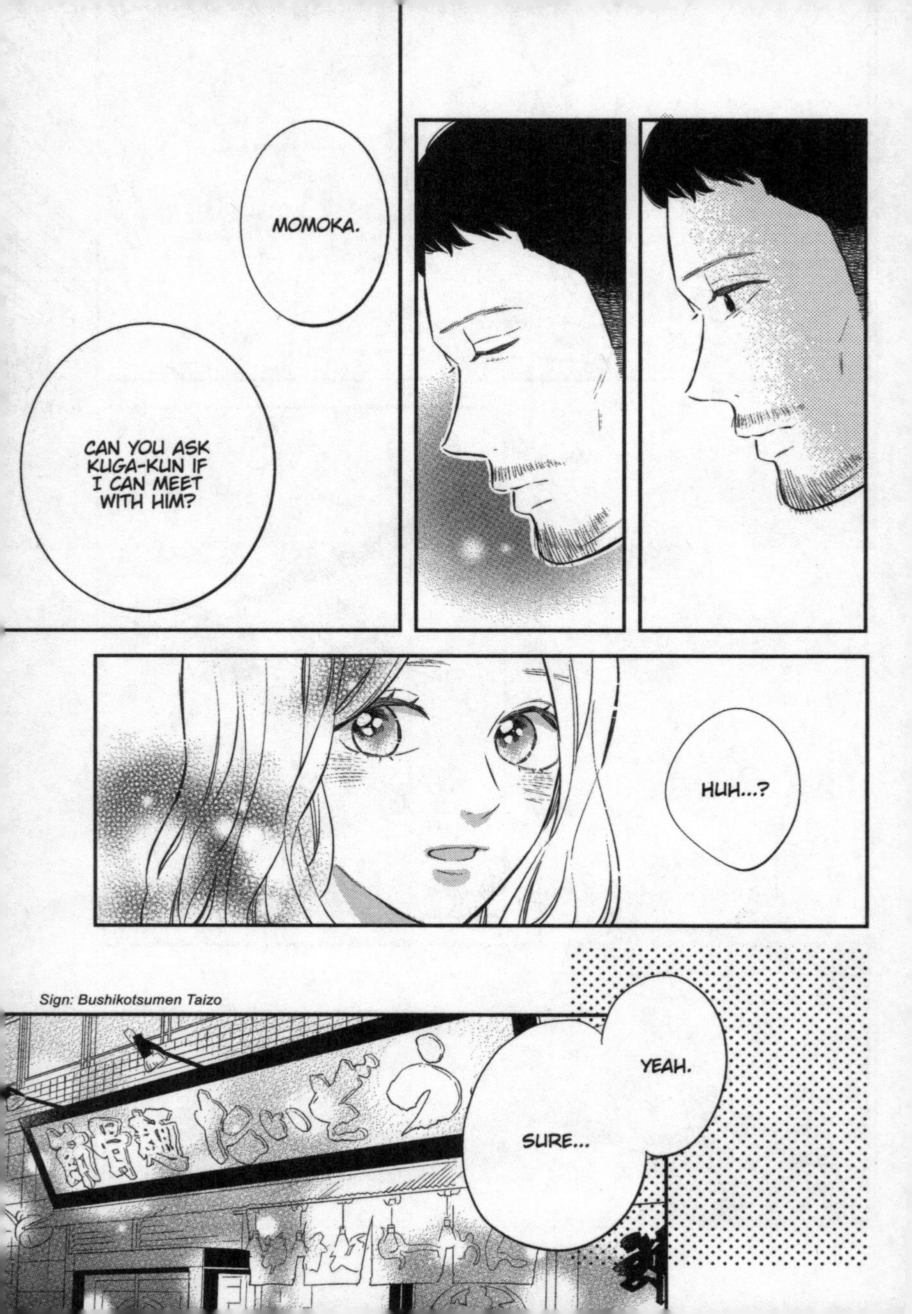
MOMOKA.
CAN YOU ASK KUGA-KUN IF I CAN MEET WITH HIM?
HUH...?
Sign: Bushikotsumen Taizo
YEAH.
SURE...

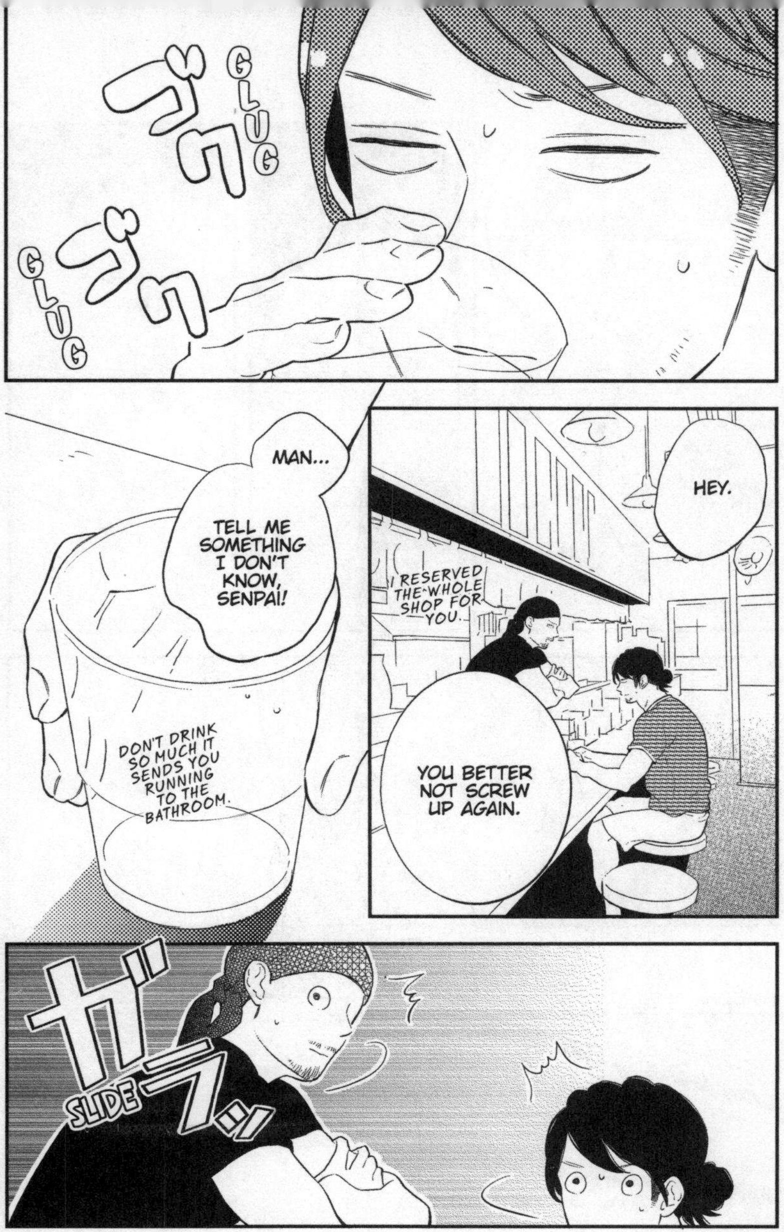
GLUG
GLUG
HEY.
I RESERVED THE WHOLE SHOP FOR YOU.
YOU BETTER NOT SCREW UP AGAIN.
MAN...
TELL ME SOMETHING I DON'T KNOW, SENPAI!
DON'T DRINK SO MUCH IT SENDS YOU RUNNING TO THE BATHROOM.
SLIDE

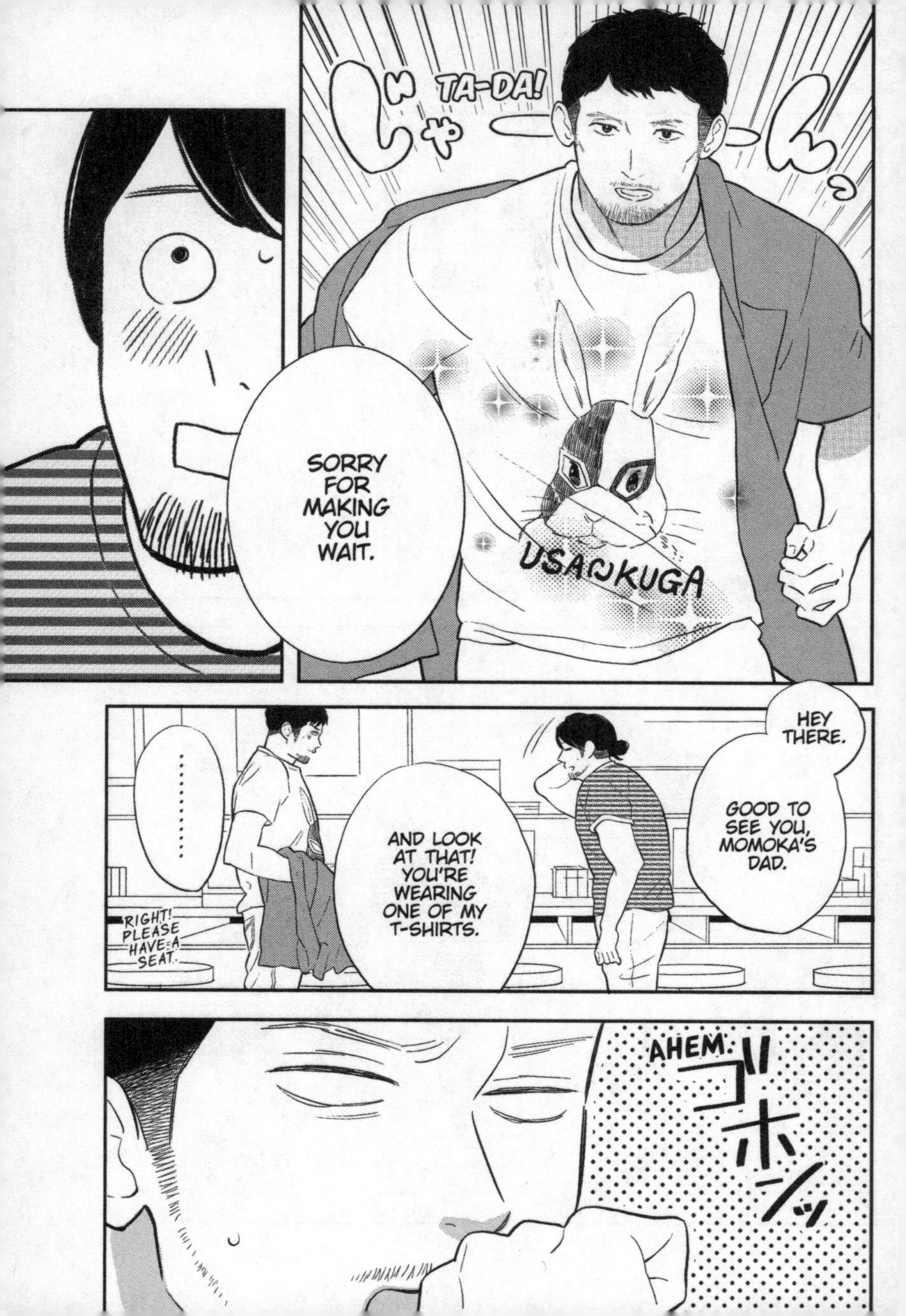
TA-DA!
じゃーんっ
SORRY FOR MAKING YOU WAIT.
HEY THERE.
GOOD TO SEE YOU, MOMOKA'S DAD.
AND LOOK AT THAT! YOU'RE WEARING ONE OF MY T-SHIRTS.
......
RIGHT! PLEASE HAVE A SEAT.
AHEM.
ゴホンッ

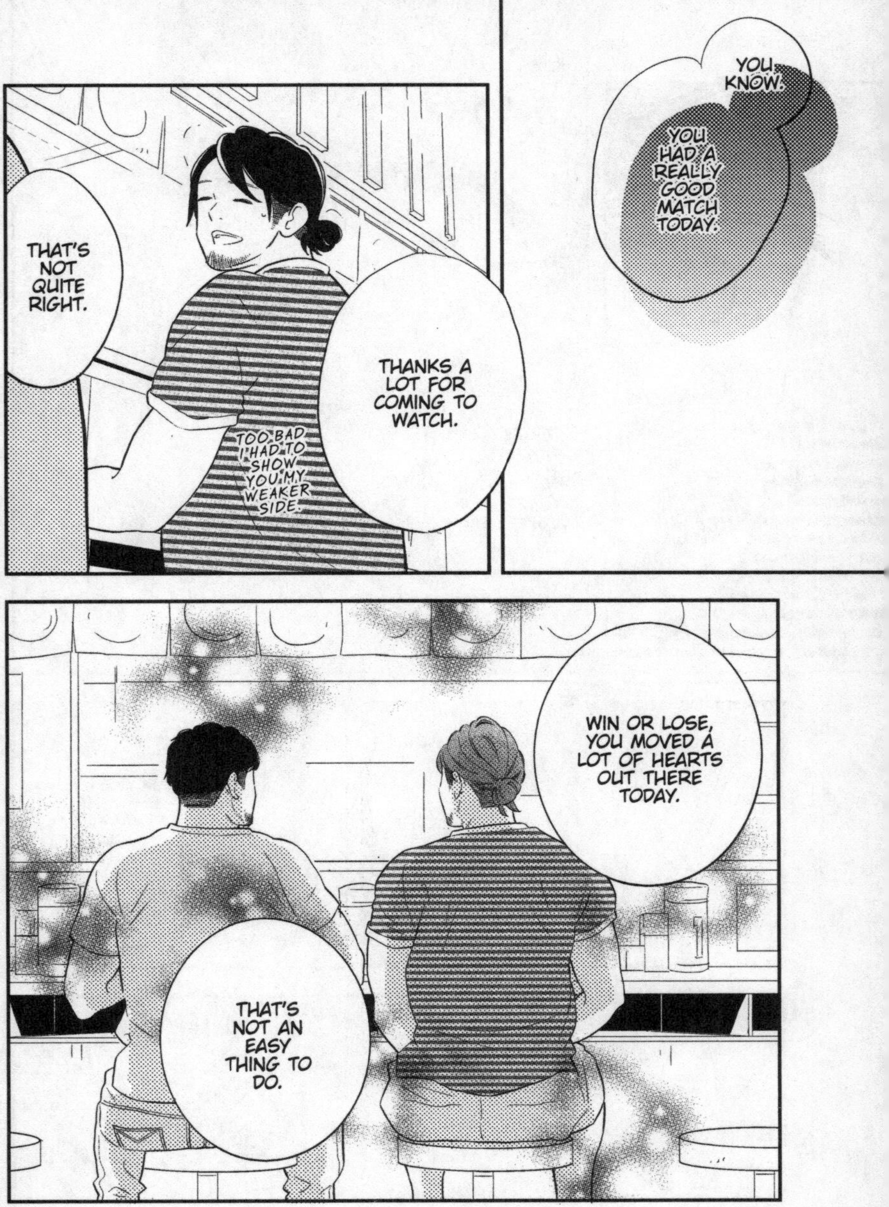
YOU KNOW.
YOU HAD A REALLY GOOD MATCH TODAY.
THANKS A LOT FOR COMING TO WATCH.
TOO BAD I HAD TO SHOW YOU MY WEAKER SIDE.
THAT'S NOT QUITE RIGHT.
WIN OR LOSE, YOU MOVED A LOT OF HEARTS OUT THERE TODAY.
THAT'S NOT AN EASY THING TO DO.

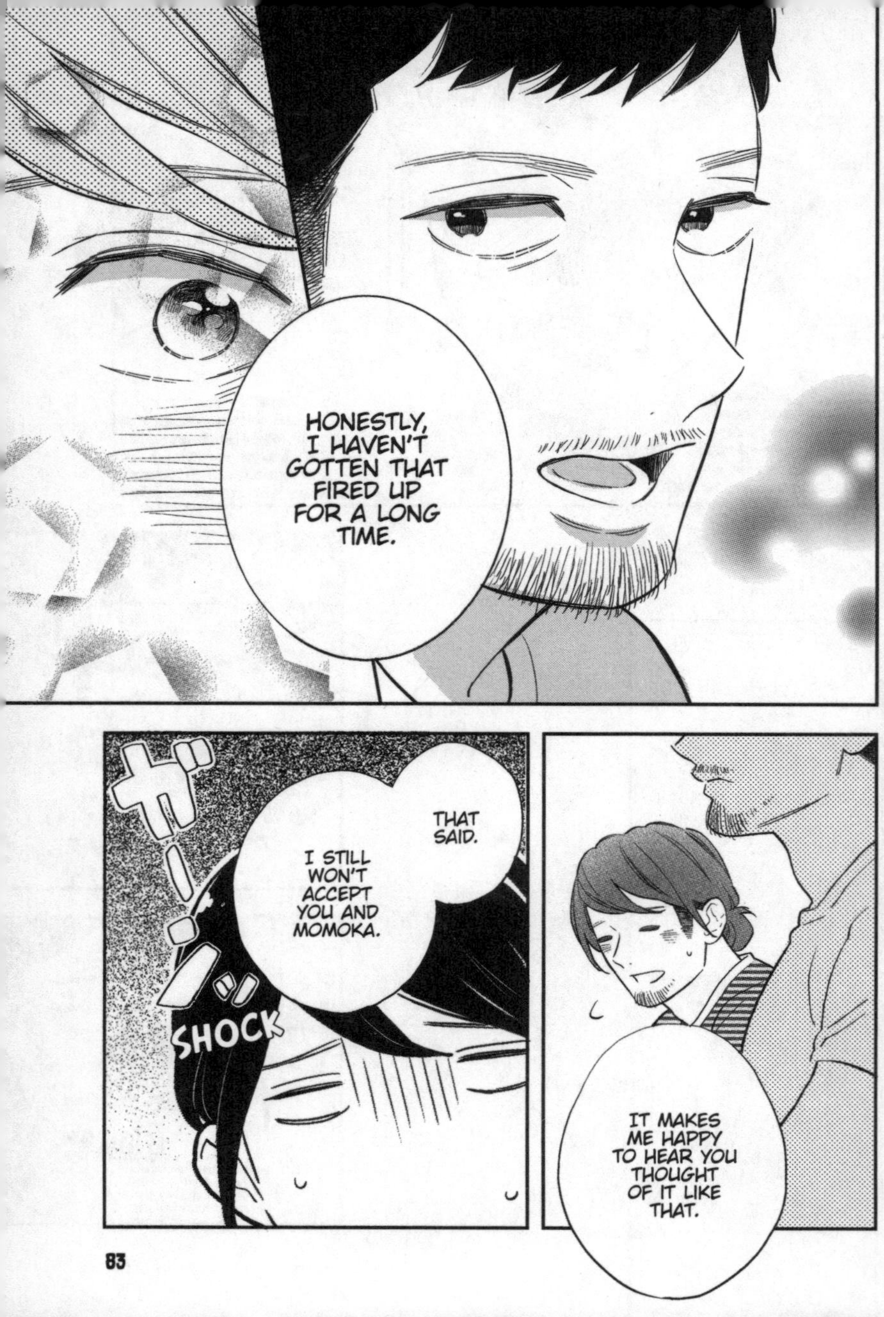
HONESTLY, I HAVEN'T GOTTEN THAT FIRED UP FOR A LONG TIME.
IT MAKES ME HAPPY TO HEAR YOU THOUGHT OF IT LIKE THAT.
THAT SAID.
I STILL WON'T ACCEPT YOU AND MOMOKA.
SHOCK

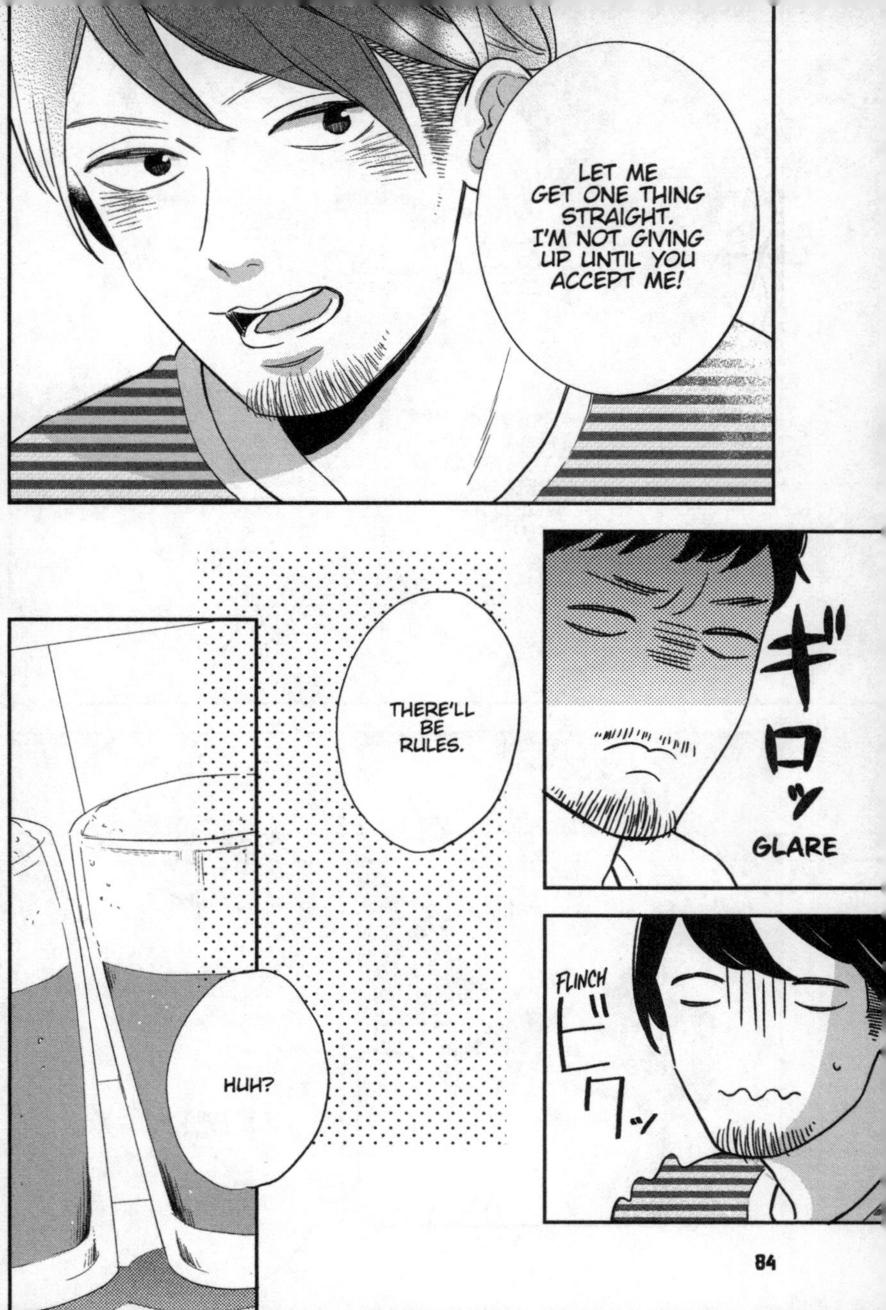
LET ME GET ONE THING STRAIGHT. I'M NOT GIVING UP UNTIL YOU ACCEPT ME!
ギロッ
GLARE
THERE'LL BE RULES.
FLINCH
ビクッ
HUH?

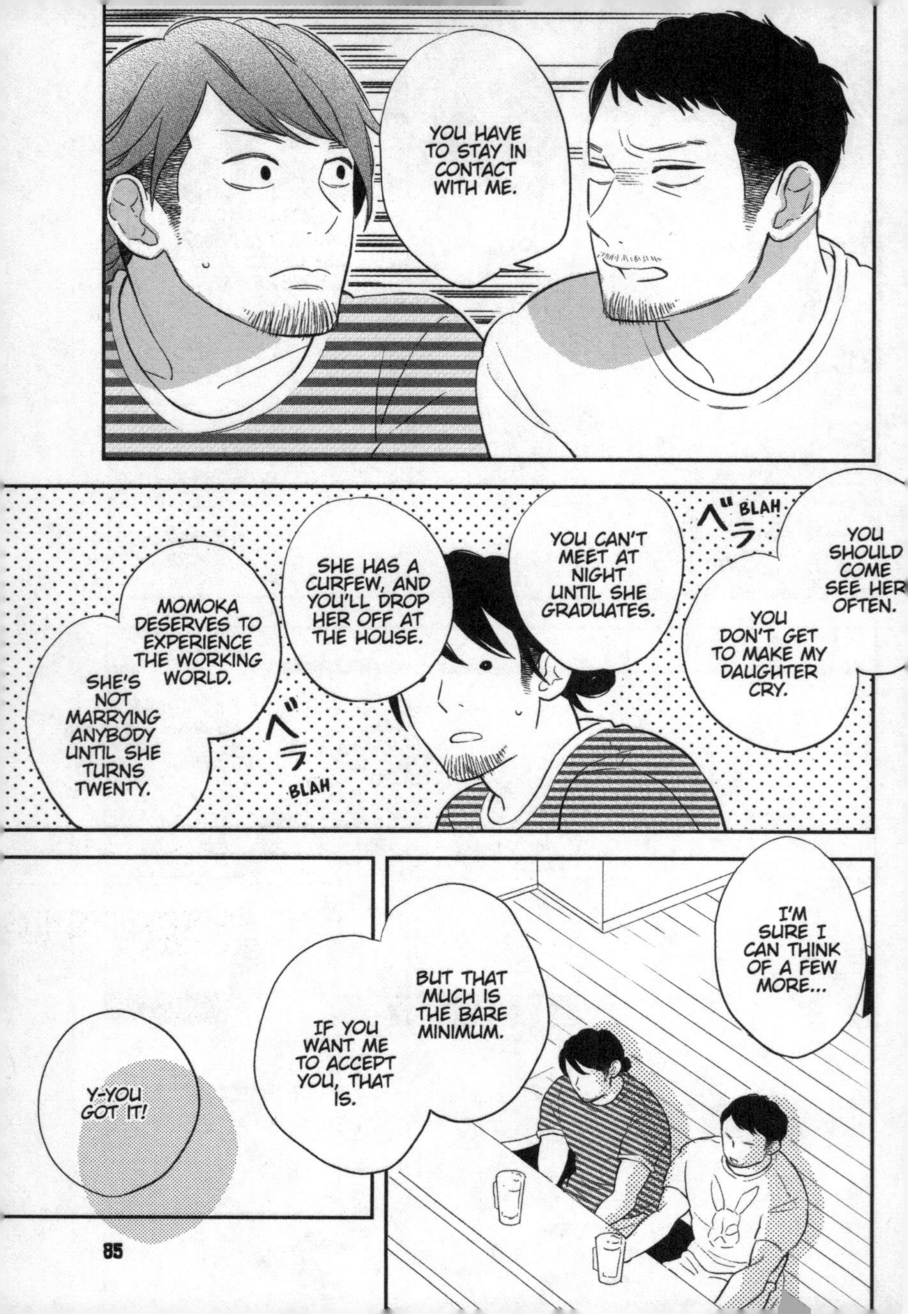
YOU HAVE TO STAY IN CONTACT WITH ME.
YOU SHOULD COME SEE HER OFTEN.
YOU DON'T GET TO MAKE MY DAUGHTER CRY.
ベラ BLAH
YOU CAN'T MEET AT NIGHT UNTIL SHE GRADUATES.
SHE HAS A CURFEW, AND YOU'LL DROP HER OFF AT THE HOUSE.
MOMOKA DESERVES TO EXPERIENCE THE WORKING WORLD.
SHE'S NOT MARRYING ANYBODY UNTIL SHE TURNS TWENTY.
ベラ BLAH
I'M SURE I CAN THINK OF A FEW MORE...
BUT THAT MUCH IS THE BARE MINIMUM.
IF YOU WANT ME TO ACCEPT YOU, THAT IS.
Y-YOU GOT IT!

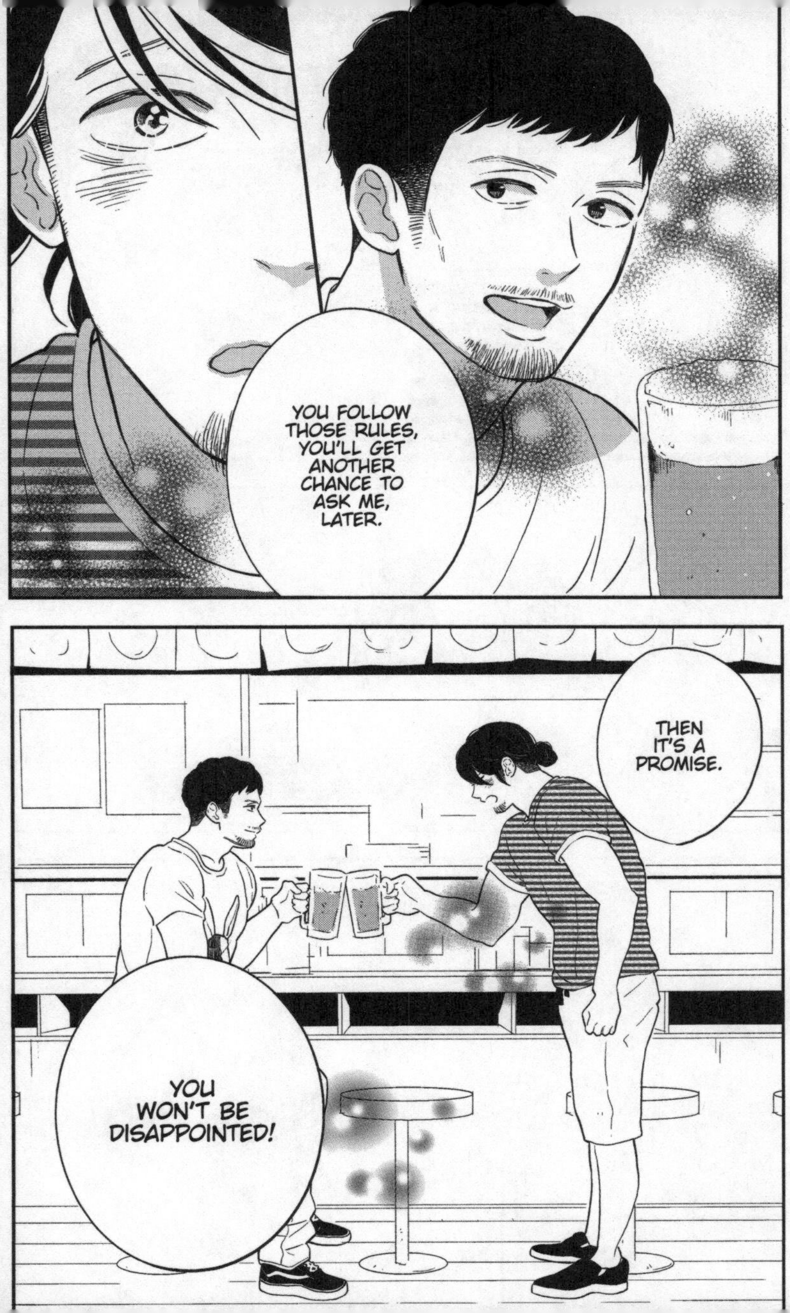
YOU FOLLOW THOSE RULES, YOU'LL GET ANOTHER CHANCE TO ASK ME, LATER.
THEN IT'S A PROMISE.
YOU WON'T BE DISAPPOINTED!

Cutie and the BEAST

Cutie and the BEAST

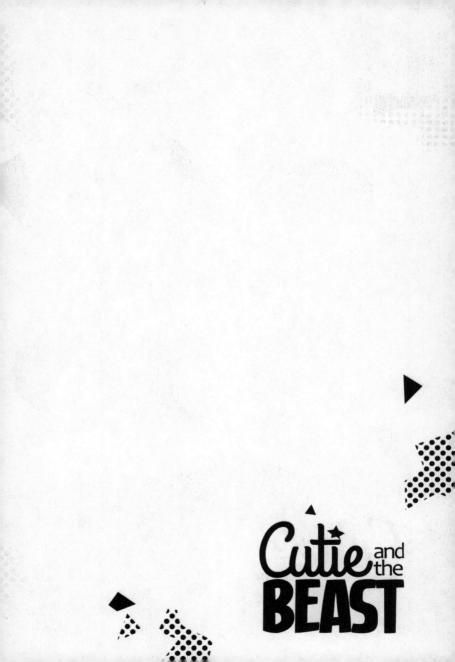

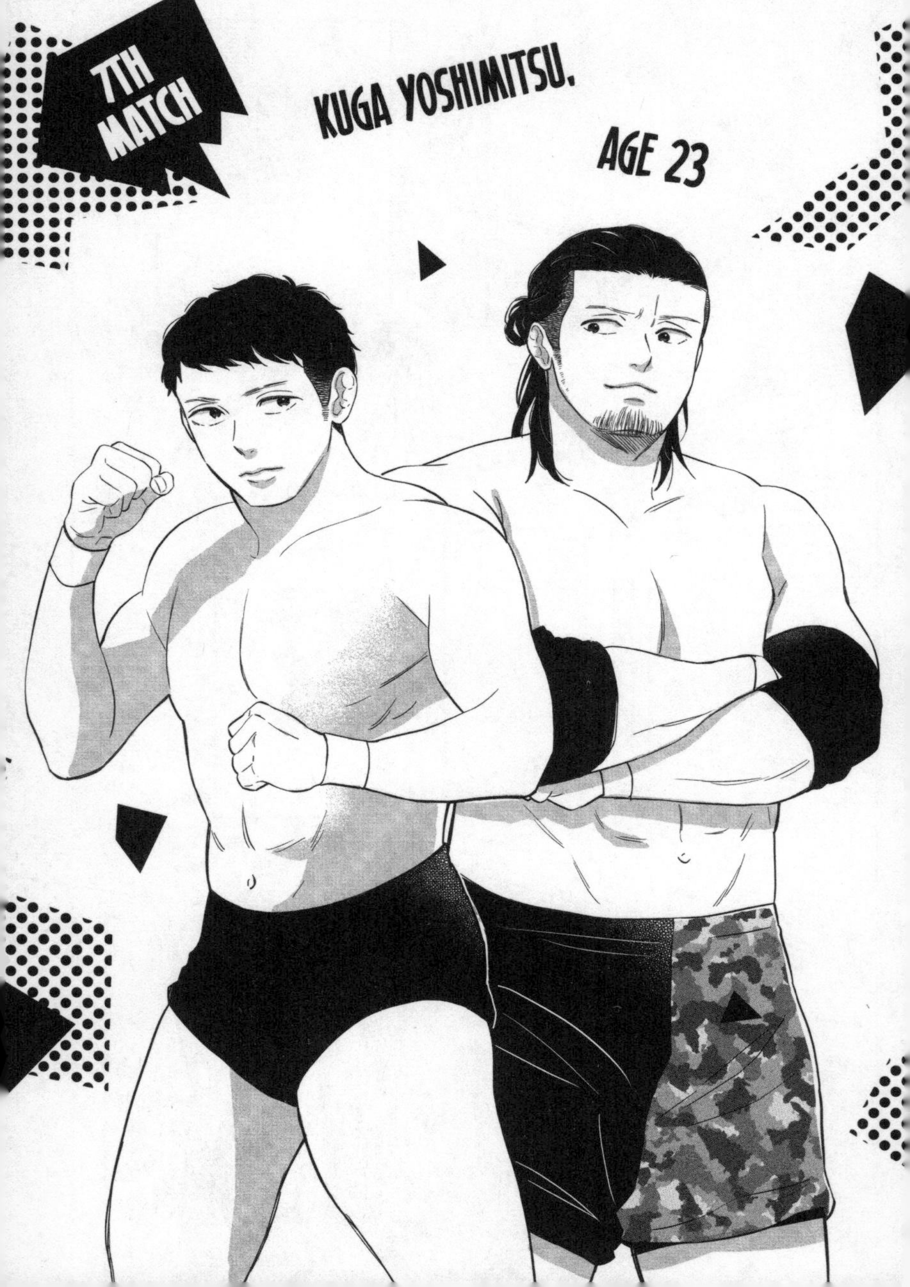
7TH MATCH
KUGA YOSHIMITSU.
AGE 23

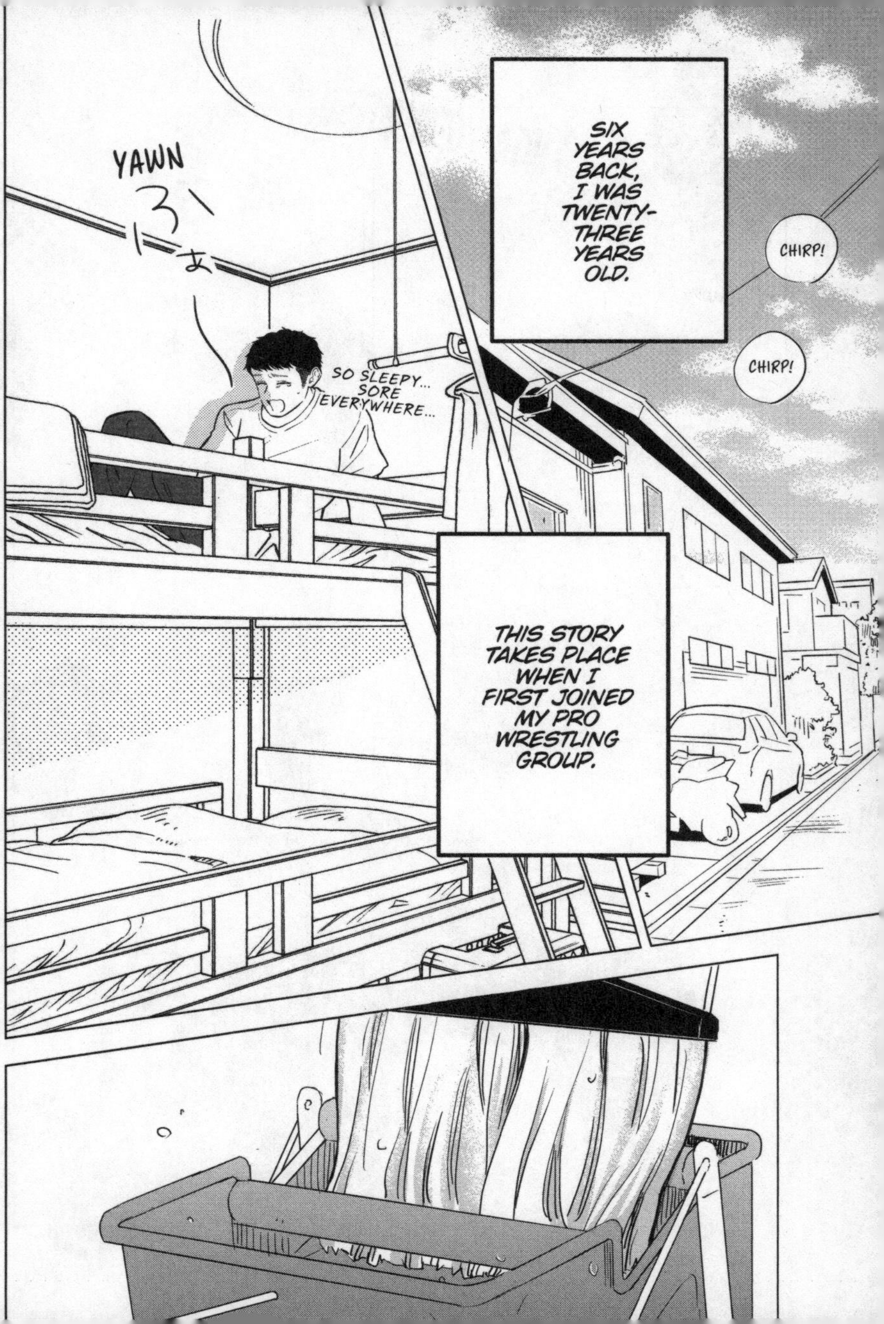
SIX YEARS BACK, I WAS TWENTY-THREE YEARS OLD.
CHIRP!
CHIRP!
YAWN
ふぁ
SO SLEEPY... SORE EVERYWHERE...
THIS STORY TAKES PLACE WHEN I FIRST JOINED MY PRO WRESTLING GROUP.

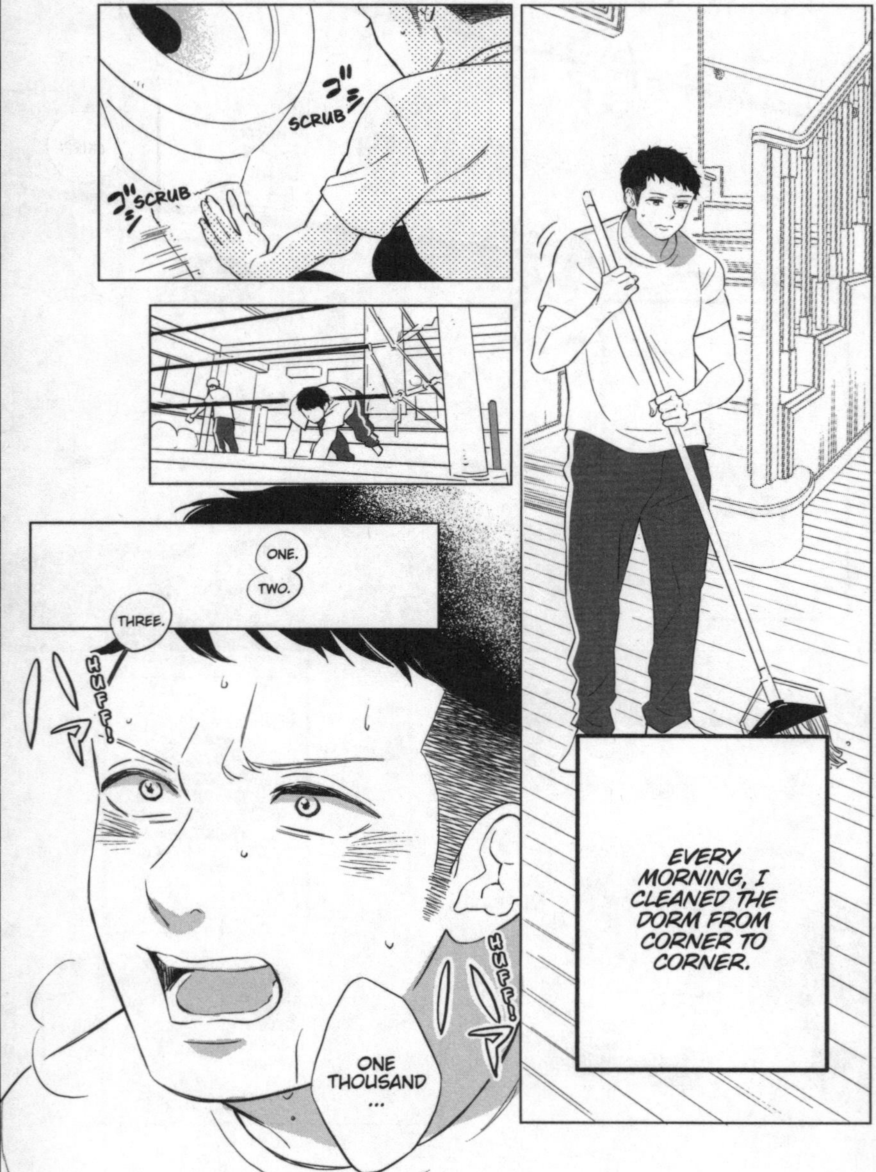
EVERY MORNING, I CLEANED THE DORM FROM CORNER TO CORNER.
SCRUB
SCRUB...
ONE.
TWO.
THREE.
HUFF!
HUFF!
ONE THOUSAND ...

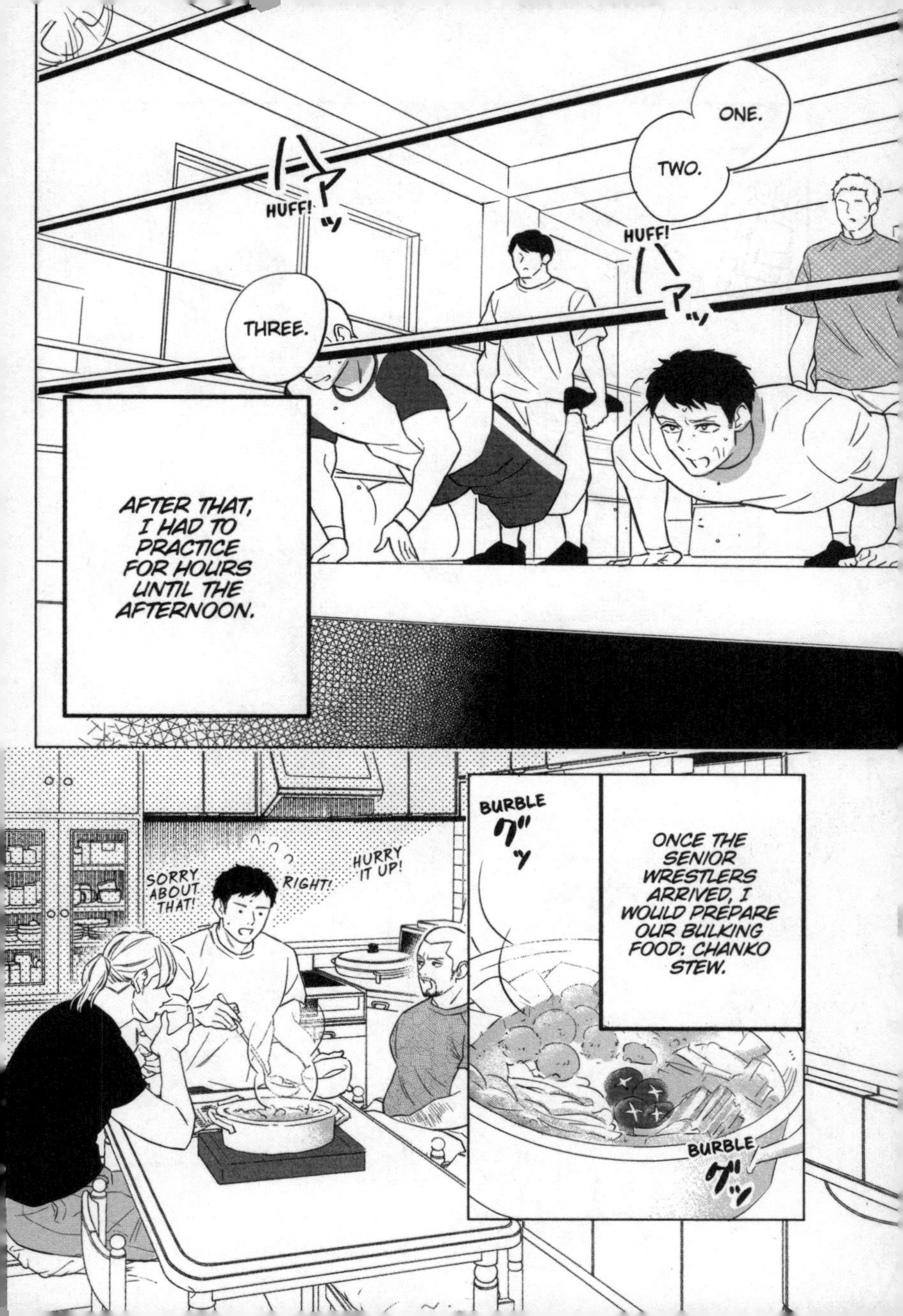
ONE.
TWO.
HUFF!
HUFF!
THREE.
AFTER THAT, I HAD TO PRACTICE FOR HOURS UNTIL THE AFTERNOON.
BURBLE
ONCE THE SENIOR WRESTLERS ARRIVED, I WOULD PREPARE OUR BULKING FOOD: CHANKO STEW.
BURBLE
HURRY IT UP!
RIGHT!
SORRY ABOUT THAT!

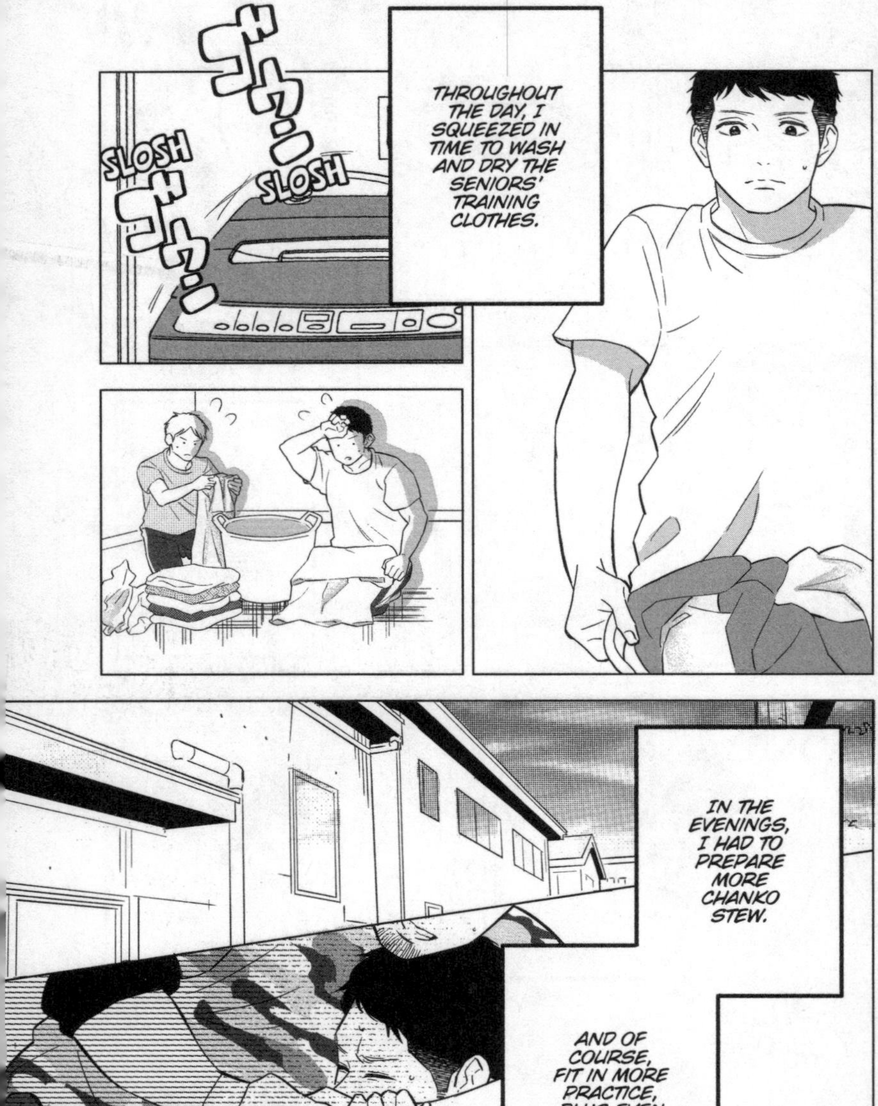
THROUGHOUT THE DAY, I SQUEEZED IN TIME TO WASH AND DRY THE SENIORS' TRAINING CLOTHES.
SLOSH
SLOSH
IN THE EVENINGS, I HAD TO PREPARE MORE CHANKO STEW.
AND OF COURSE, FIT IN MORE PRACTICE, PLUS EVEN MORE LAUNDRY.

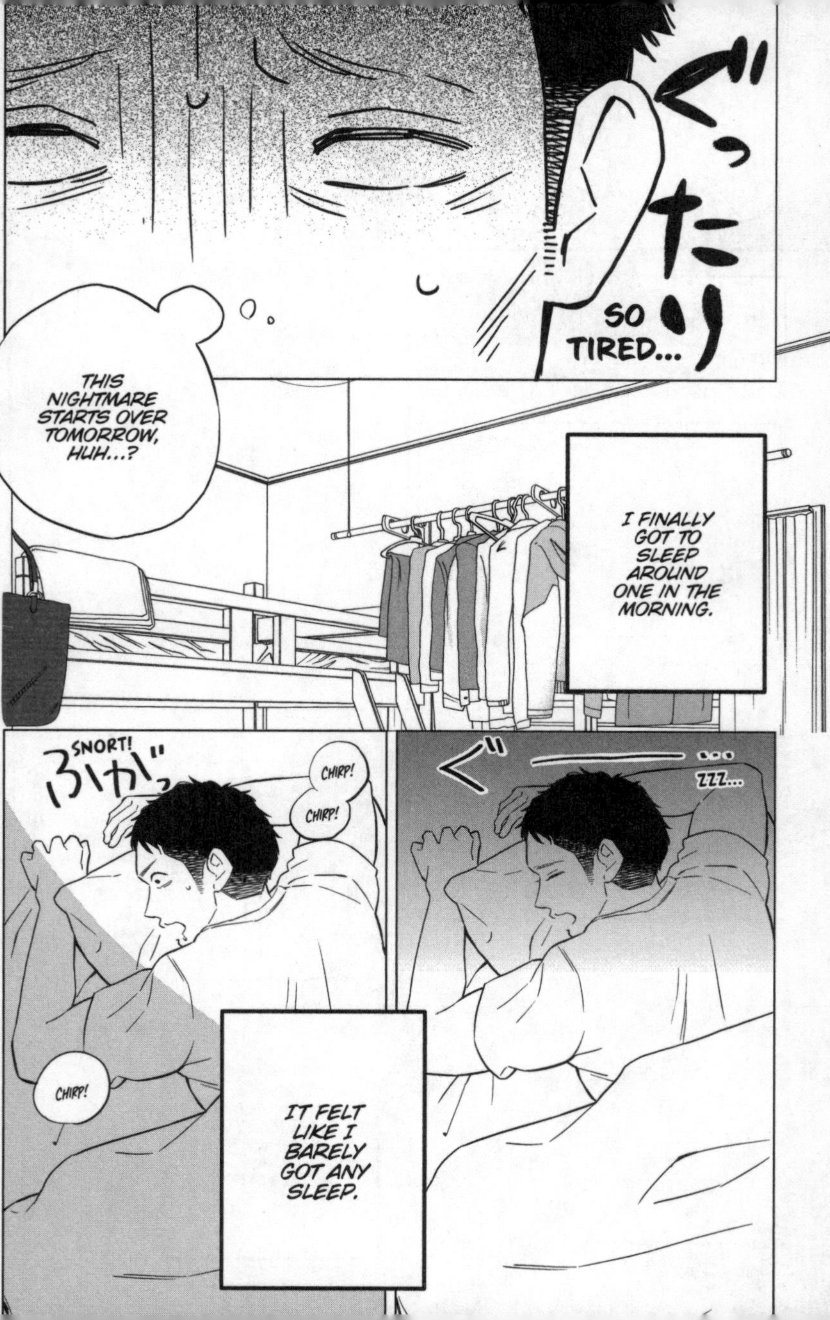
ぐったり
SO TIRED...
THIS NIGHTMARE STARTS OVER TOMORROW, HUH...?
I FINALLY GOT TO SLEEP AROUND ONE IN THE MORNING.
ぐー...
ZZZ...
ふがっ
SNORT!
CHIRP!
CHIRP!
CHIRP!
IT FELT LIKE I BARELY GOT ANY SLEEP.

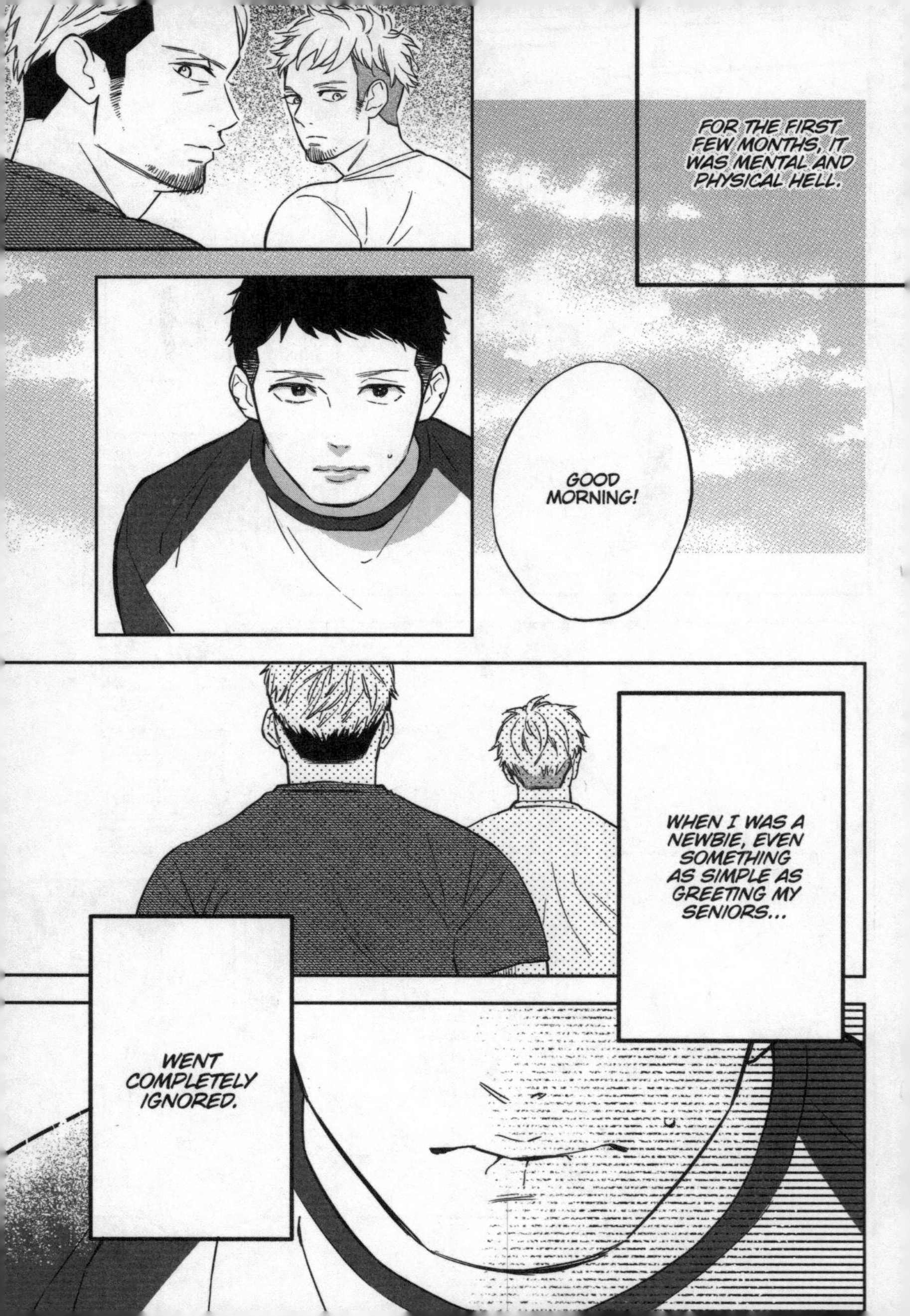
FOR THE FIRST FEW MONTHS, IT WAS MENTAL AND PHYSICAL HELL.
GOOD MORNING!
WHEN I WAS A NEWBIE, EVEN SOMETHING AS SIMPLE AS GREETING MY SENIORS...
WENT COMPLETELY IGNORED.

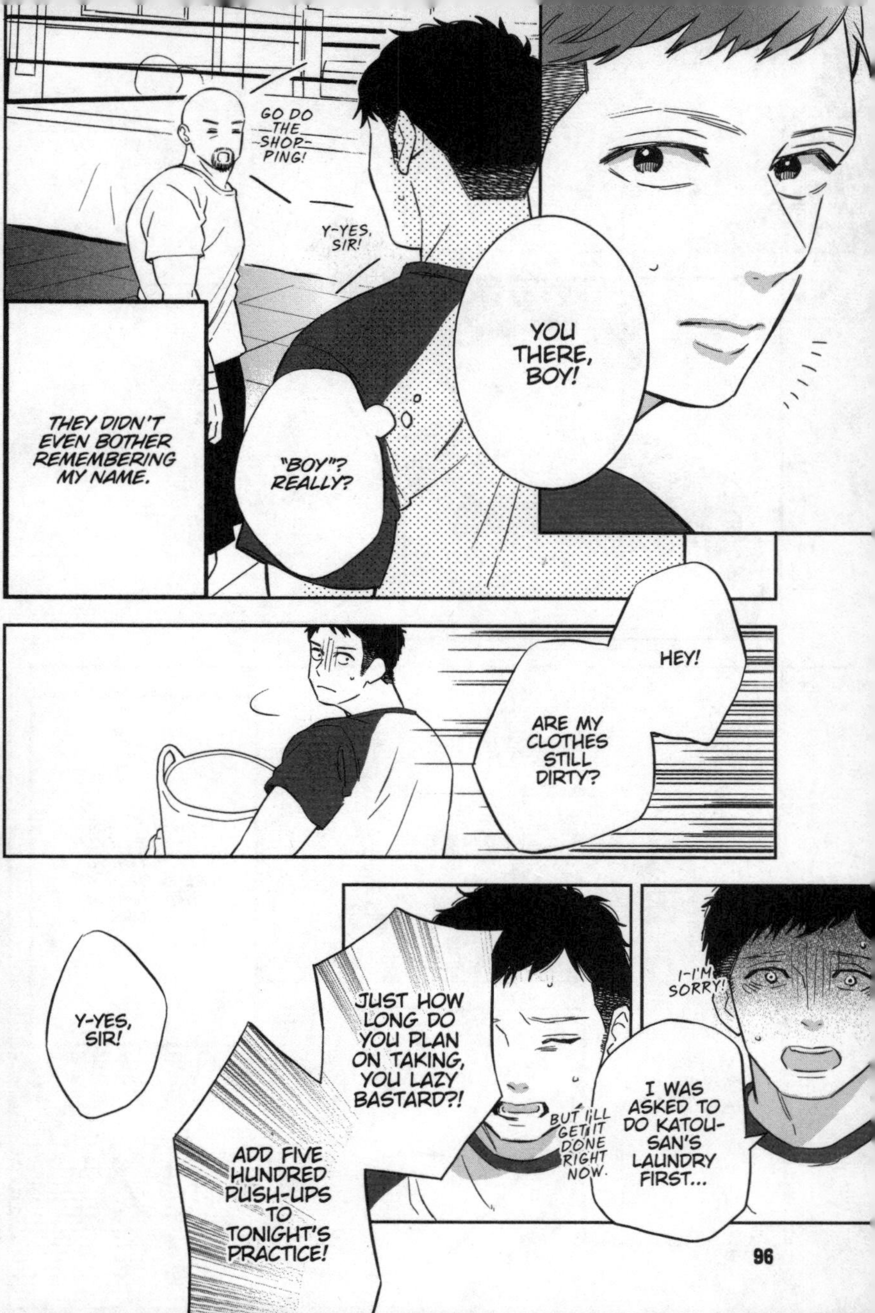
YOU THERE, BOY!
GO DO THE SHOPPING!
Y-YES, SIR!
"BOY"? REALLY?
THEY DIDN'T EVEN BOTHER REMEMBERING MY NAME.
HEY!
ARE MY CLOTHES STILL DIRTY?
I-I'M SORRY!
I WAS ASKED TO DO KATOU-SAN'S LAUNDRY FIRST...
BUT I'LL GET IT DONE RIGHT NOW.
JUST HOW LONG DO YOU PLAN ON TAKING, YOU LAZY BASTARD?!
ADD FIVE HUNDRED PUSH-UPS TO TONIGHT'S PRACTICE!
Y-YES, SIR!

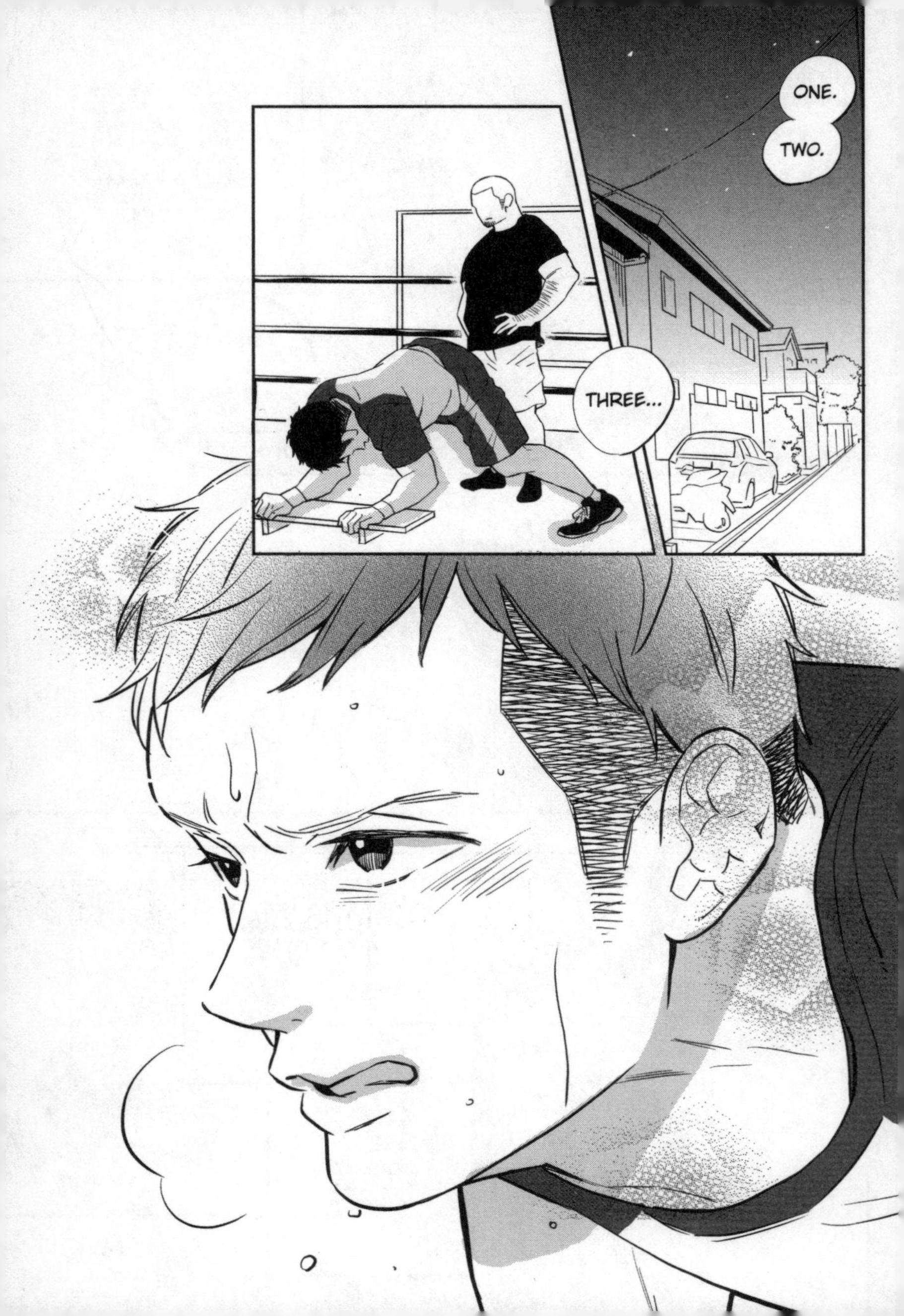
ONE.
TWO.
THREE...

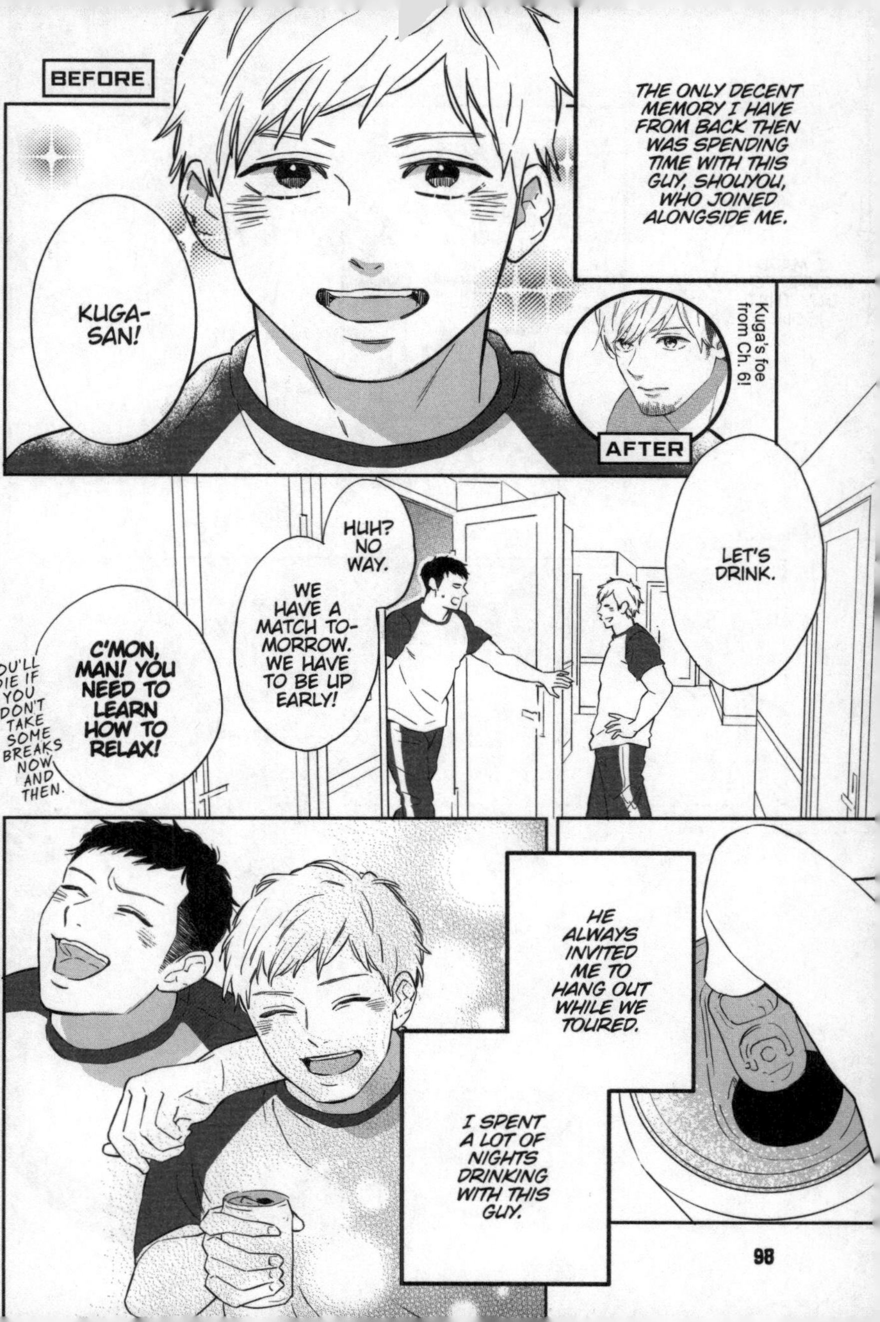
THE ONLY DECENT MEMORY I HAVE FROM BACK THEN WAS SPENDING TIME WITH THIS GUY, SHOUYOU, WHO JOINED ALONGSIDE ME.
BEFORE
KUGA-SAN!
AFTER
Kuga's foe from Ch. 6!
LET'S DRINK.
HUH? NO WAY.
WE HAVE A MATCH TO-MORROW. WE HAVE TO BE UP EARLY!
C'MON, MAN! YOU NEED TO LEARN HOW TO RELAX!
YOU'LL DIE IF YOU DON'T TAKE SOME BREAKS NOW AND THEN.
HE ALWAYS INVITED ME TO HANG OUT WHILE WE TOURED.
I SPENT A LOT OF NIGHTS DRINKING WITH THIS GUY.

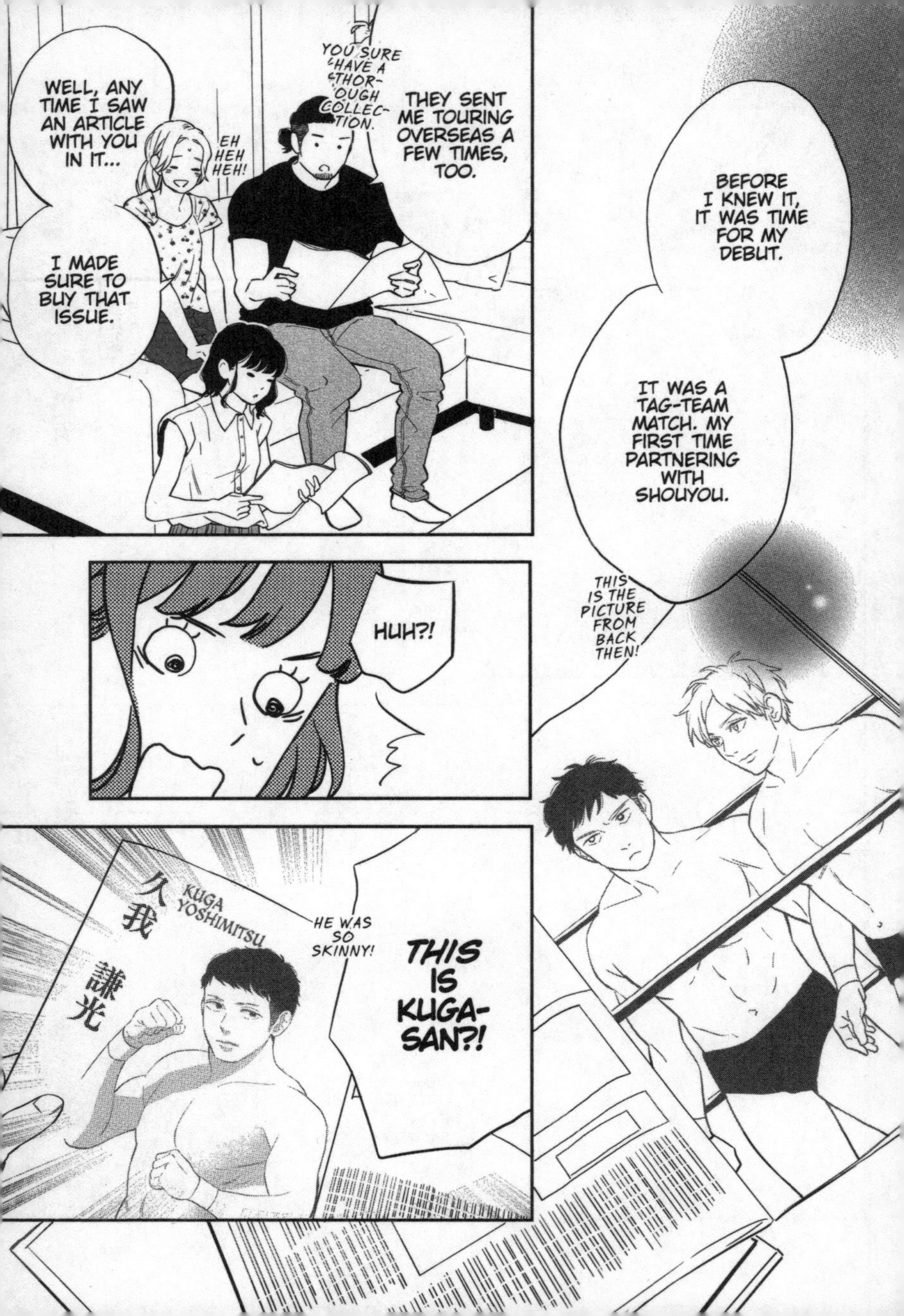
BEFORE I KNEW IT, IT WAS TIME FOR MY DEBUT.
IT WAS A TAG-TEAM MATCH. MY FIRST TIME PARTNERING WITH SHOUYOU.
THIS IS THE PICTURE FROM BACK THEN!
YOU SURE HAVE A THOR-OUGH COLLEC-TION.
THEY SENT ME TOURING OVERSEAS A FEW TIMES, TOO.
EH HEH HEH!
WELL, ANY TIME I SAW AN ARTICLE WITH YOU IN IT...
I MADE SURE TO BUY THAT ISSUE.
HUH?!
THIS IS KUGA-SAN?!
HE WAS SO SKINNY!
KUGA YOSHIMITSU
久我 謙光

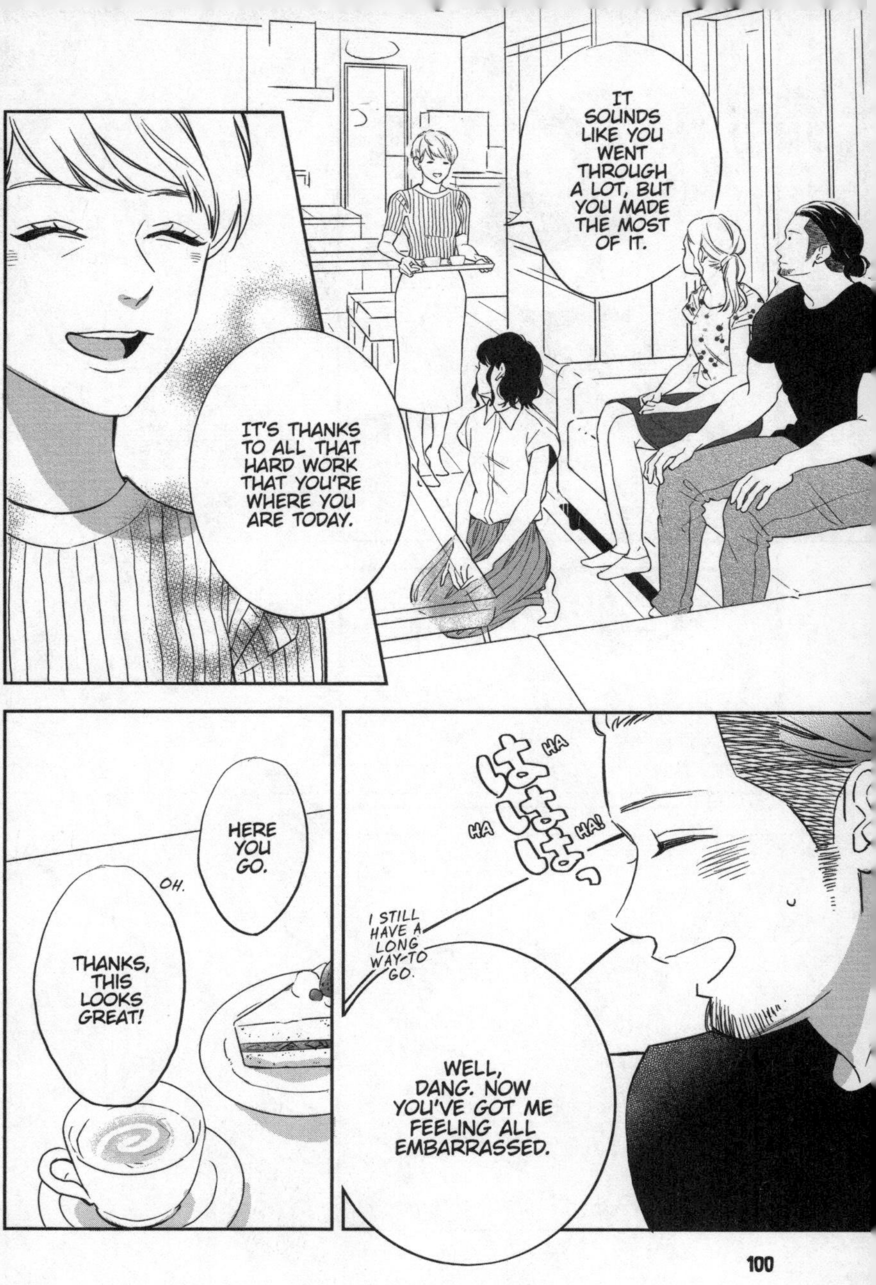
IT SOUNDS LIKE YOU WENT THROUGH A LOT, BUT YOU MADE THE MOST OF IT.
IT'S THANKS TO ALL THAT HARD WORK THAT YOU'RE WHERE YOU ARE TODAY.
はははっ
HA HA HA!
I STILL HAVE A LONG WAY TO GO.
WELL, DANG. NOW YOU'VE GOT ME FEELING ALL EMBARRASSED.
HERE YOU GO.
OH.
THANKS, THIS LOOKS GREAT!

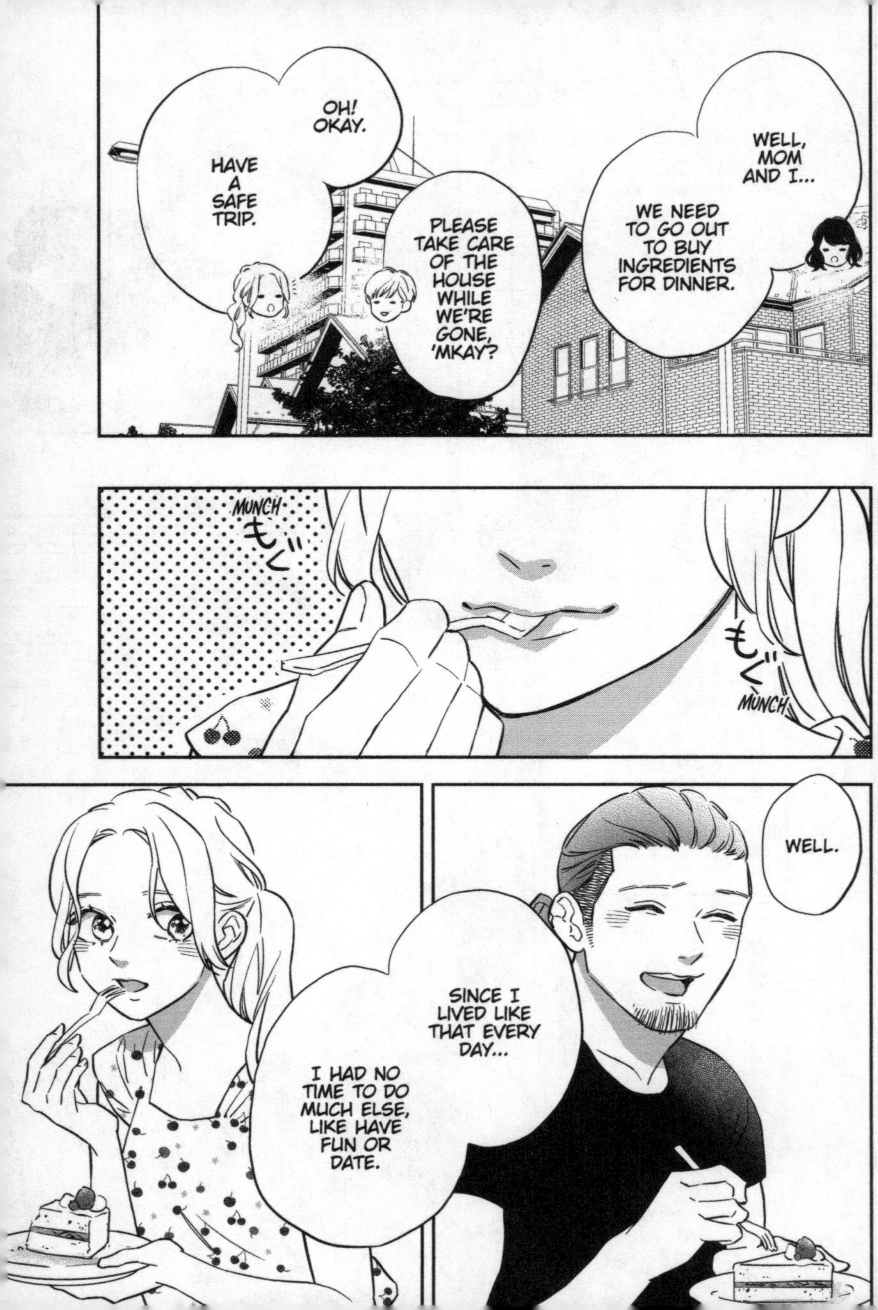
WELL, MOM AND I...
WE NEED TO GO OUT TO BUY INGREDIENTS FOR DINNER.
PLEASE TAKE CARE OF THE HOUSE WHILE WE'RE GONE, 'MKAY?
OH! OKAY.
HAVE A SAFE TRIP.
もぐ
MUNCH
MUNCH
もぐ
WELL.
SINCE I LIVED LIKE THAT EVERY DAY...
I HAD NO TIME TO DO MUCH ELSE, LIKE HAVE FUN OR DATE.

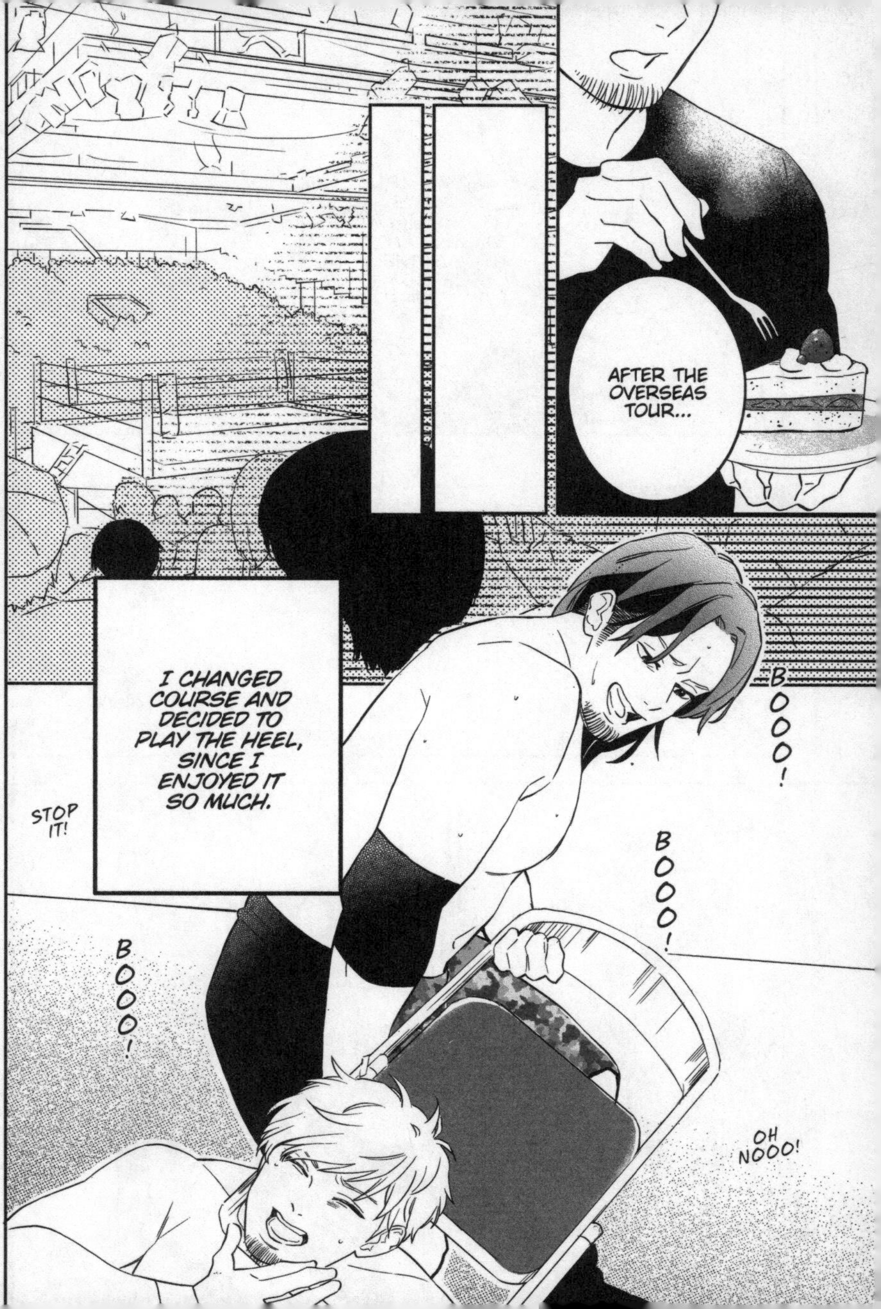
AFTER THE OVERSEAS TOUR...
BOOOO!
I CHANGED COURSE AND DECIDED TO PLAY THE HEEL, SINCE I ENJOYED IT SO MUCH.
STOP IT!
BOOOO!
BOOOO!
OH NOOO!

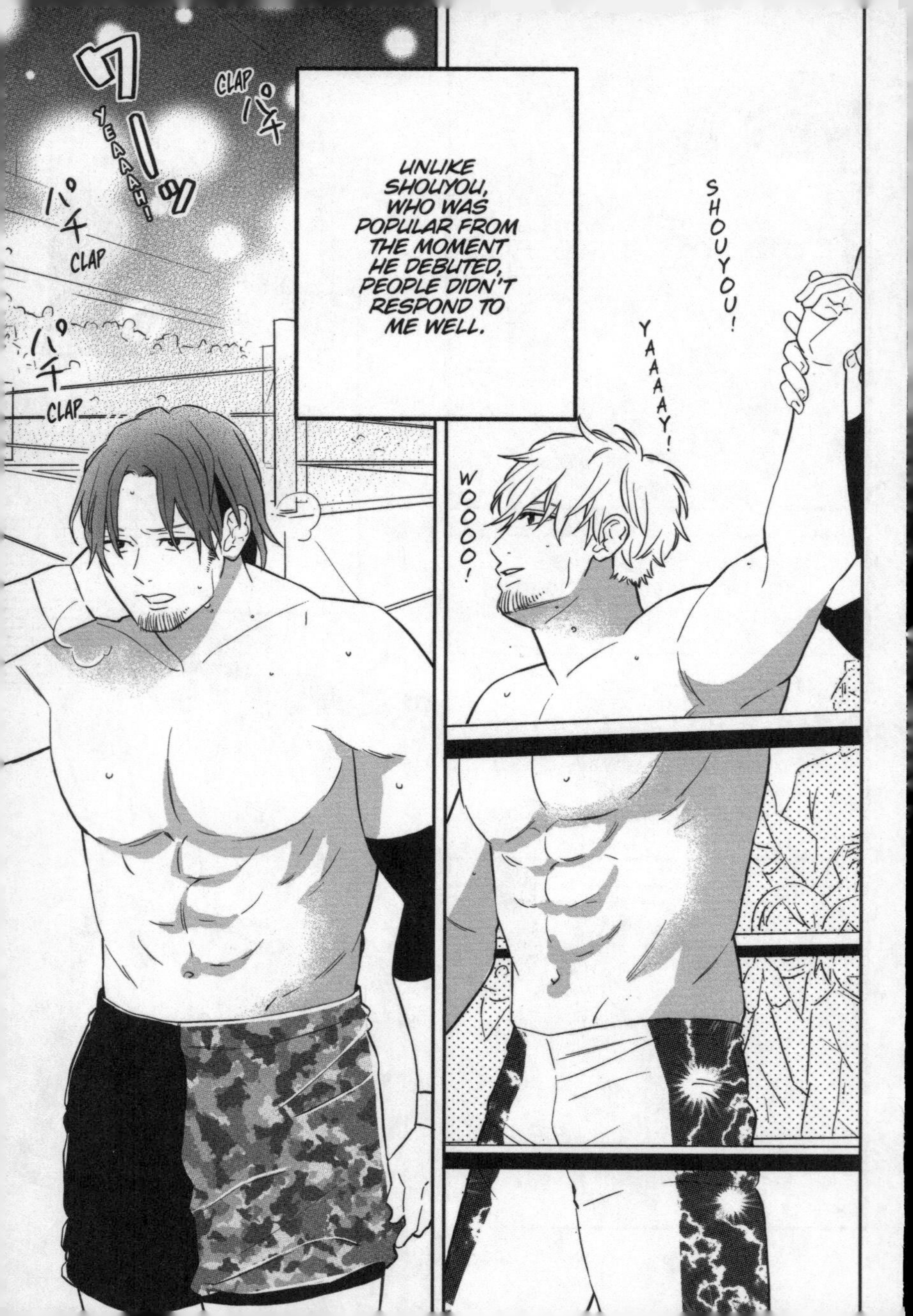
UNLIKE SHOUYOU, WHO WAS POPULAR FROM THE MOMENT HE DEBUTED, PEOPLE DIDN'T RESPOND TO ME WELL.
SHOUYOU!
YAAAAY!
WOOOOO!
ワーッ
YEAAAAH!
パチ
CLAP
パチ
CLAP
パチ
CLAP

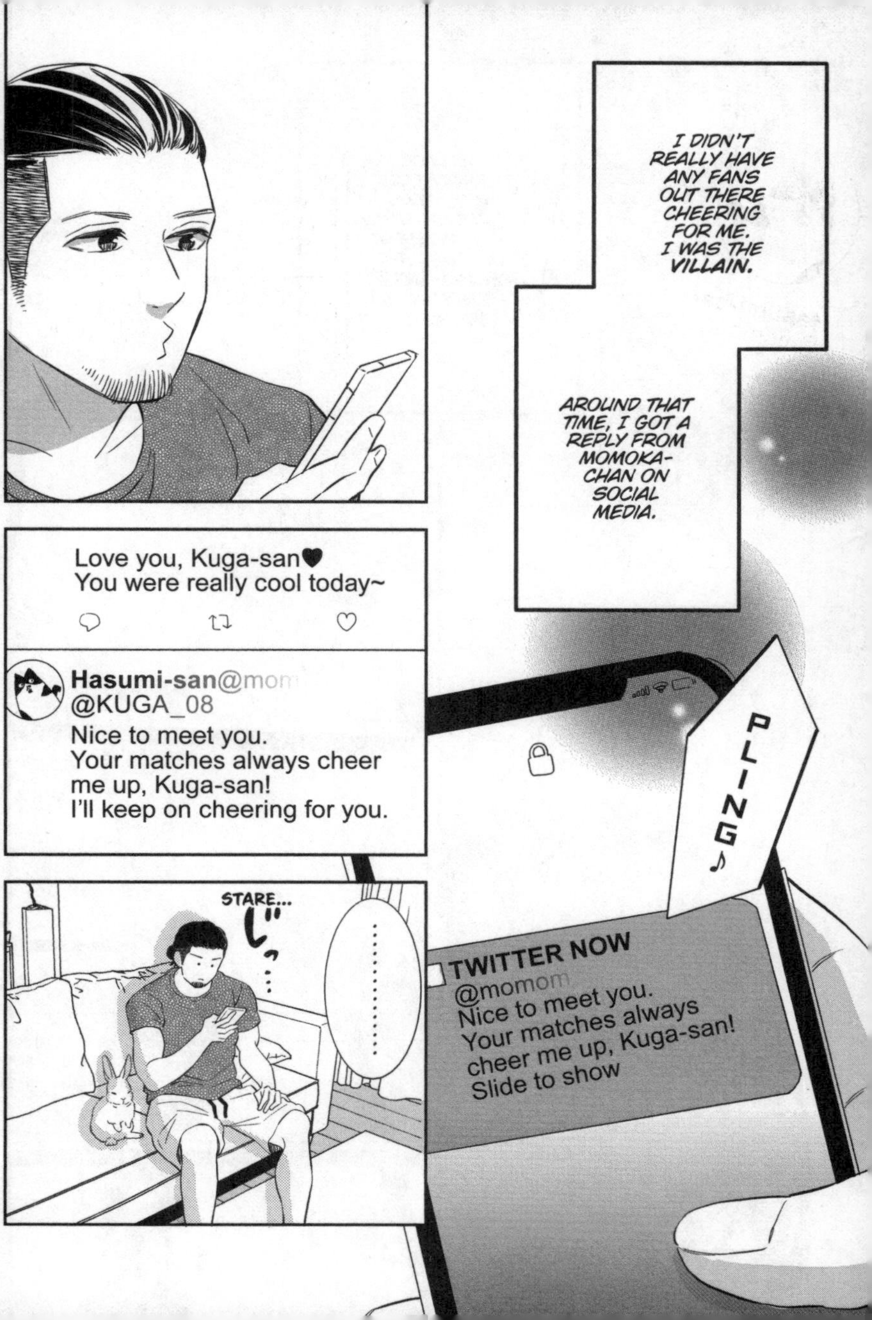
I DIDN'T REALLY HAVE ANY FANS OUT THERE CHEERING FOR ME. I WAS THE VILLAIN.
AROUND THAT TIME, I GOT A REPLY FROM MOMOKA-CHAN ON SOCIAL MEDIA.
PLING♪
TWITTER NOW
@momom
Nice to meet you.
Your matches always cheer me up, Kuga-san!
Slide to show
Love you, Kuga-san♥
You were really cool today~
Hasumi-san@mom
@KUGA_08
Nice to meet you.
Your matches always cheer me up, Kuga-san!
I'll keep on cheering for you.
STARE...
じっ...
......

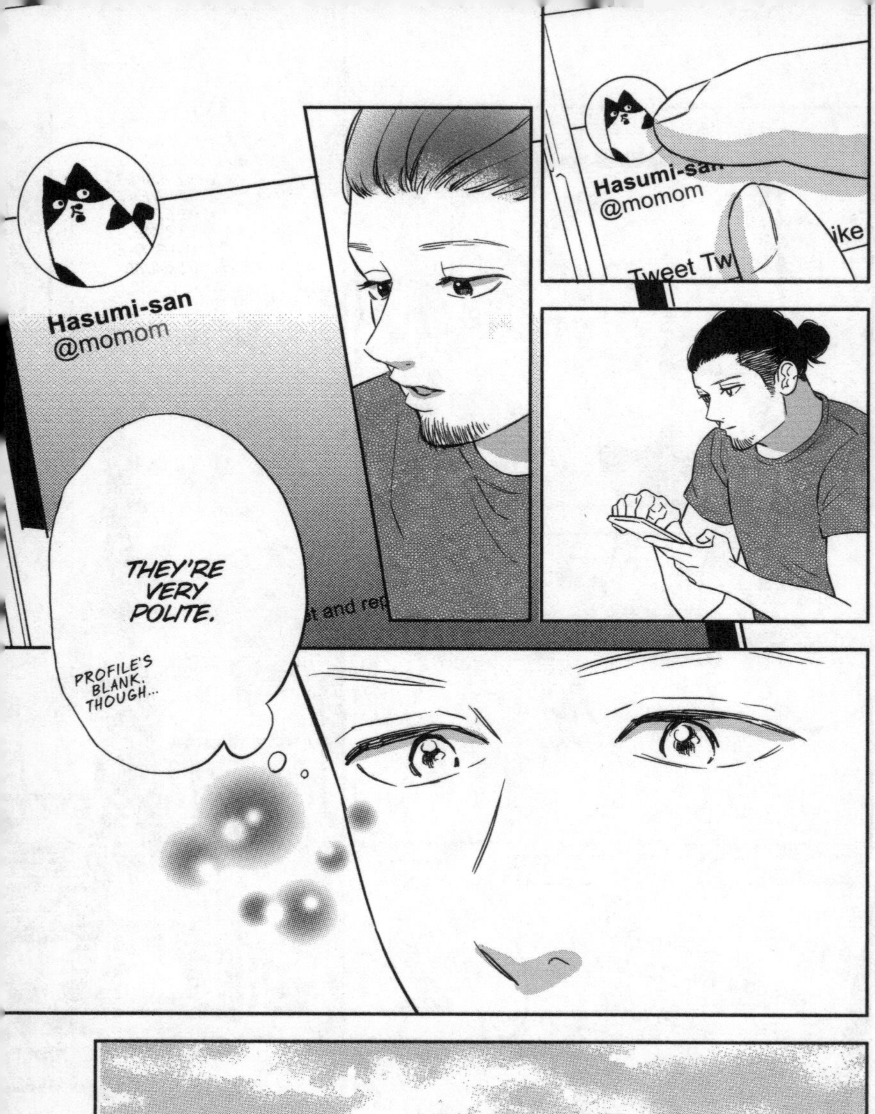
Hasumi-san
@momom
ike
Tweet Tw
Hasumi-san
@momom
et and rep
THEY'RE VERY POLITE.
PROFILE'S BLANK, THOUGH...

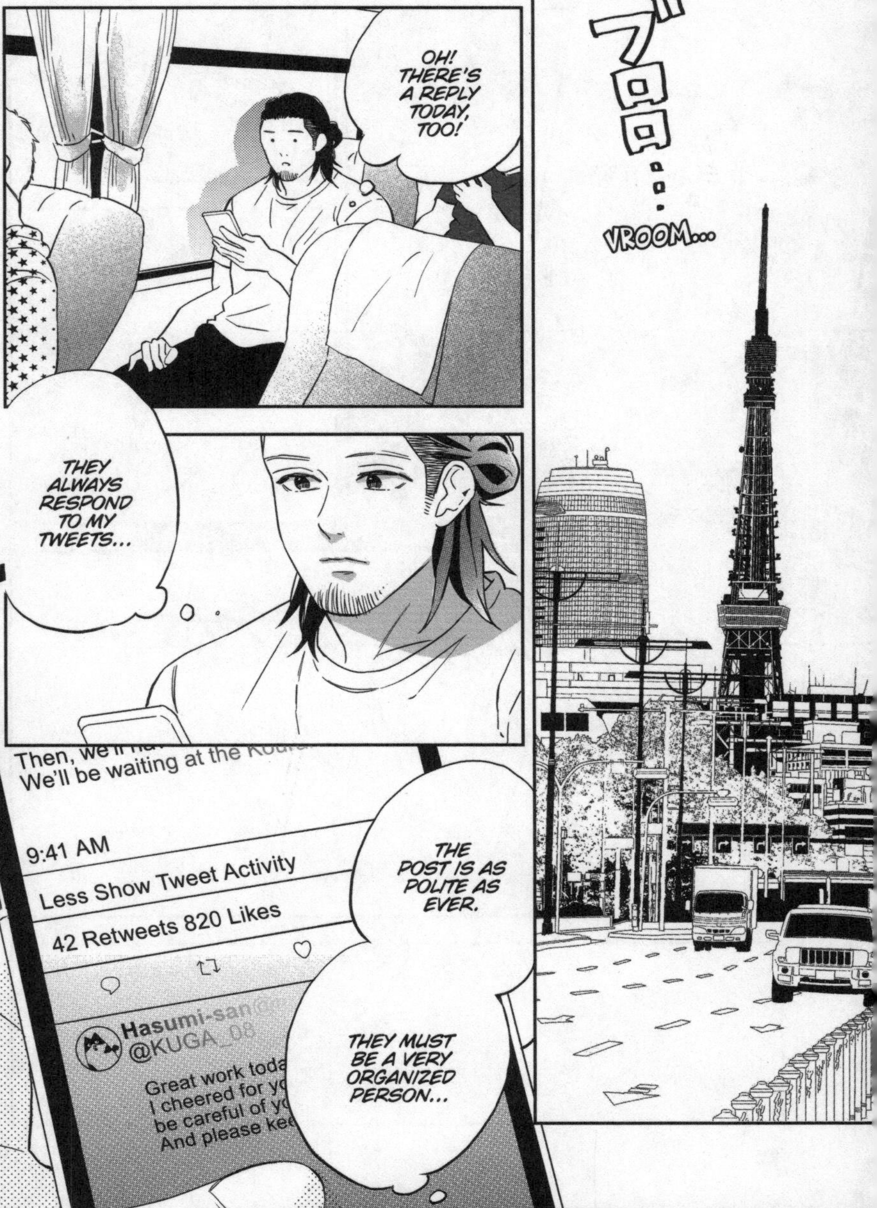
ブロロ…
VROOM…
OH! THERE'S A REPLY TODAY, TOO!
THEY ALWAYS RESPOND TO MY TWEETS…
9:41 AM
Less Show Tweet Activity
42 Retweets 820 Likes
@KUGA_08
THE POST IS AS POLITE AS EVER.
THEY MUST BE A VERY ORGANIZED PERSON…

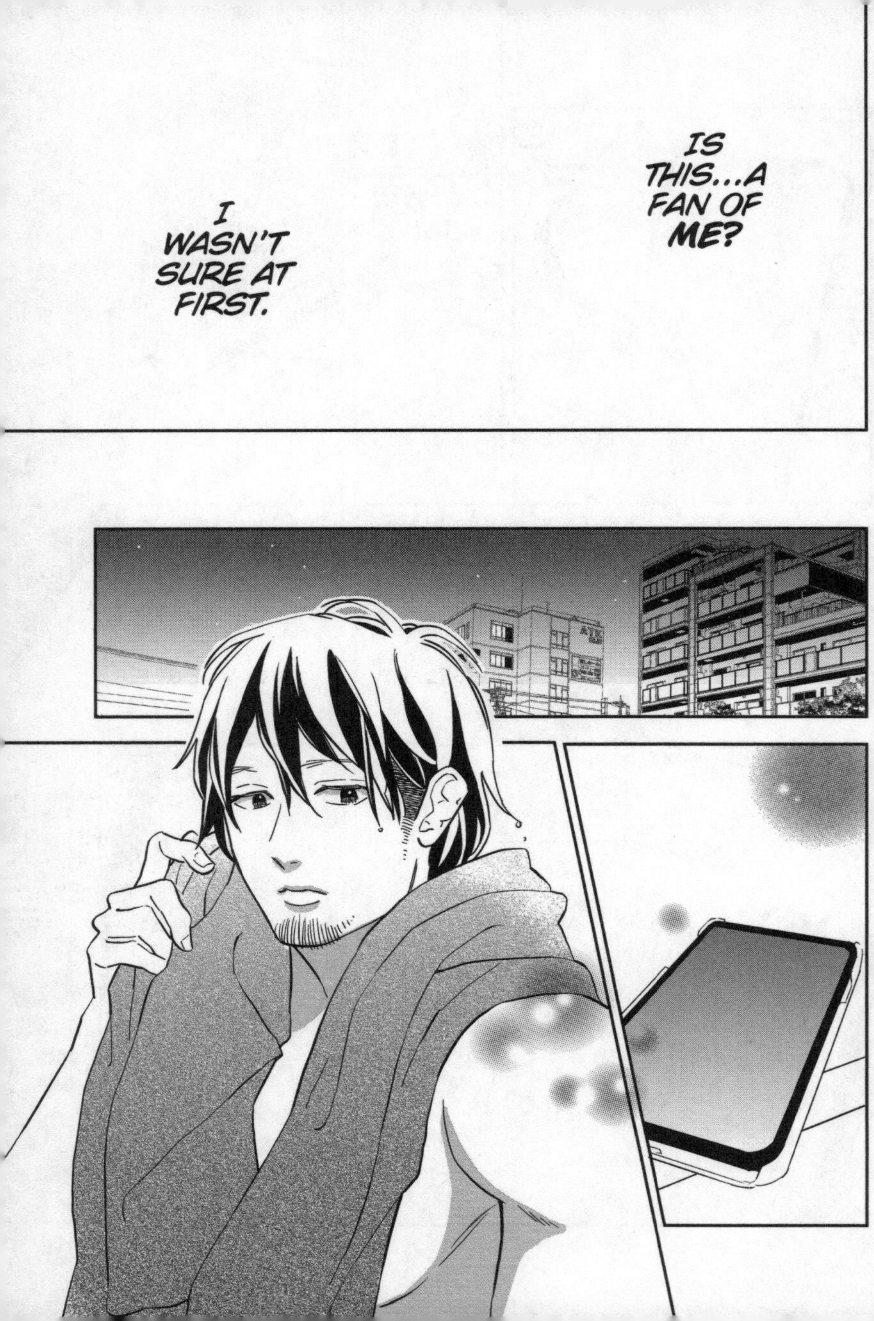
IS THIS...A FAN OF ME?
I WASN'T SURE AT FIRST.

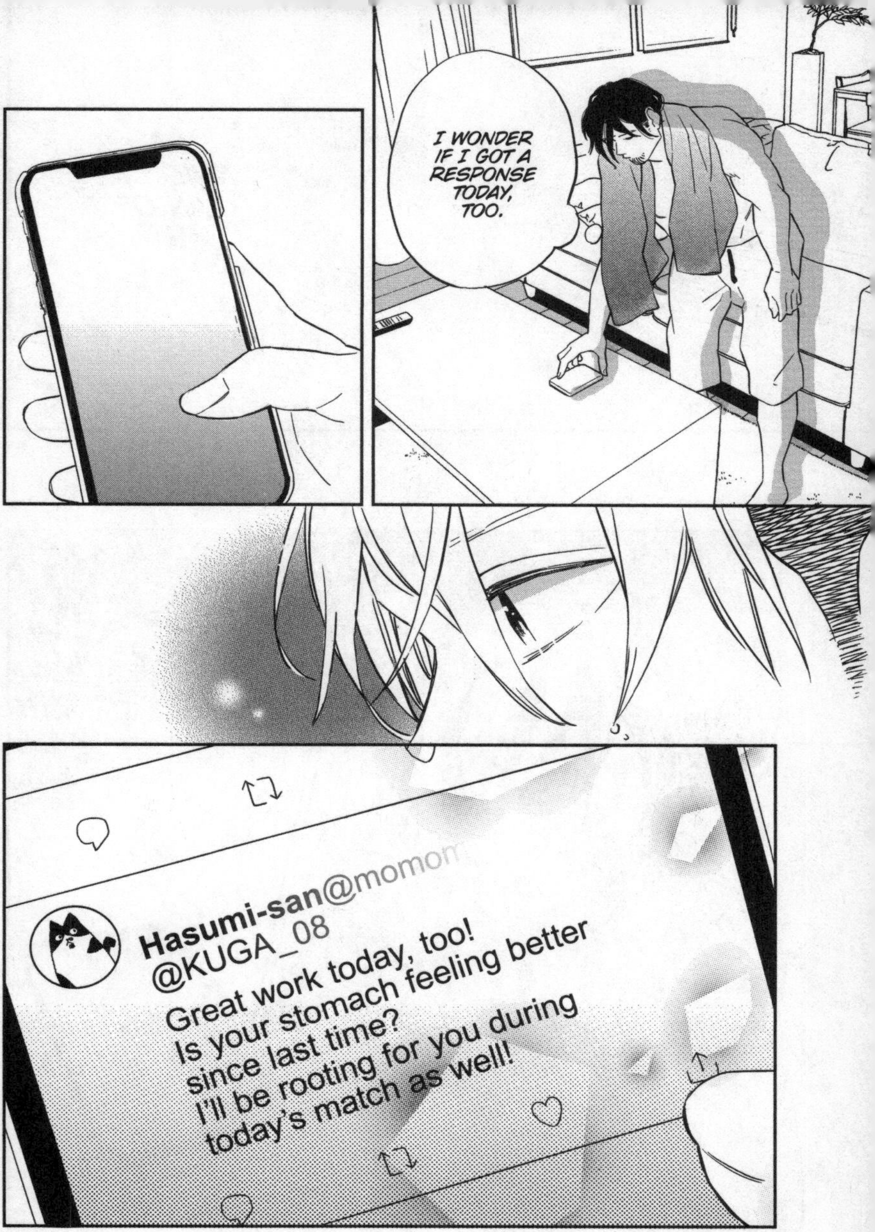
I WONDER IF I GOT A RESPONSE TODAY, TOO.
Hasumi-san@momon
@KUGA_08
Great work today, too!
Is your stomach feeling better since last time?
I'll be rooting for you during today's match as well!

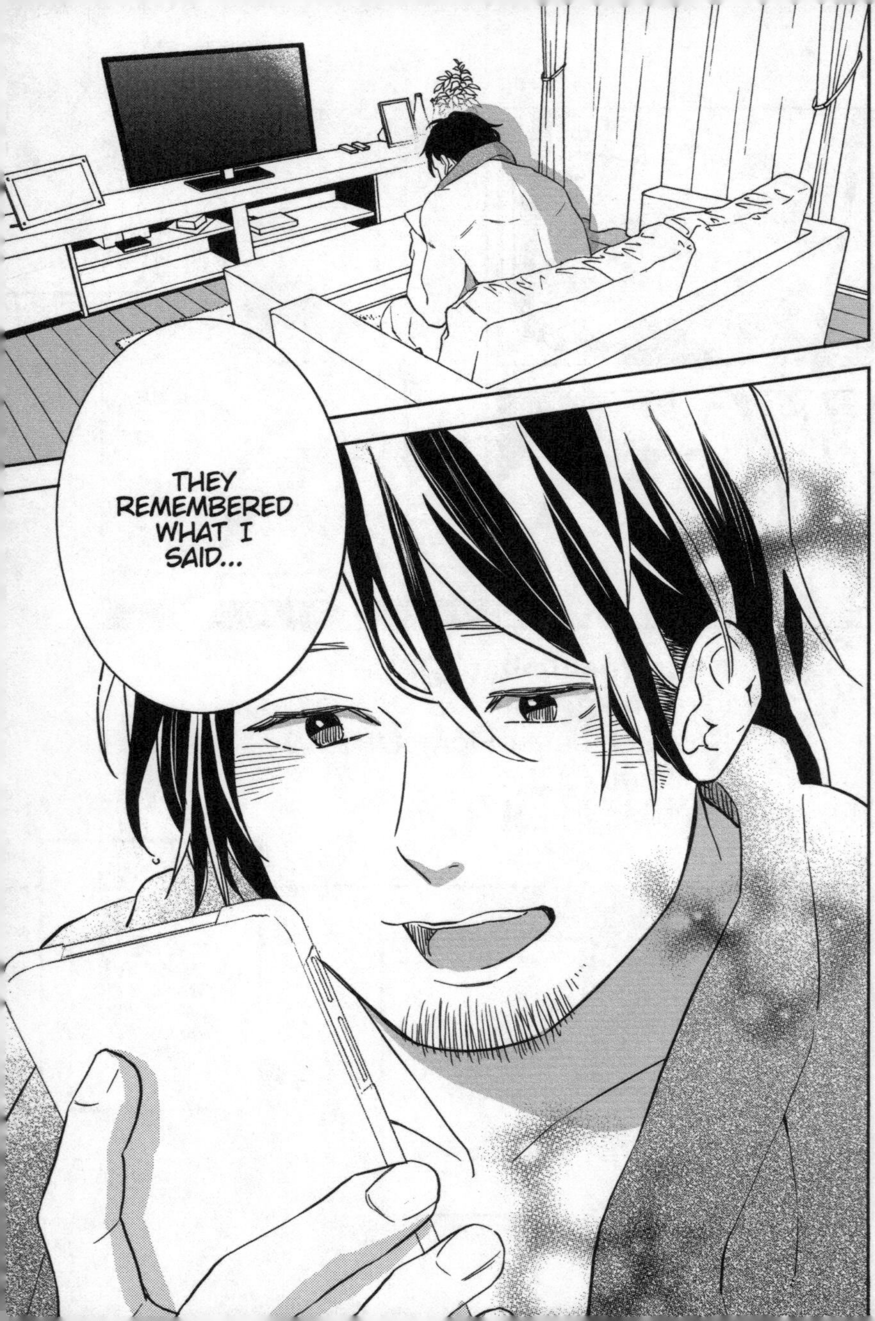
THEY REMEMBERED WHAT I SAID...

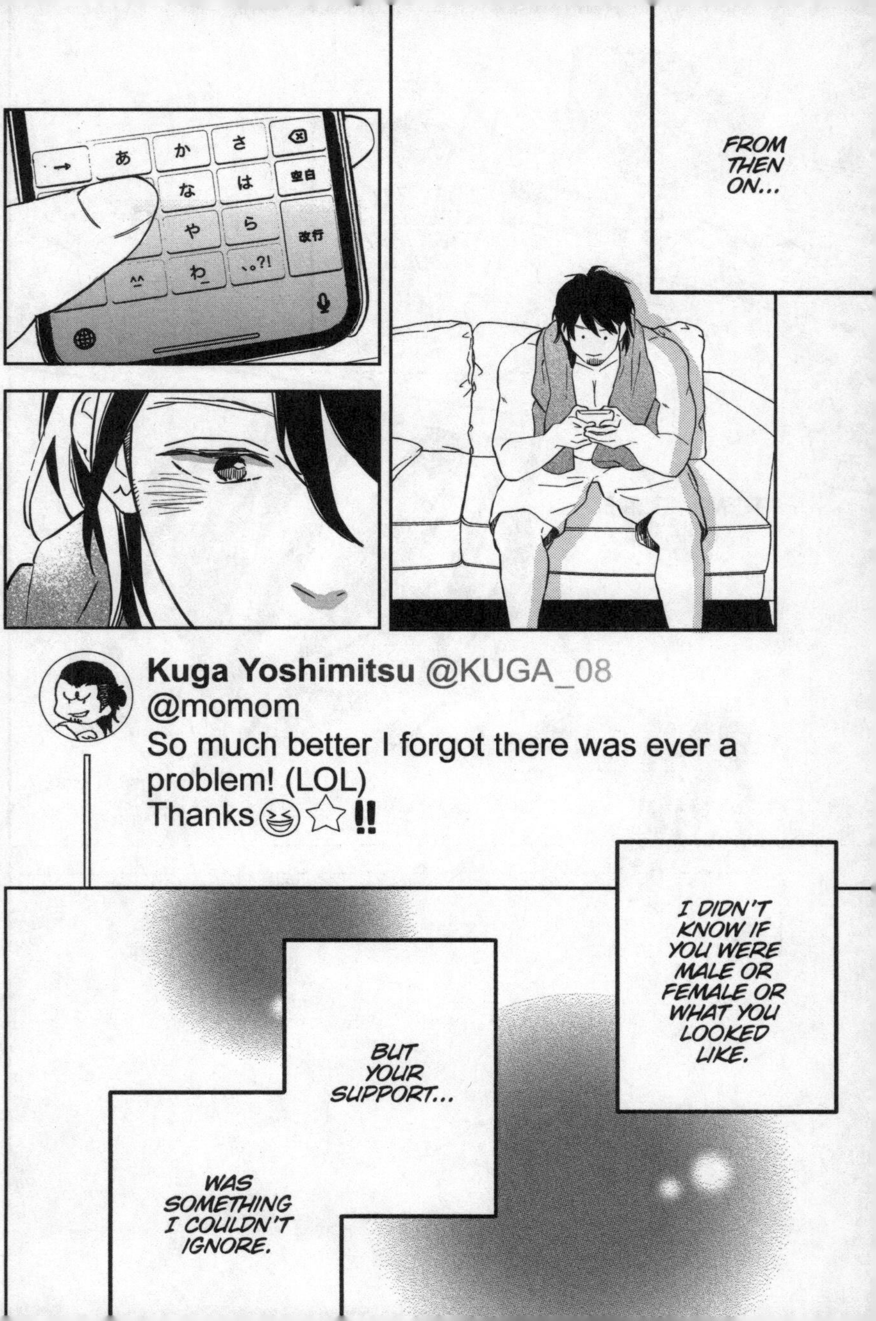
FROM THEN ON...
Kuga Yoshimitsu @KUGA_08
@momom
So much better I forgot there was ever a problem! (LOL)
Thanks😆☆!!
I DIDN'T KNOW IF YOU WERE MALE OR FEMALE OR WHAT YOU LOOKED LIKE.
BUT YOUR SUPPORT...
WAS SOMETHING I COULDN'T IGNORE.

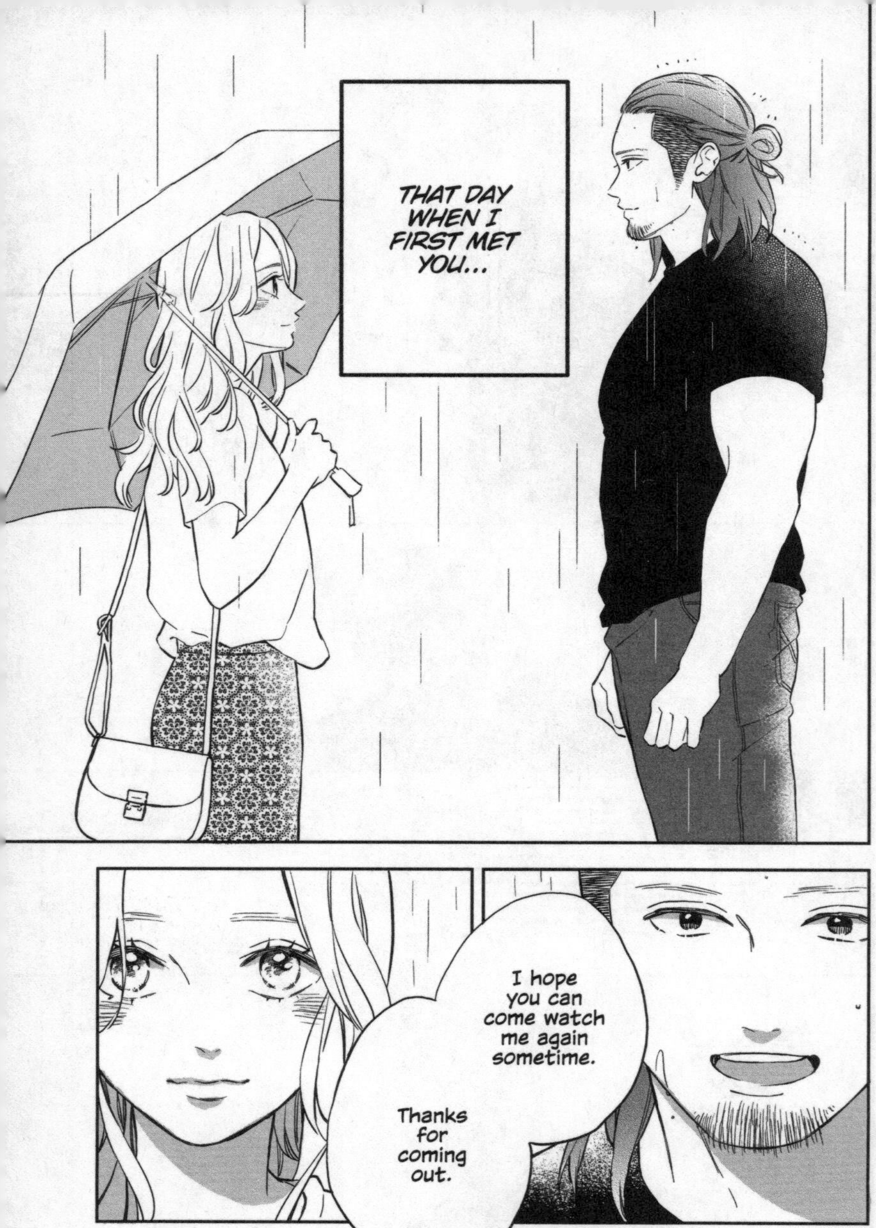
THAT DAY WHEN I FIRST MET YOU...
I hope you can come watch me again sometime.
Thanks for coming out.

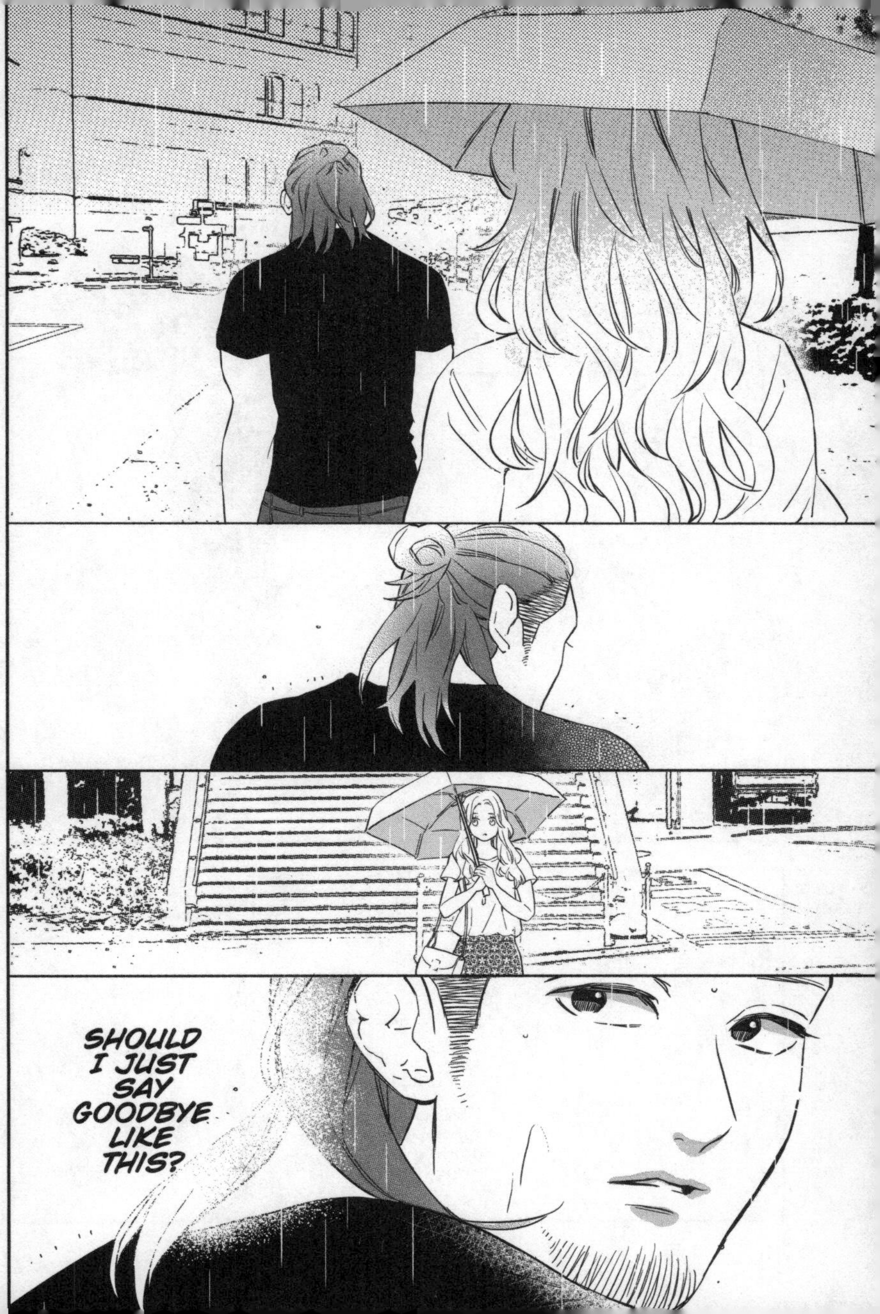
SHOULD I JUST SAY GOODBYE LIKE THIS?

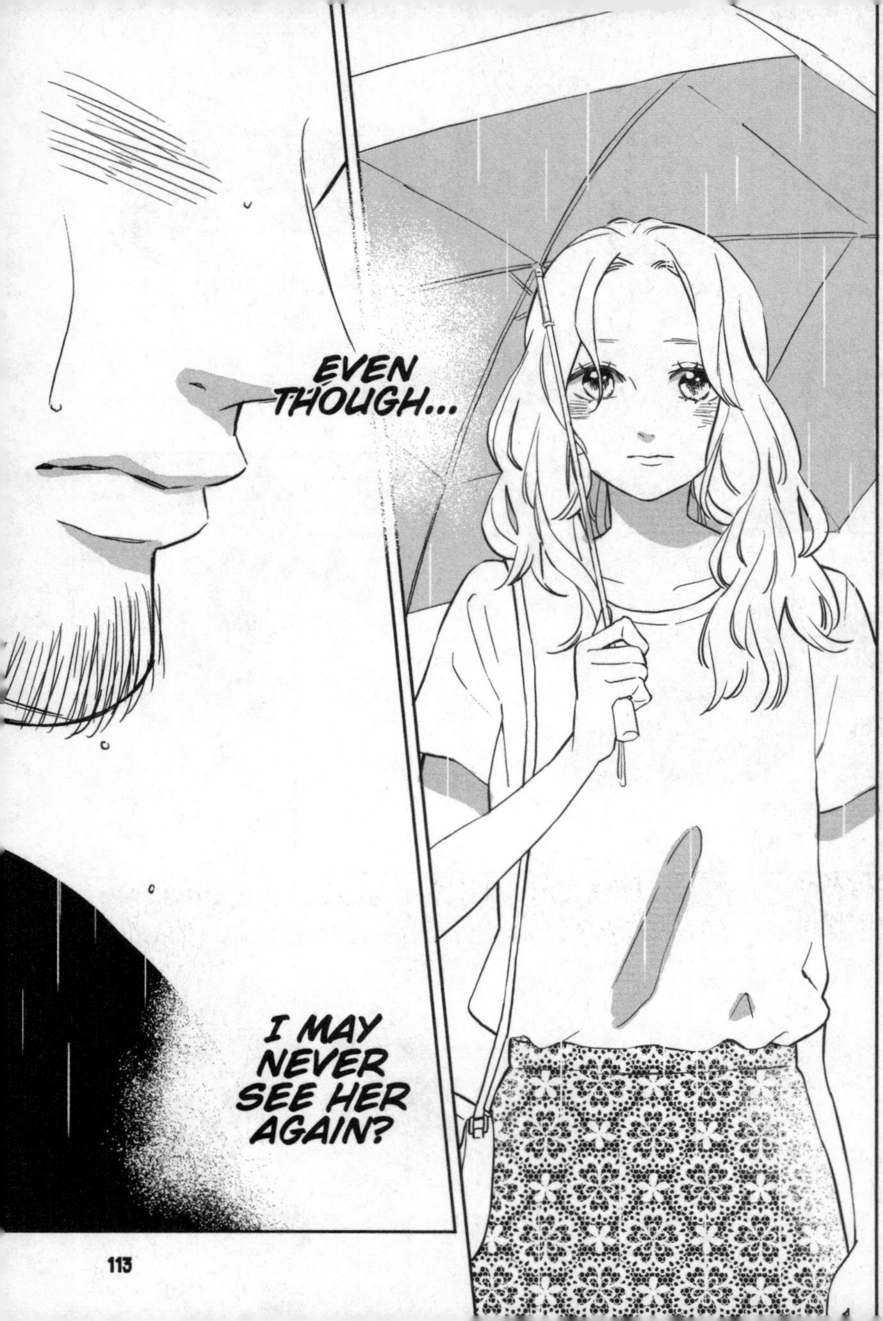
EVEN THOUGH...
I MAY NEVER SEE HER AGAIN?

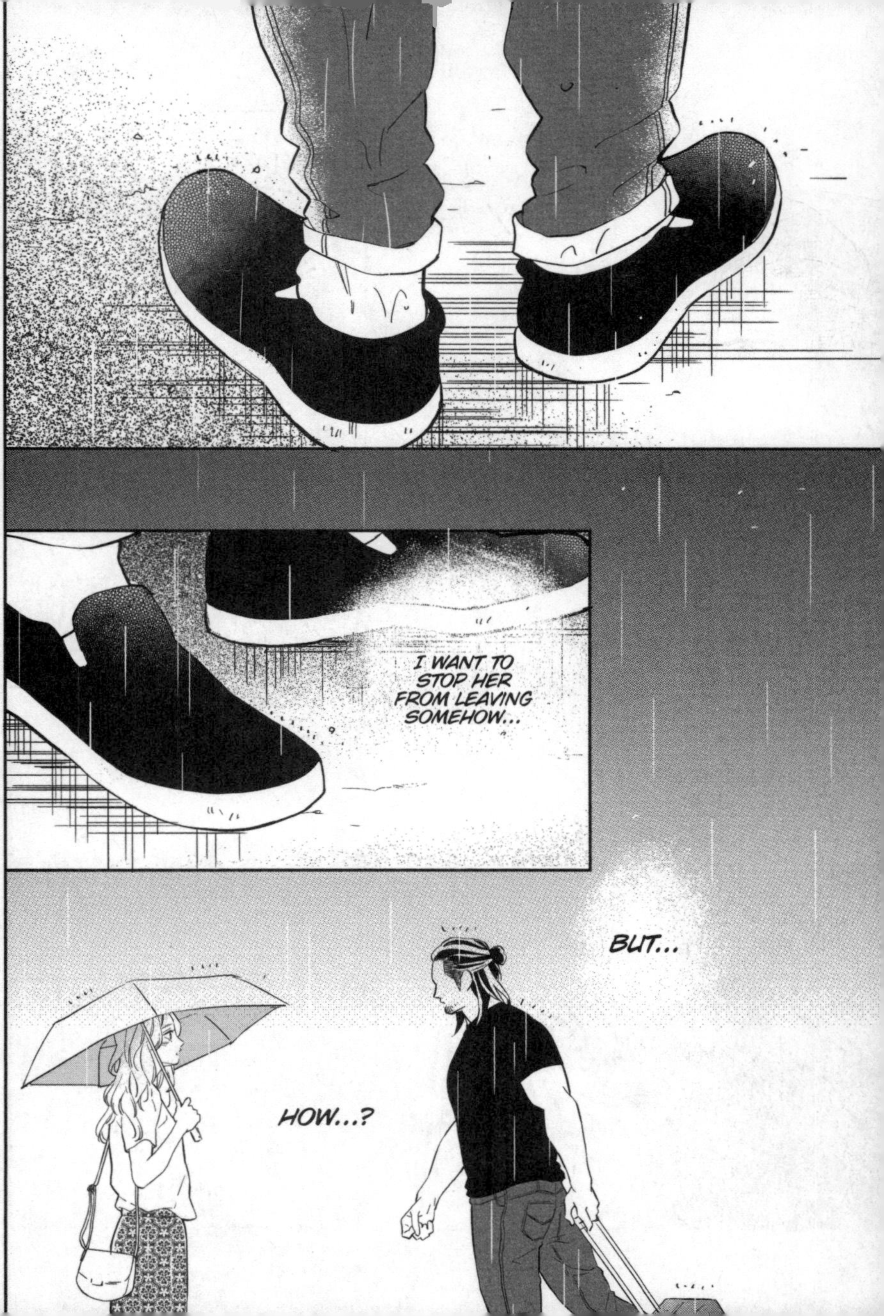
I WANT TO STOP HER FROM LEAVING SOMEHOW...
BUT...
HOW...?

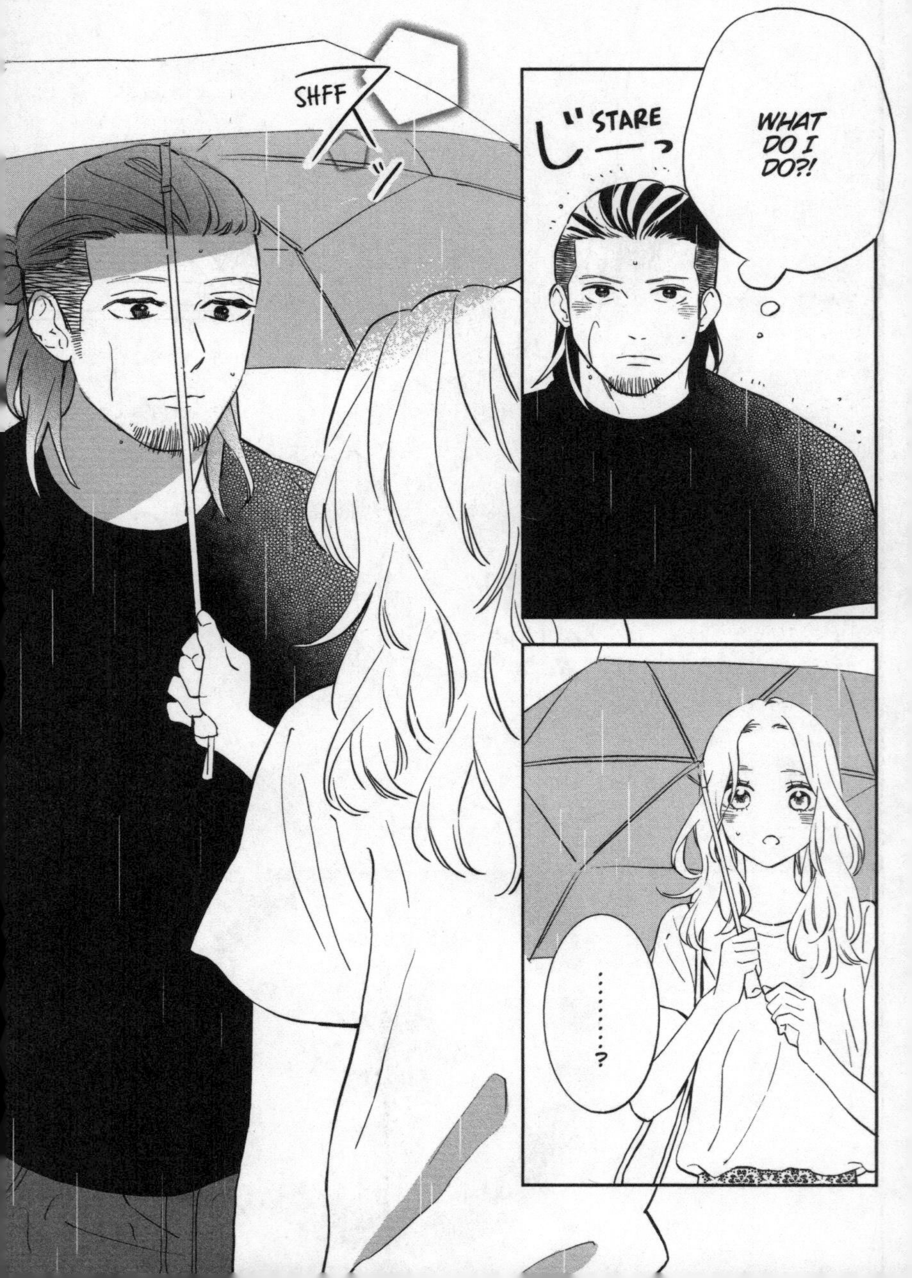

じーっ
STARE
WHAT DO I DO?!
......?
スッ
SHFF

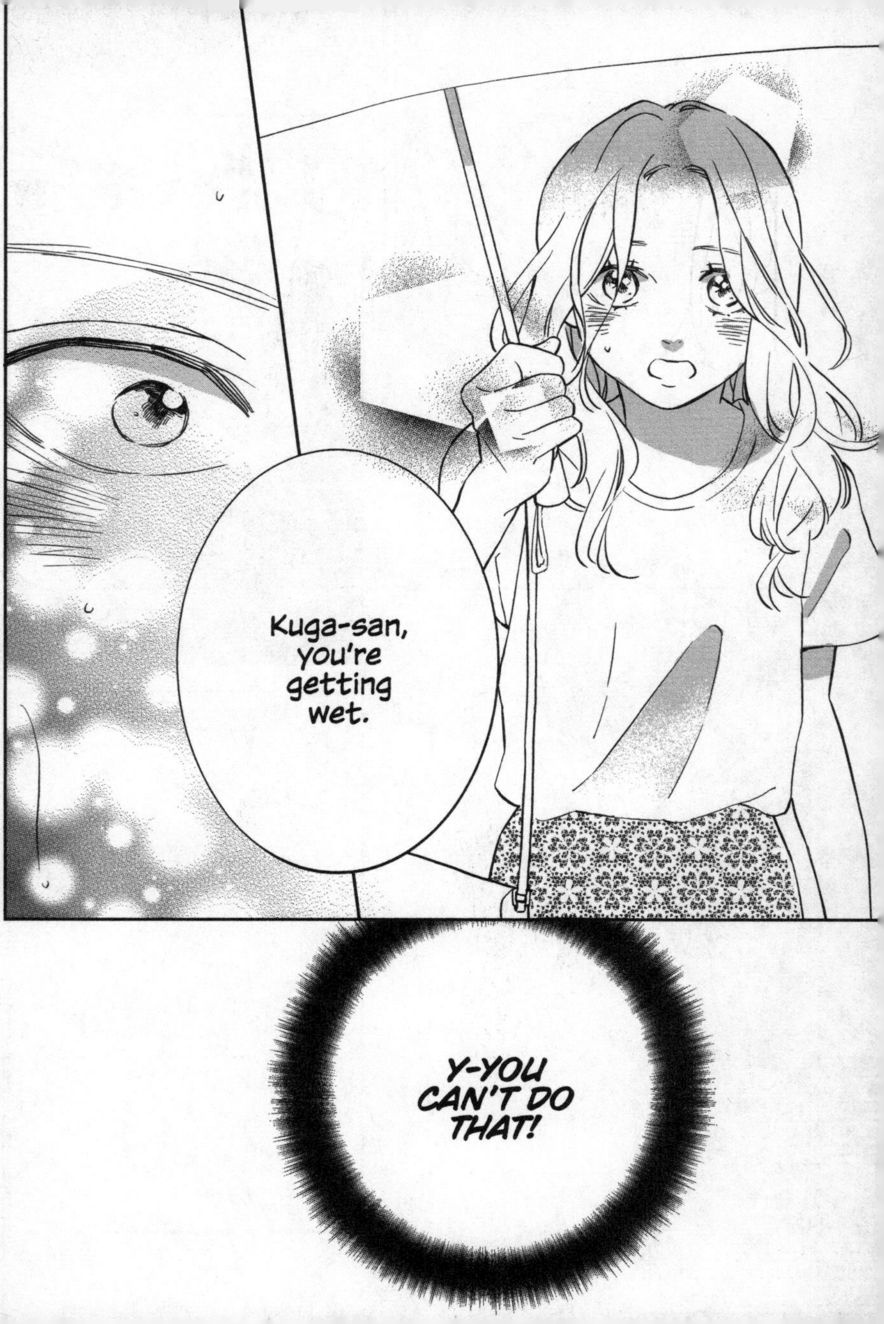
Kuga-san, you're getting wet.
Y-YOU CAN'T DO THAT!

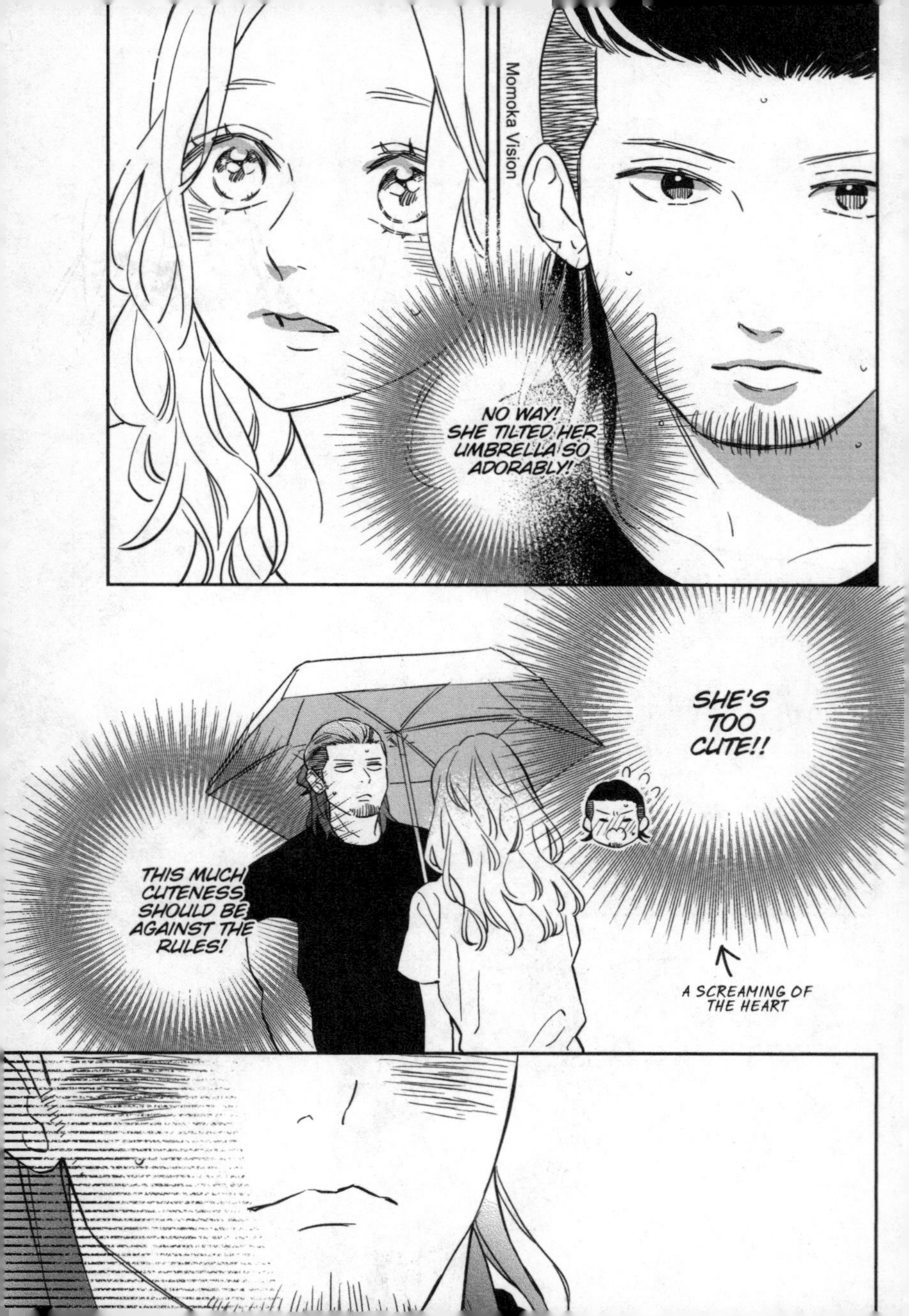
Momoka Vision
NO WAY! SHE TILTED HER UMBRELLA SO ADORABLY!
SHE'S TOO CUTE!!
A SCREAMING OF THE HEART
THIS MUCH CUTENESS SHOULD BE AGAINST THE RULES!

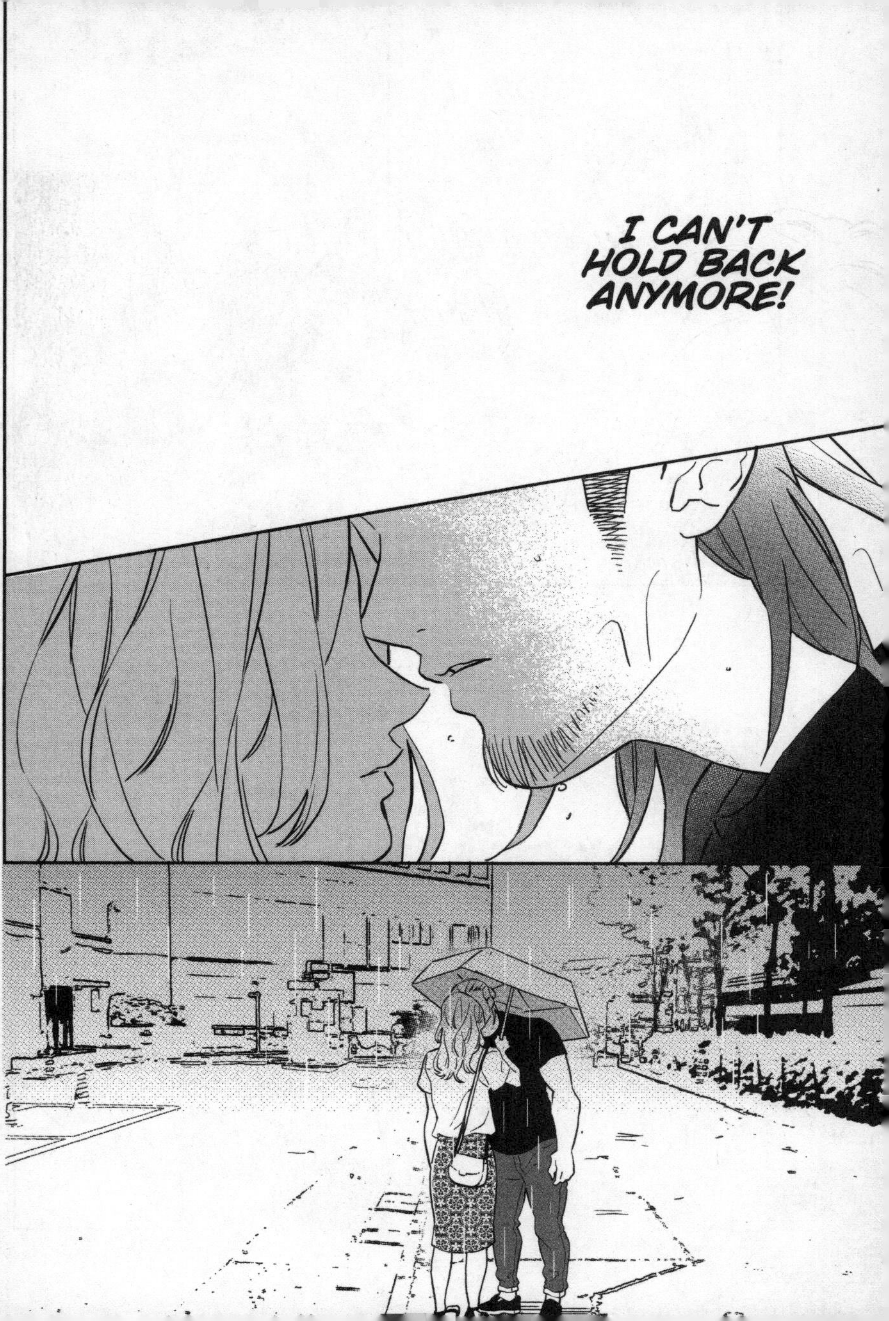
I CAN'T
HOLD BACK
ANYMORE!

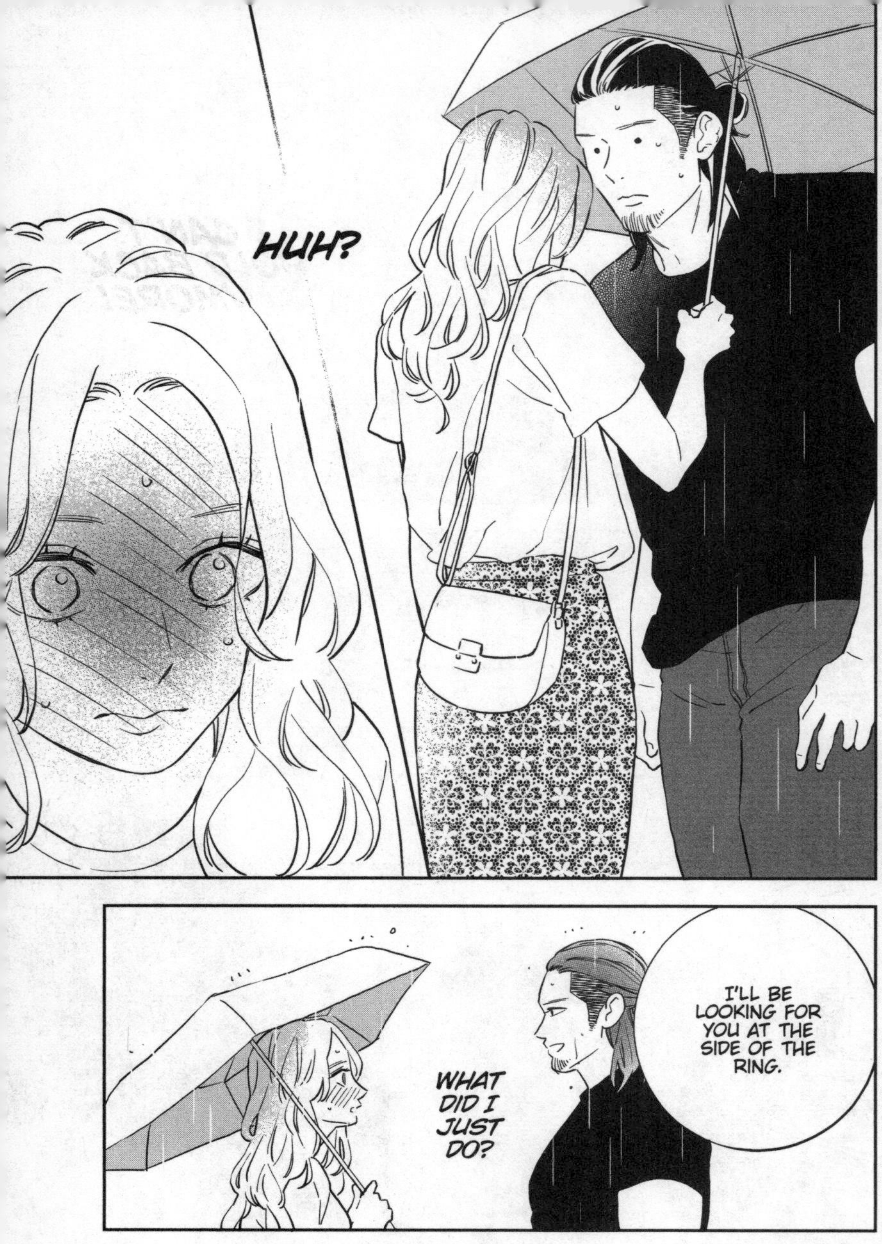
HUH?
I'LL BE LOOKING FOR YOU AT THE SIDE OF THE RING.
WHAT DID I JUST DO?

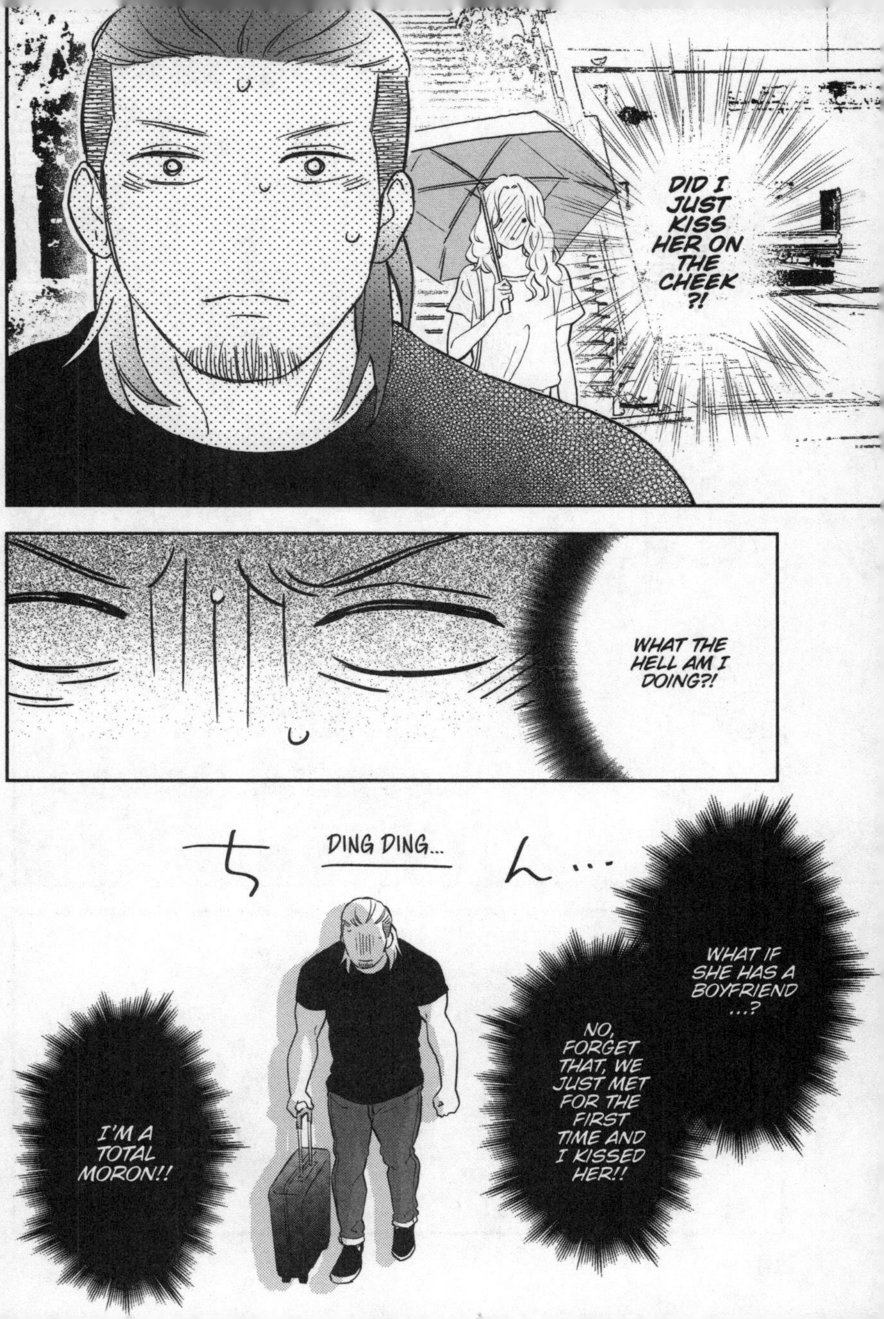
DID I JUST KISS HER ON THE CHEEK?!
WHAT THE HELL AM I DOING?!
ちん…
DING DING...
WHAT IF SHE HAS A BOYFRIEND...?
NO, FORGET THAT, WE JUST MET FOR THE FIRST TIME AND I KISSED HER!!
I'M A TOTAL MORON!!

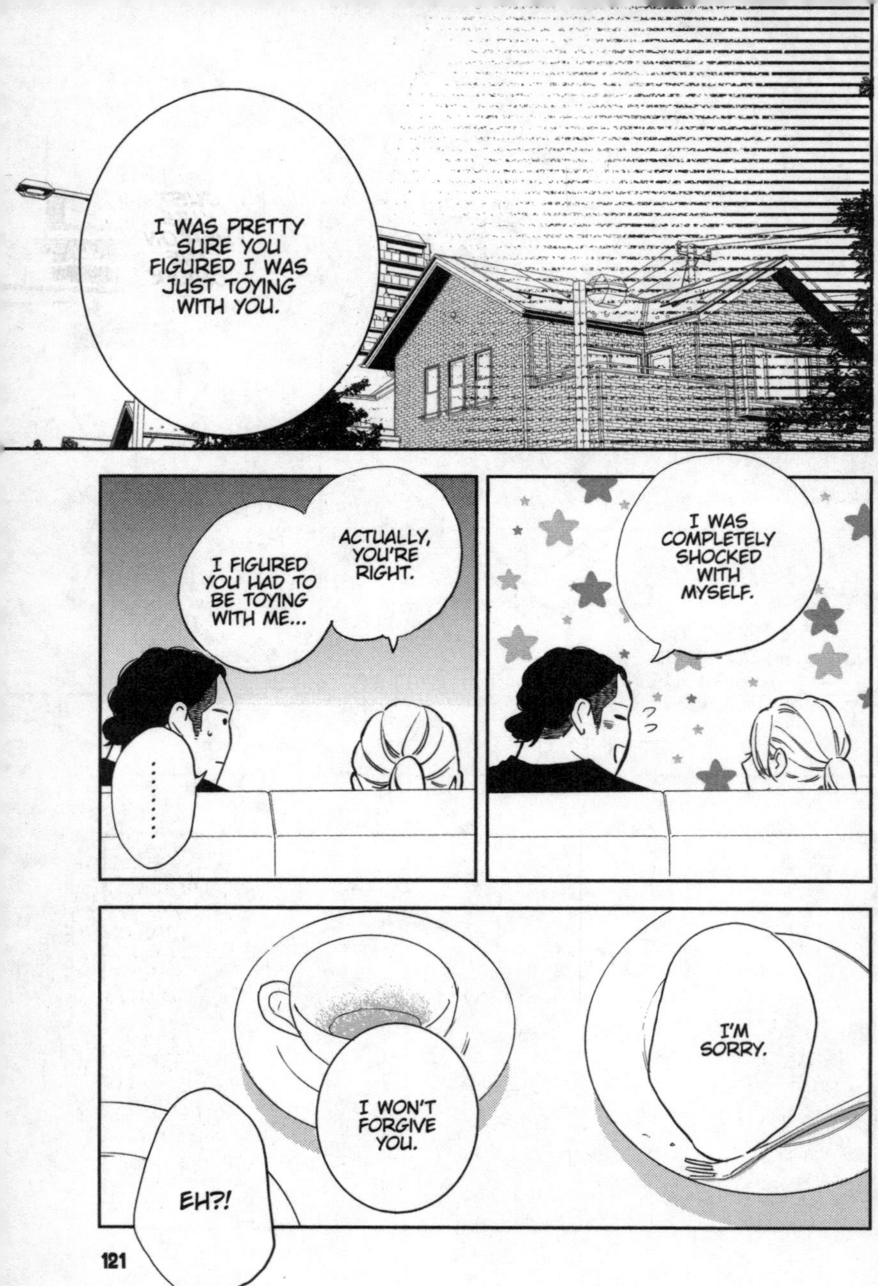
I WAS PRETTY SURE YOU FIGURED I WAS JUST TOYING WITH YOU.
I WAS COMPLETELY SHOCKED WITH MYSELF.
ACTUALLY, YOU'RE RIGHT.
I FIGURED YOU HAD TO BE TOYING WITH ME...
......
I'M SORRY.
I WON'T FORGIVE YOU.
EH?!

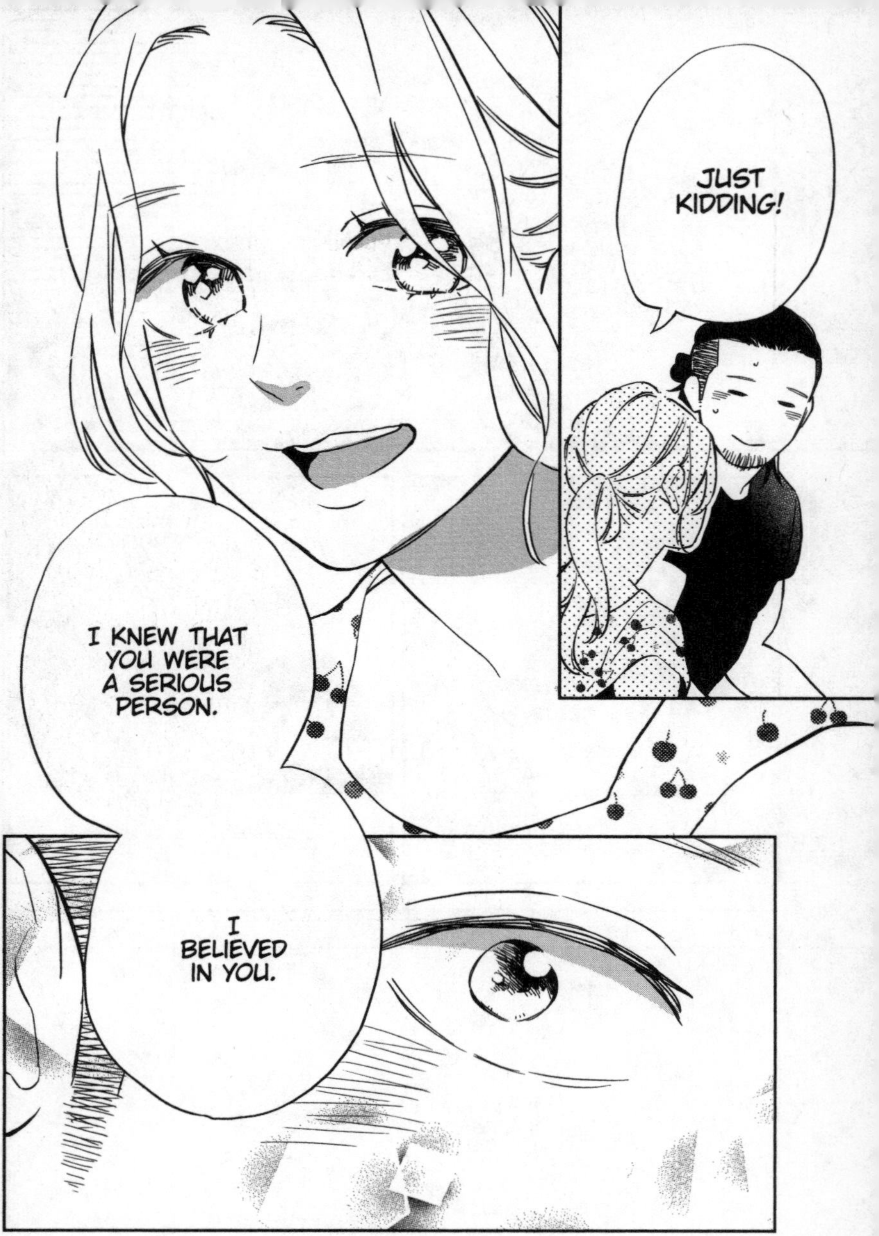
JUST KIDDING!
I KNEW THAT YOU WERE A SERIOUS PERSON.
I BELIEVED IN YOU.

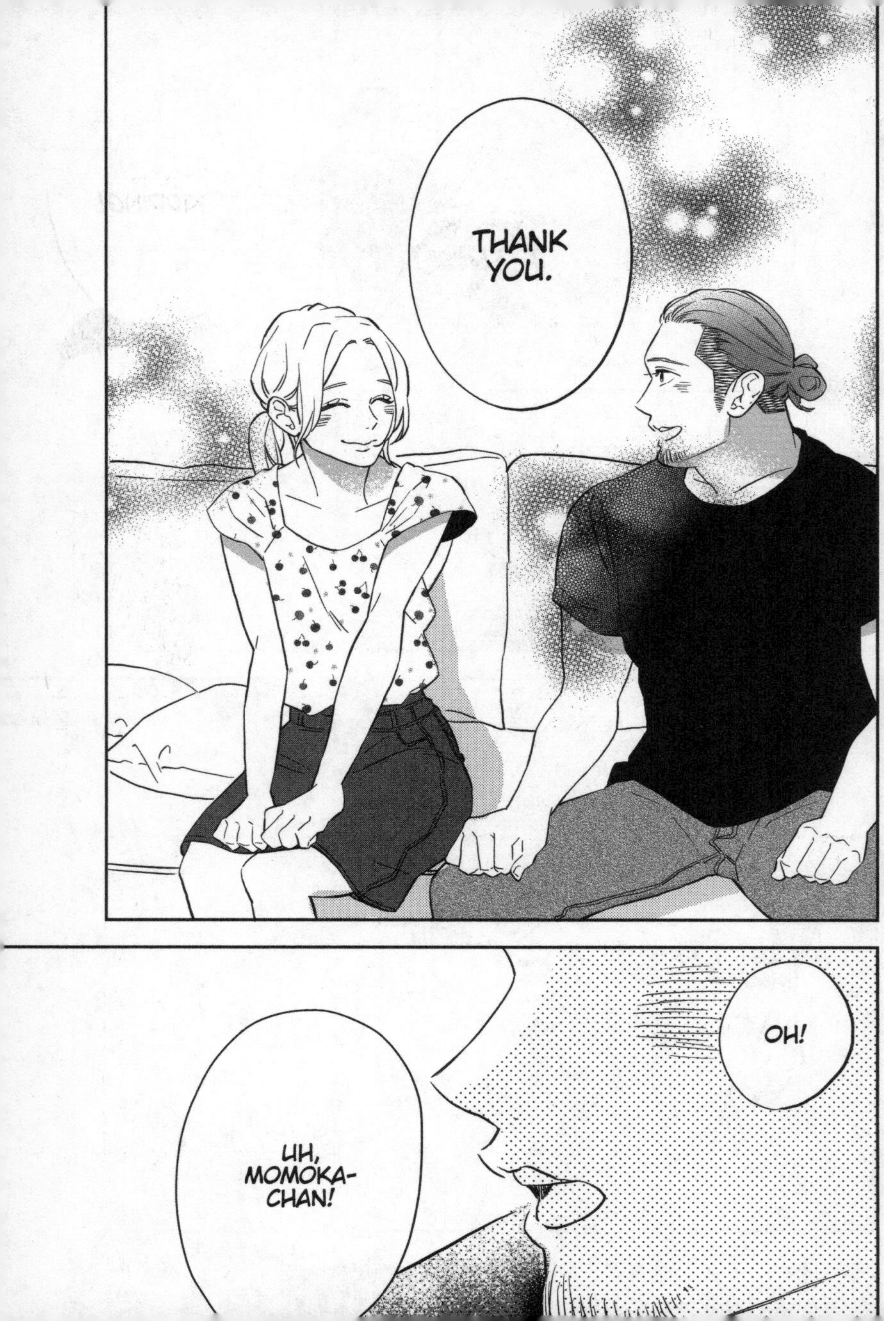
THANK YOU.
OH!
UH, MOMOKA-CHAN!

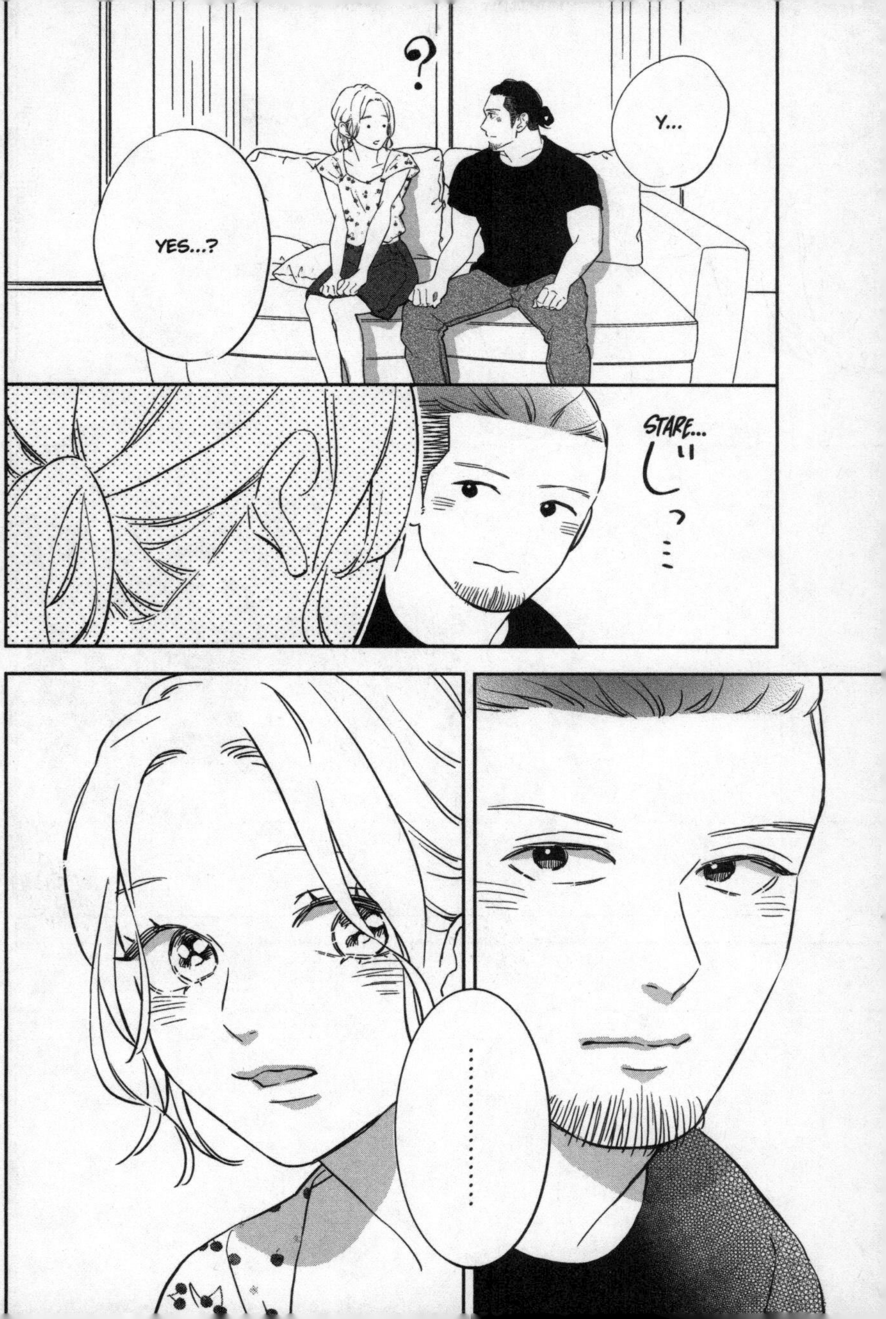
Y...
YES...?
STARE...
じぃっ…
......

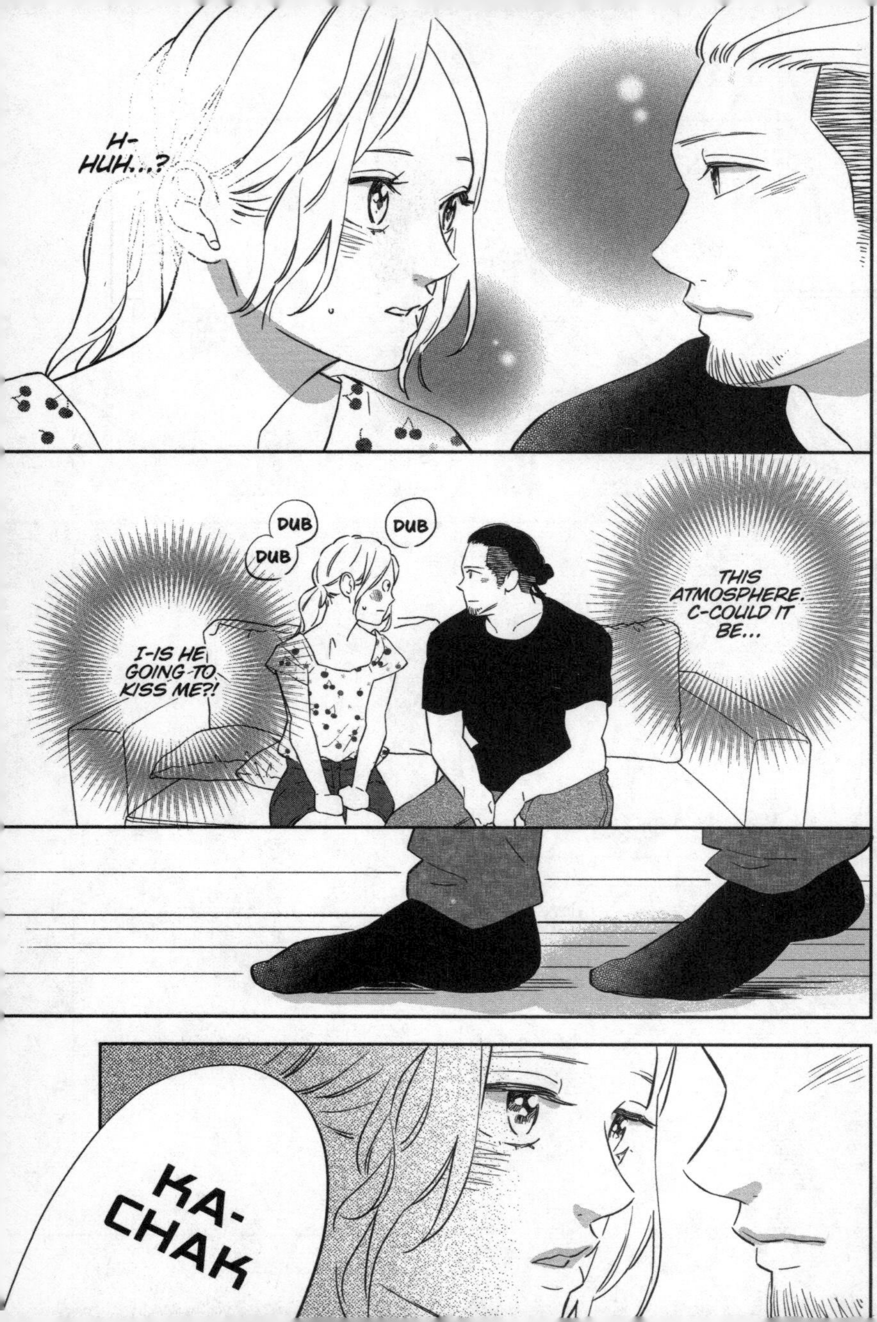
H-HUH...?
THIS ATMOSPHERE. C-COULD IT BE...
DUB
DUB
DUB
I-IS HE GOING TO KISS ME?!
KA-CHAK

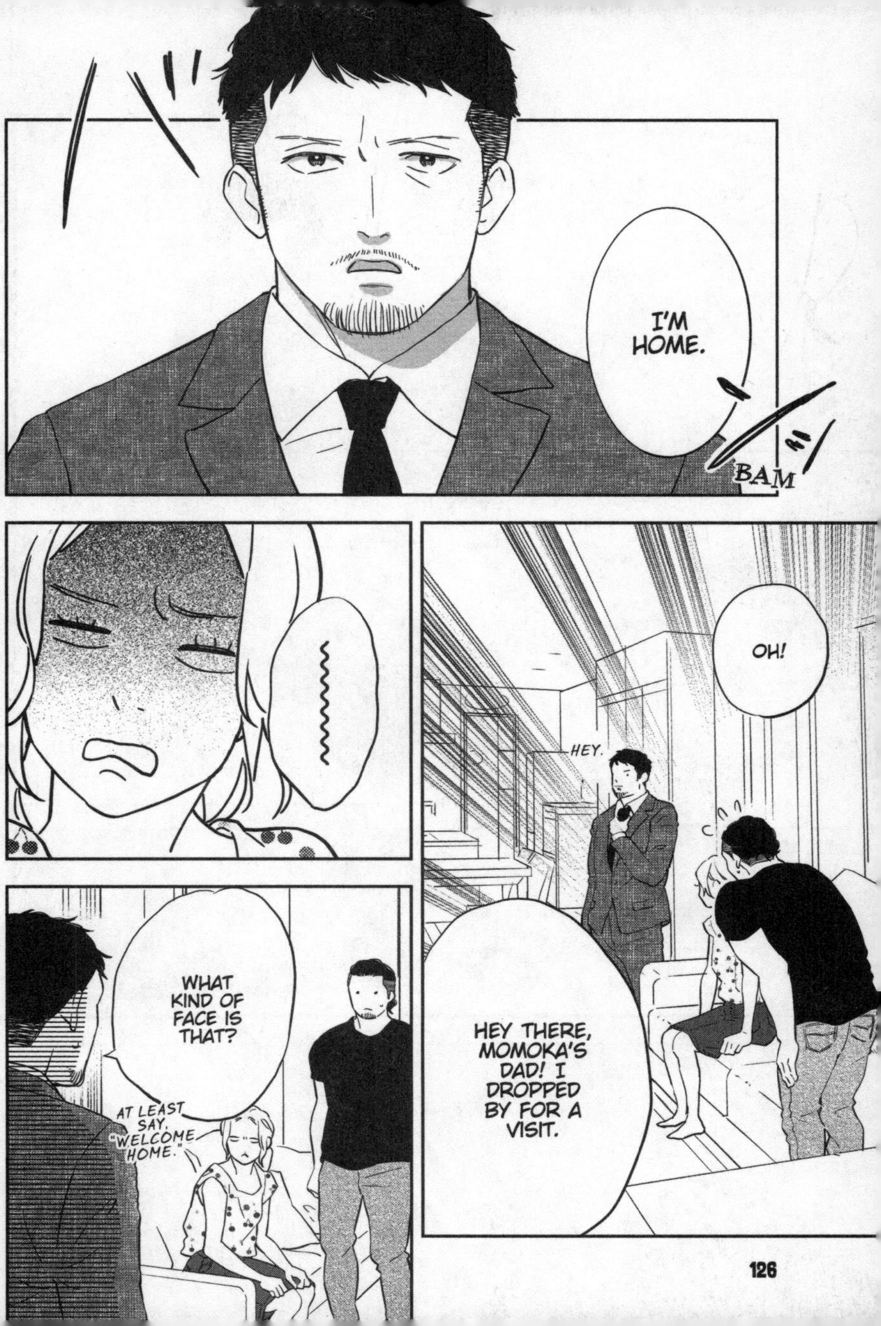
I'M HOME.
BAM
OH!
HEY.
HEY THERE, MOMOKA'S DAD! I DROPPED BY FOR A VISIT.
WHAT KIND OF FACE IS THAT?
AT LEAST SAY, "WELCOME HOME."

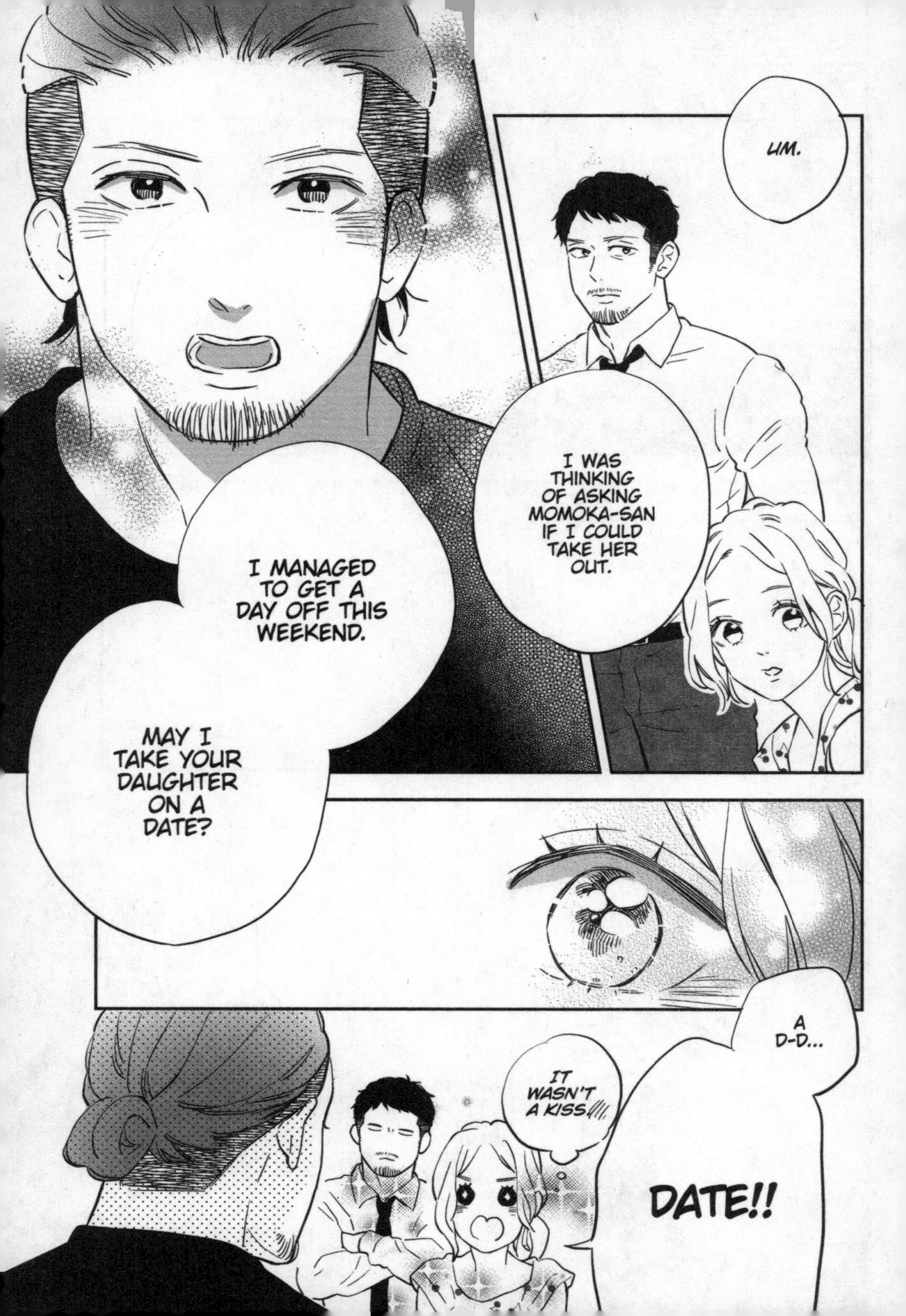
UM.
I WAS THINKING OF ASKING MOMOKA-SAN IF I COULD TAKE HER OUT.
I MANAGED TO GET A DAY OFF THIS WEEKEND.
MAY I TAKE YOUR DAUGHTER ON A DATE?
A D-D...
IT WASN'T A KISS
DATE!!

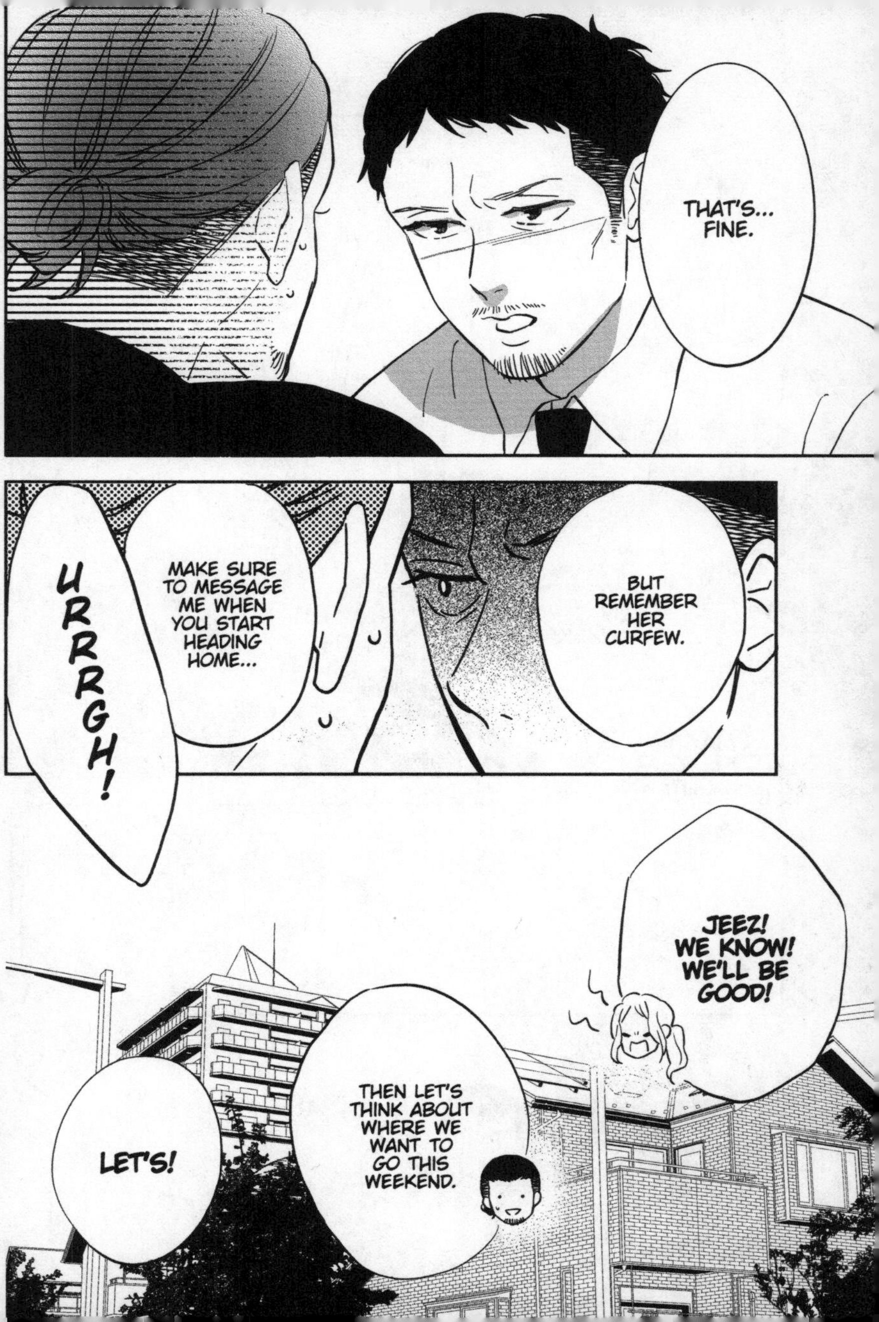
THAT'S... FINE.
BUT REMEMBER HER CURFEW.
MAKE SURE TO MESSAGE ME WHEN YOU START HEADING HOME...
URRRGH!
JEEZ! WE KNOW! WE'LL BE GOOD!
THEN LET'S THINK ABOUT WHERE WE WANT TO GO THIS WEEKEND.
LET'S!

Cutie and the BEAST

Cutie and the BEAST

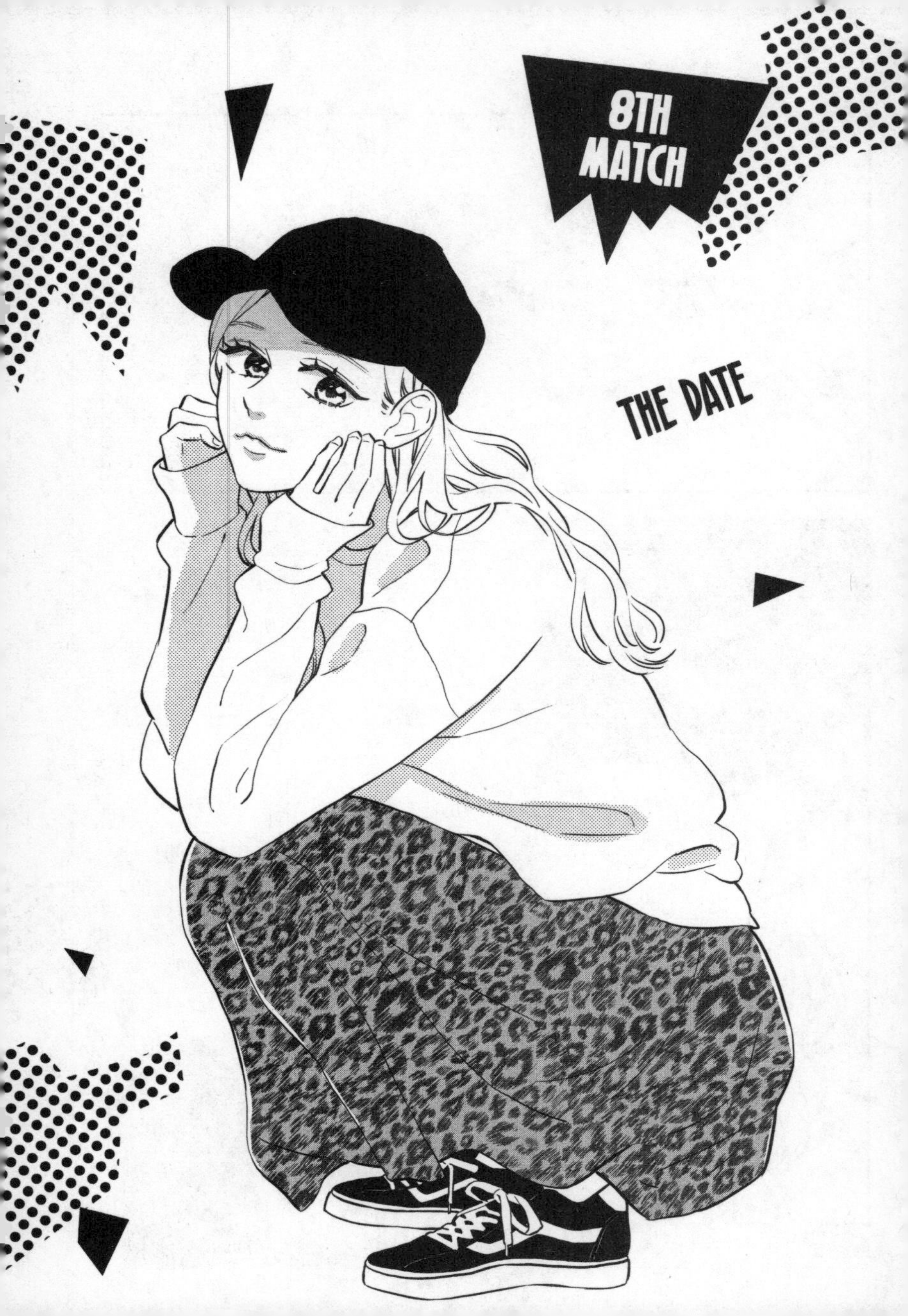
8TH MATCH
THE DATE

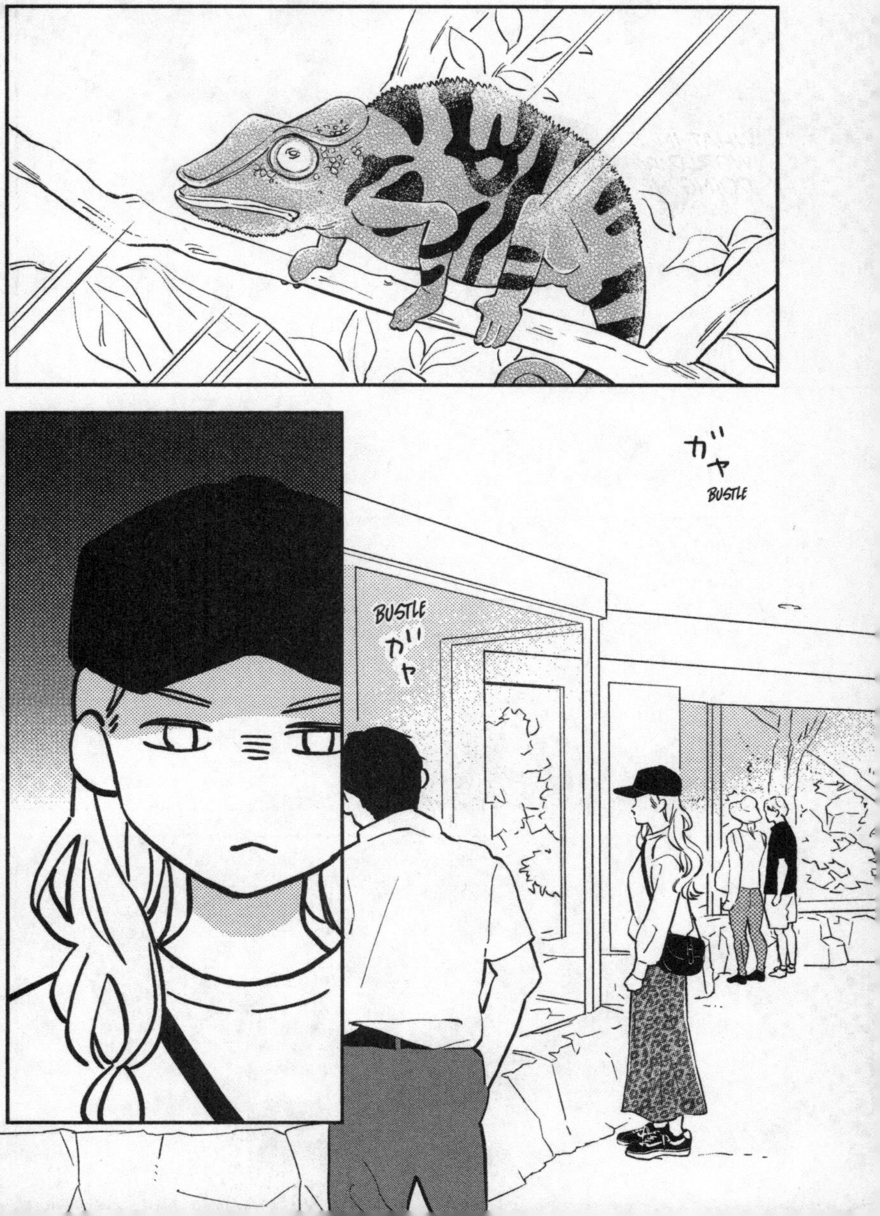
ガヤ
BUSTLE
BUSTLE
ガヤ

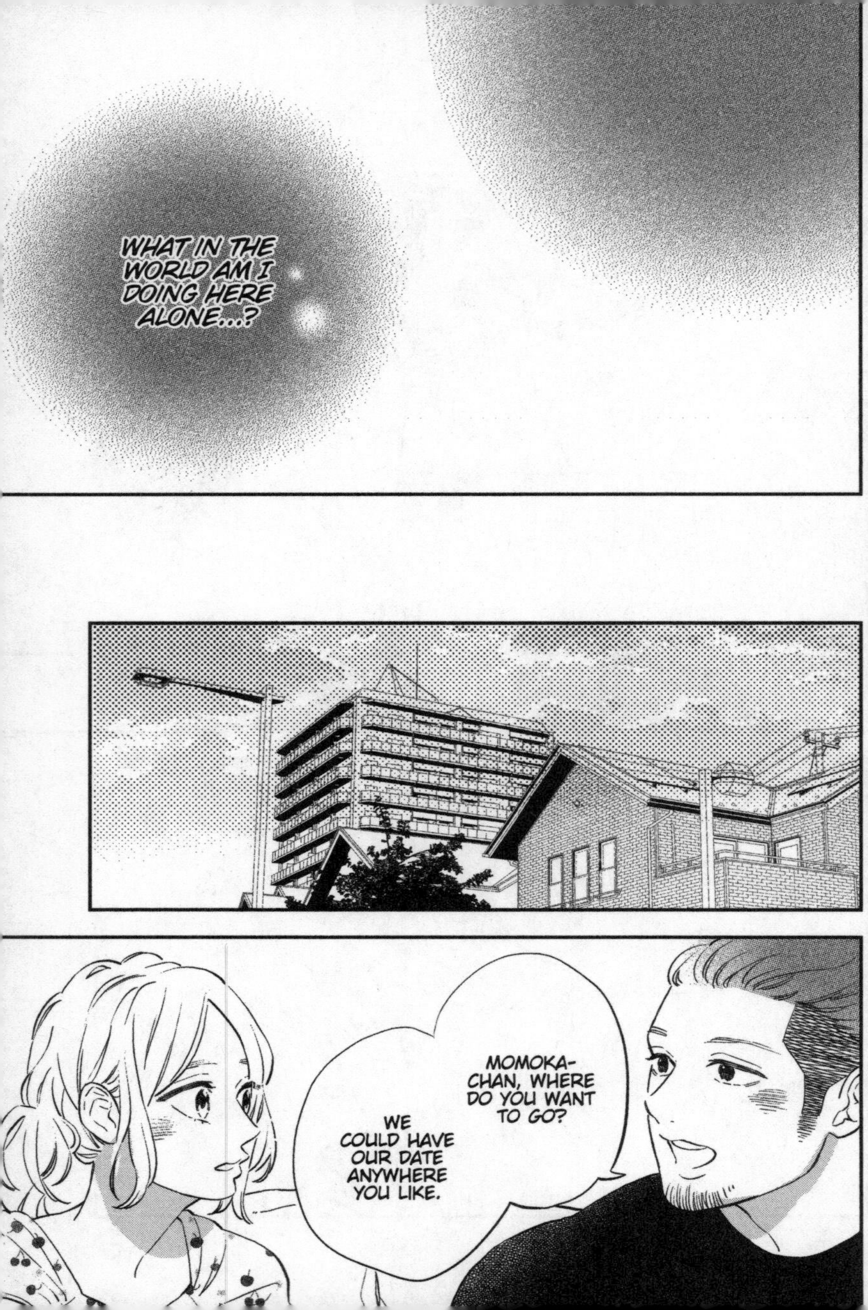
WHAT IN THE WORLD AM I DOING HERE ALONE...?
MOMOKA-CHAN, WHERE DO YOU WANT TO GO?
WE COULD HAVE OUR DATE ANYWHERE YOU LIKE.

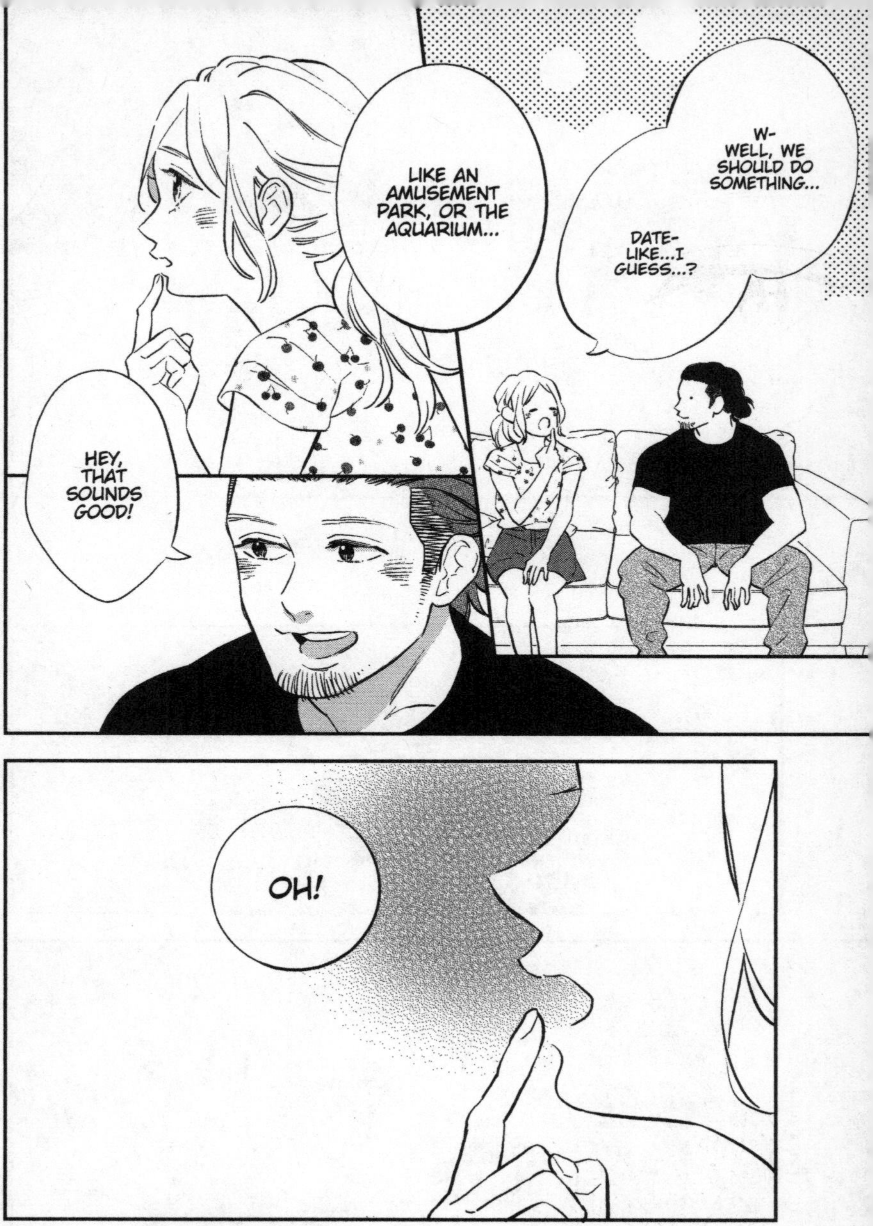
W-WELL, WE SHOULD DO SOMETHING...
DATE-LIKE...I GUESS...?
LIKE AN AMUSEMENT PARK, OR THE AQUARIUM...
HEY, THAT SOUNDS GOOD!
OH!

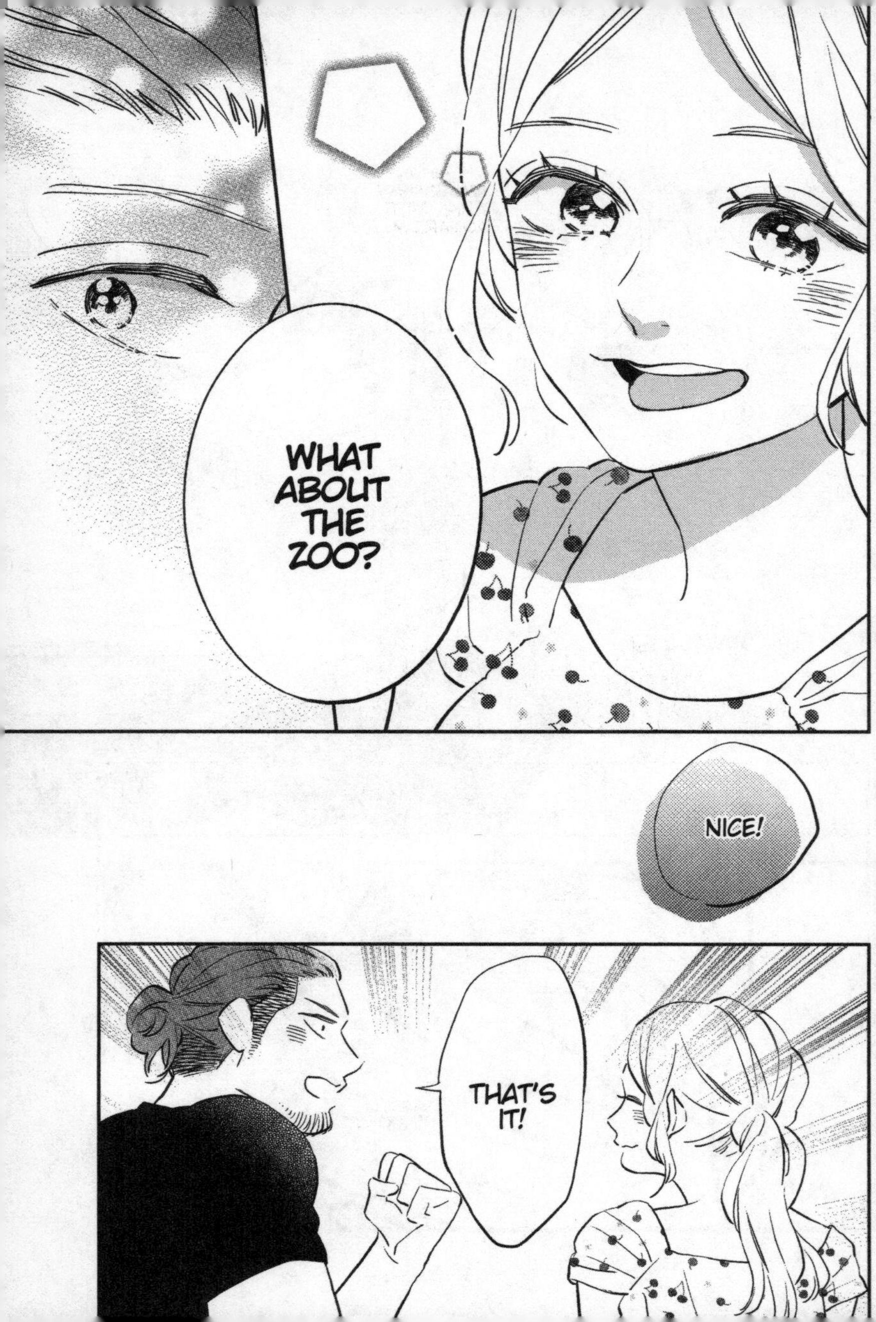
WHAT ABOUT THE ZOO?
NICE!
THAT'S IT!

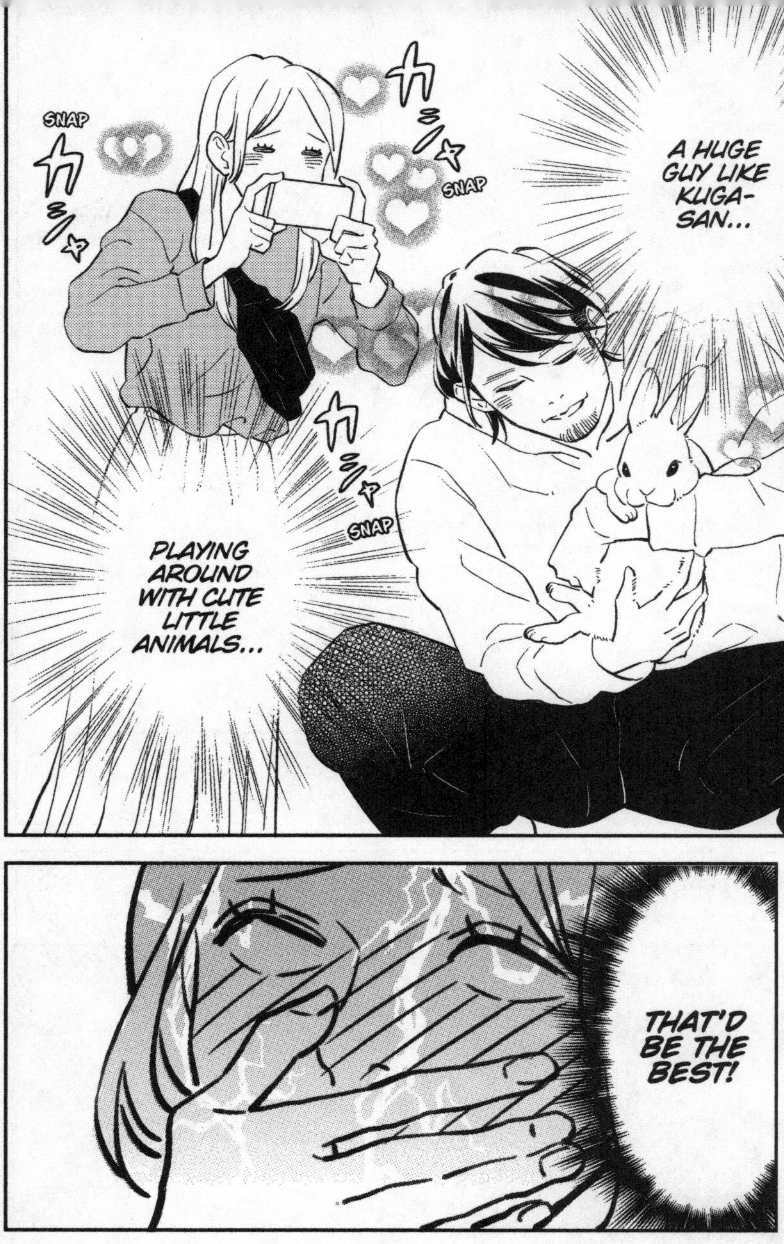
A HUGE GUY LIKE KUGA-SAN...
SNAP
SNAP
SNAP
PLAYING AROUND WITH CUTE LITTLE ANIMALS...
THAT'D BE THE BEST!

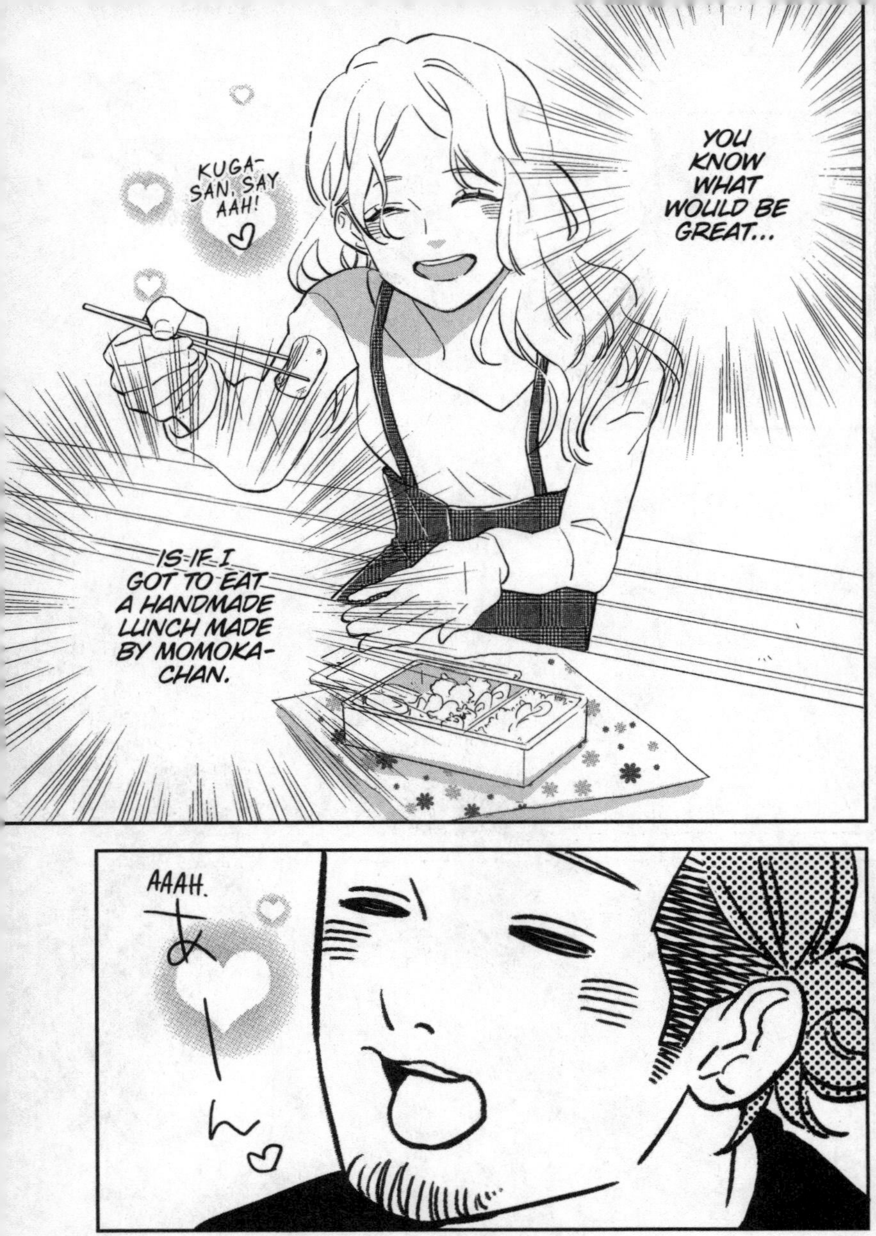
YOU KNOW WHAT WOULD BE GREAT...
KUGA-SAN, SAY AAH! ♡
IS IF I GOT TO EAT A HANDMADE LUNCH MADE BY MOMOKA-CHAN.
AAAH.
あーん♡

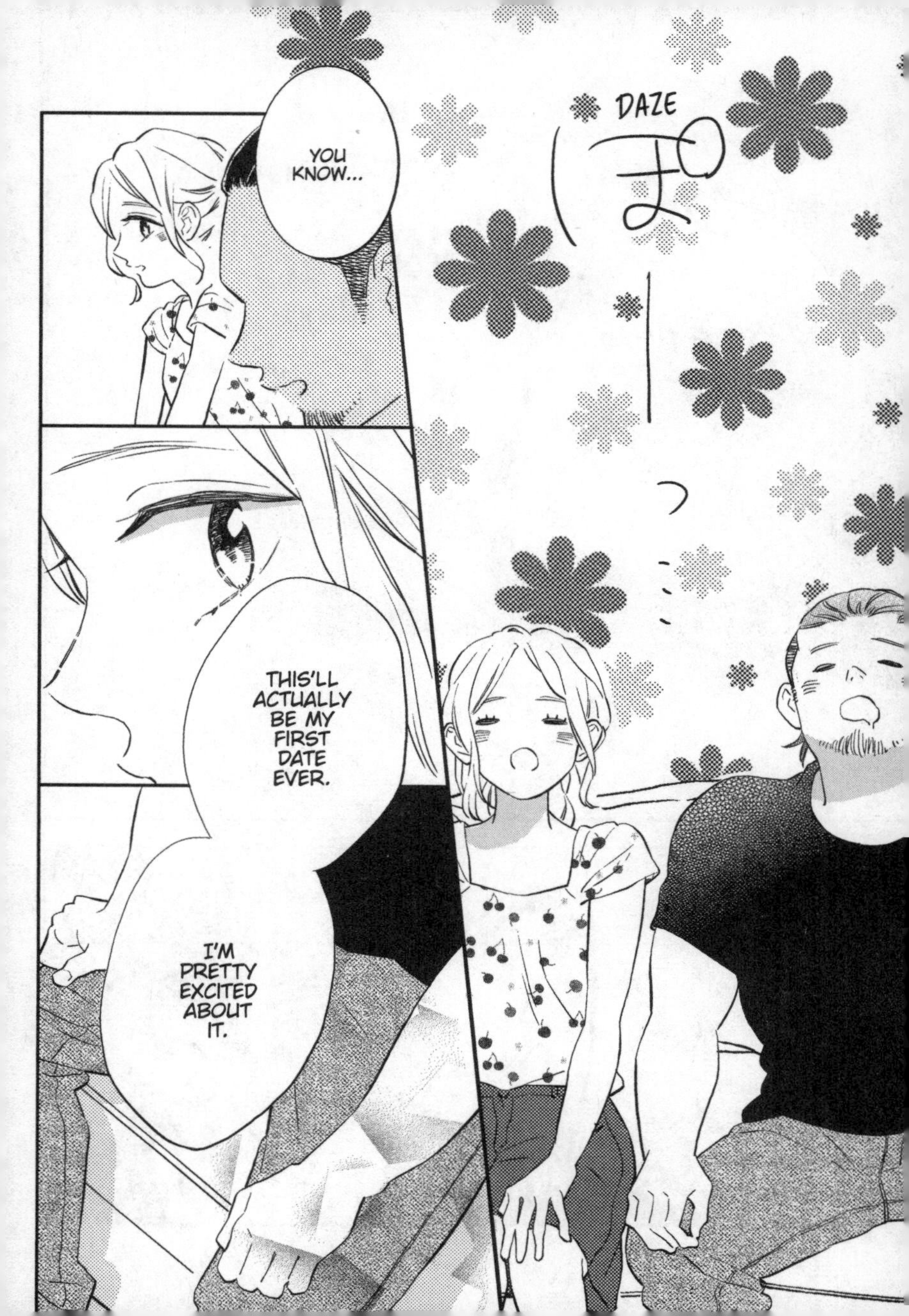
DAZE
ぽーっ…
YOU KNOW...
THIS'LL ACTUALLY BE MY FIRST DATE EVER.
I'M PRETTY EXCITED ABOUT IT.

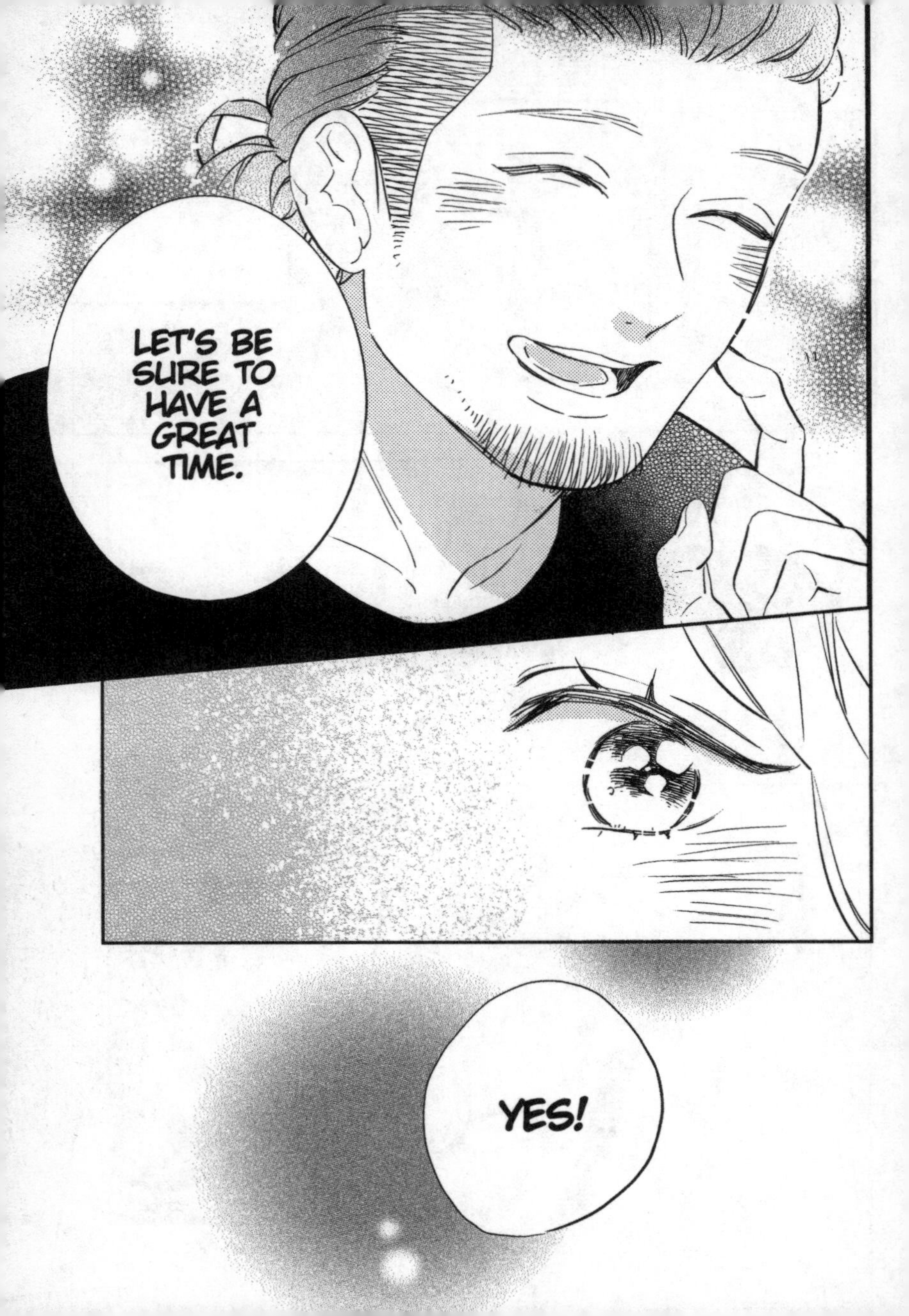
LET'S BE SURE TO HAVE A GREAT TIME.
YES!

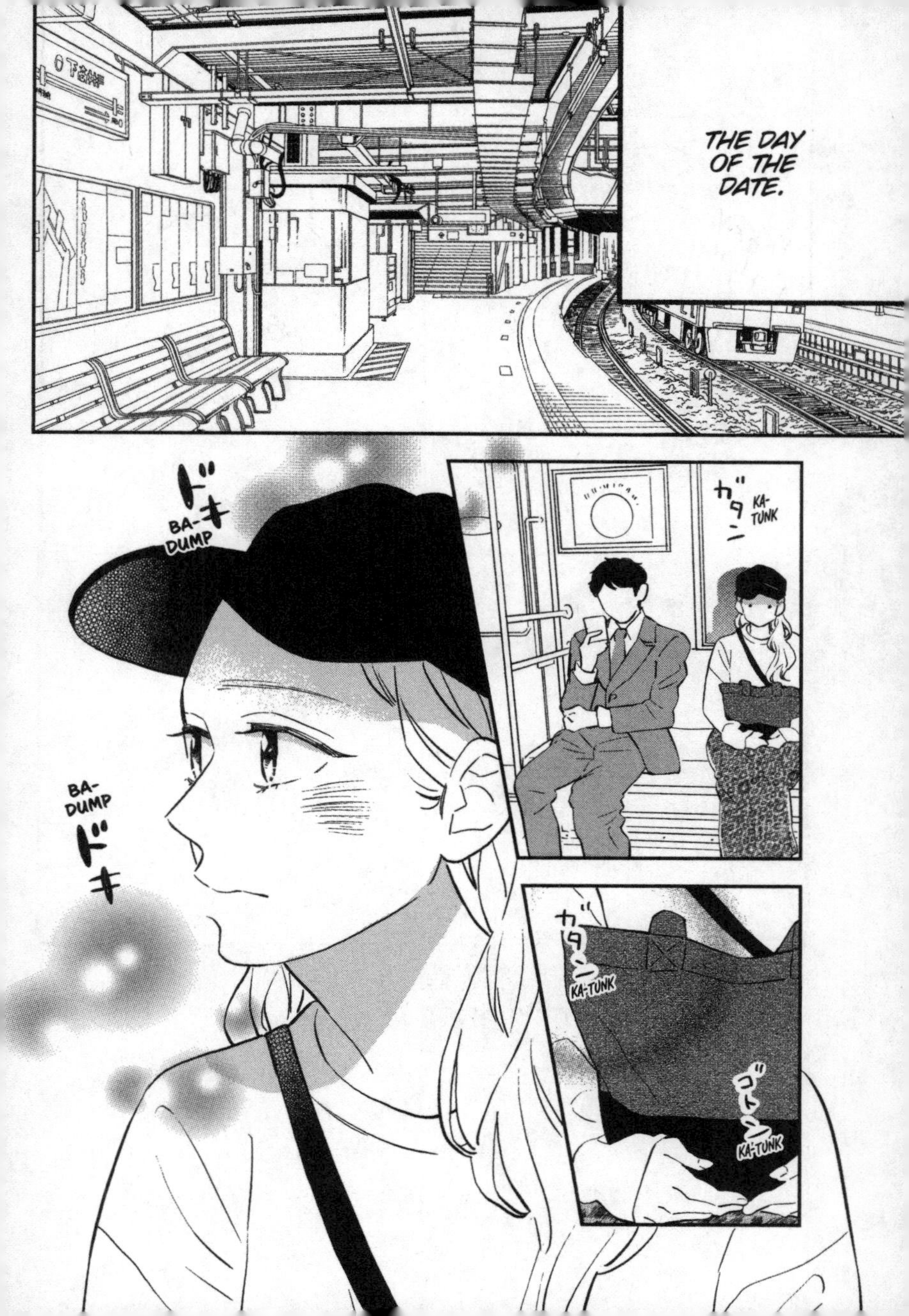
THE DAY OF THE DATE.
ガタン KA-TUNK
ガタン KA-TUNK
ゴトン KA-TUNK
ドキ BA-DUMP
BA-DUMP ドキ

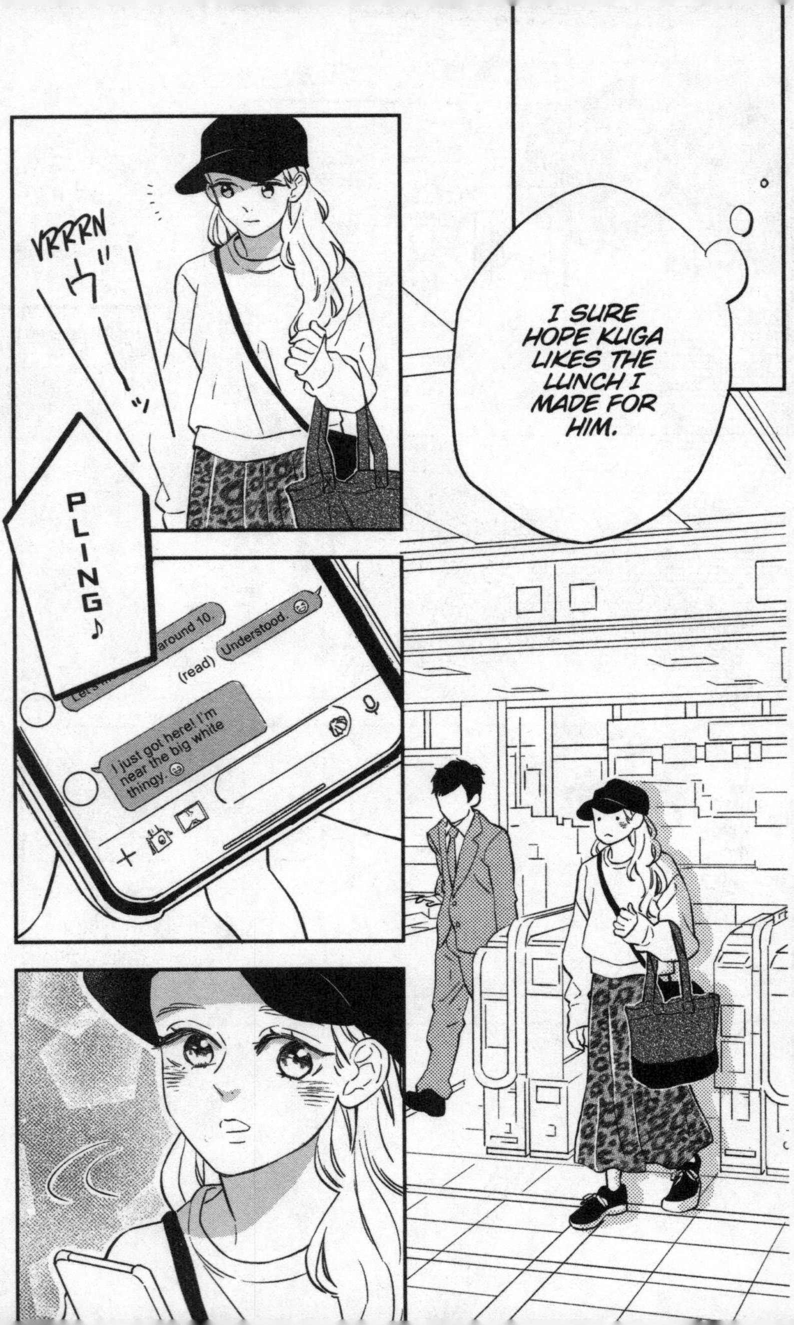
I SURE HOPE KUGA LIKES THE LUNCH I MADE FOR HIM.
VRRRN
ヴーッ
PLING♪
around 10.
Understood.
(read)
I just got here! I'm near the big white thingy.

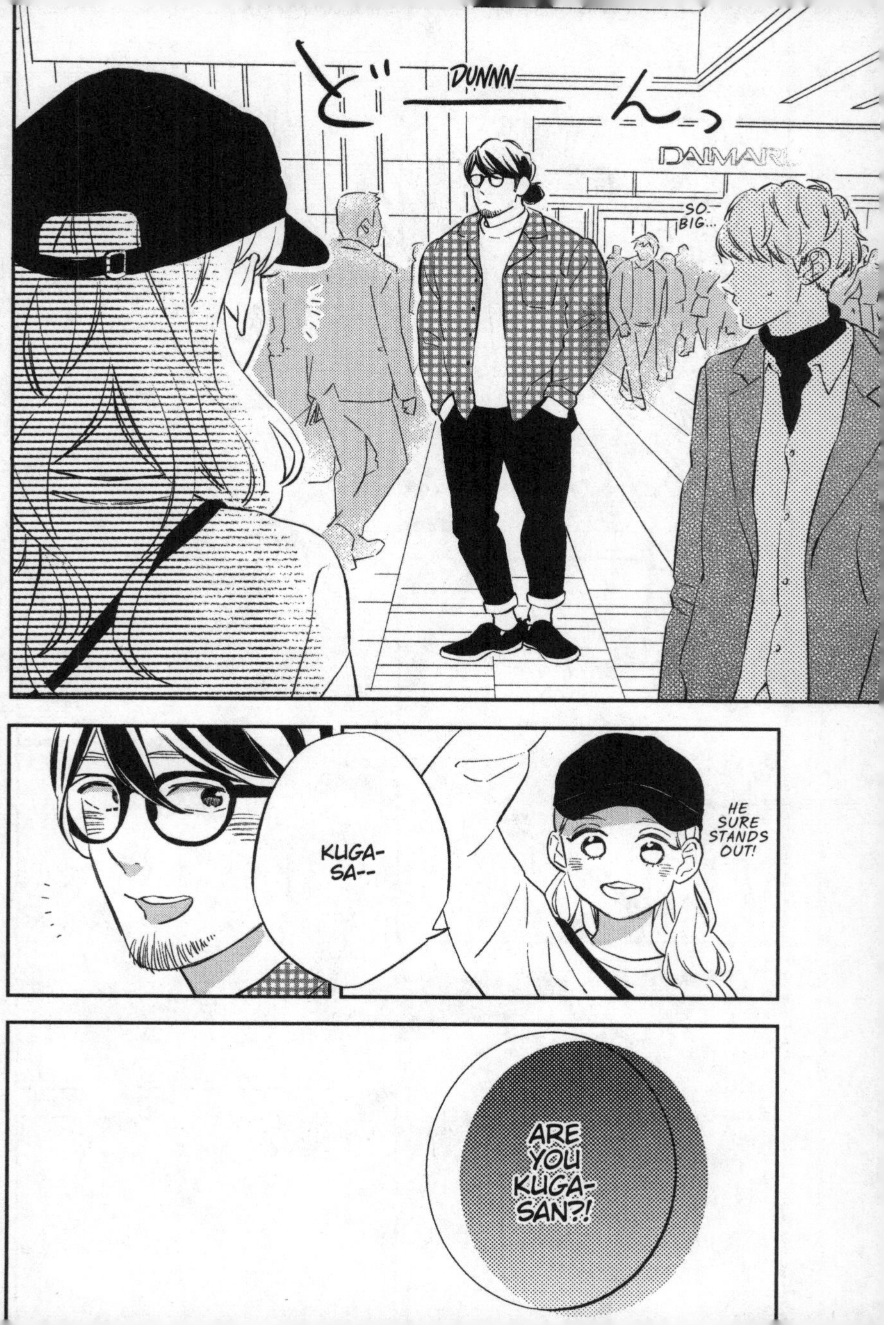
どーーんっ
DUNNN
SO BIG...
HE SURE STANDS OUT!
KUGA-SA--
ARE YOU KUGA-SAN?!

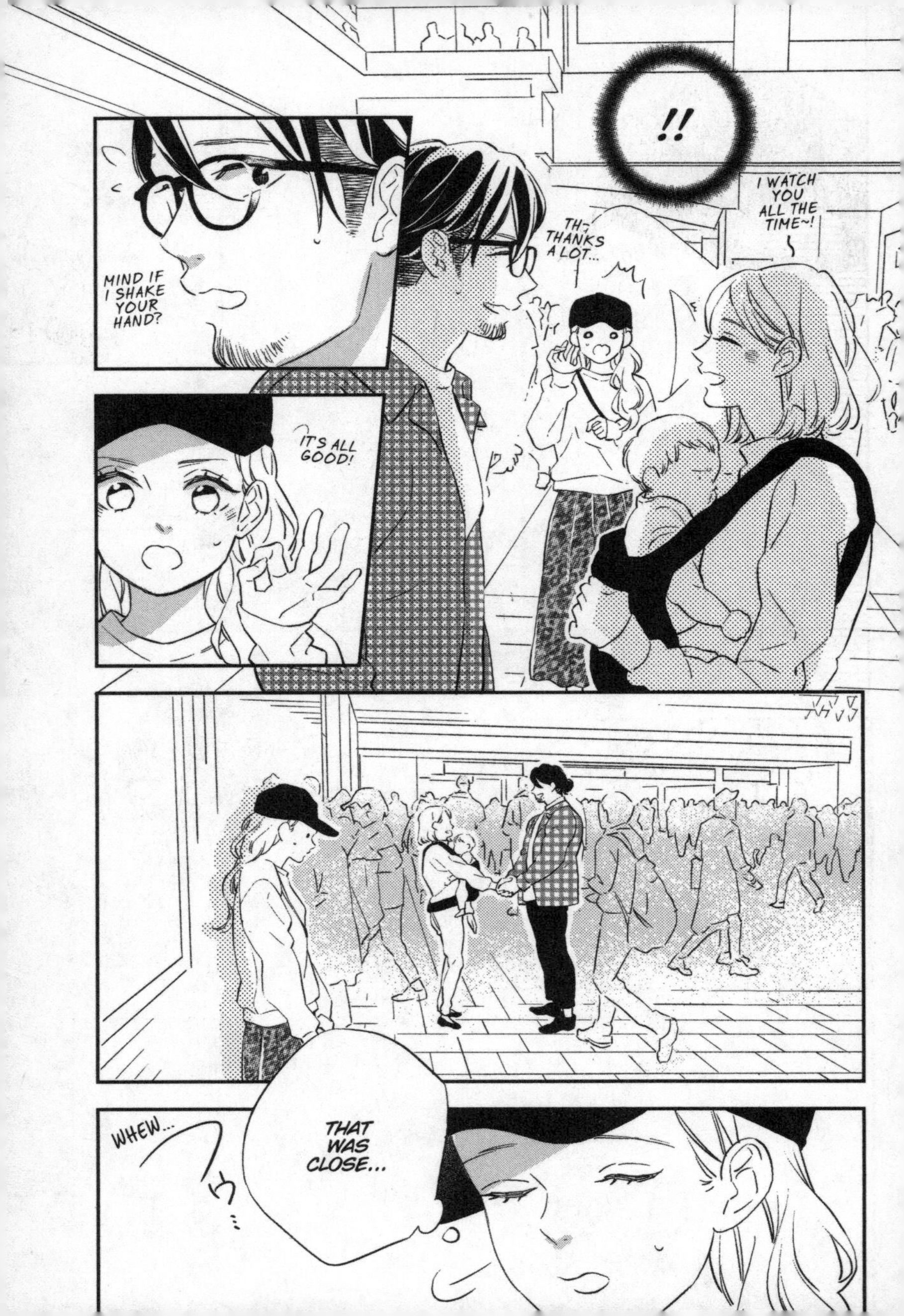
!!
I WATCH YOU ALL THE TIME~!
TH-THANKS A LOT...
MIND IF I SHAKE YOUR HAND?
IT'S ALL GOOD!
THAT WAS CLOSE...
WHEW...

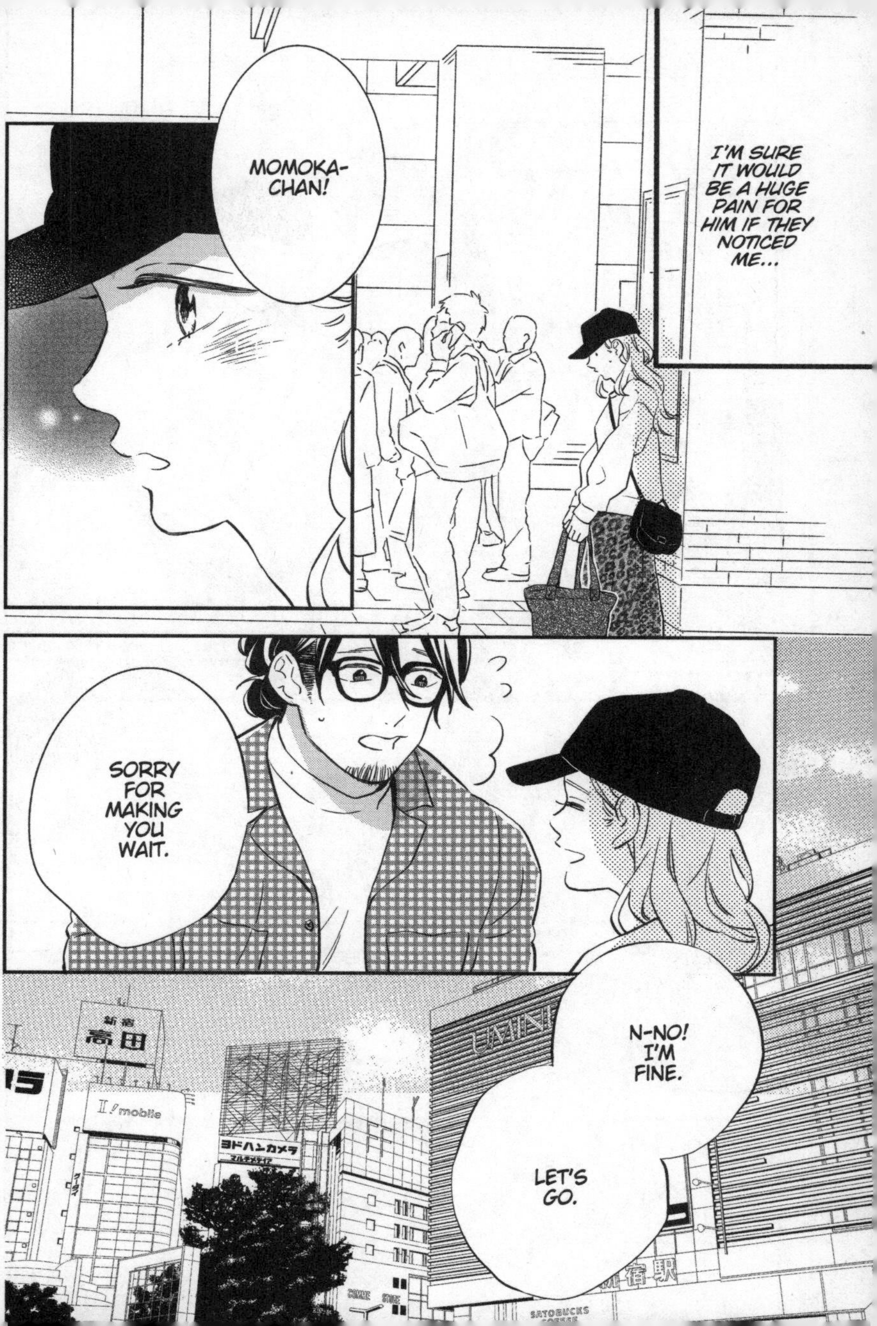

I'M SURE IT WOULD BE A HUGE PAIN FOR HIM IF THEY NOTICED ME...
MOMOKA-CHAN!
SORRY FOR MAKING YOU WAIT.
N-NO! I'M FINE.
LET'S GO.
SATOBUCKS

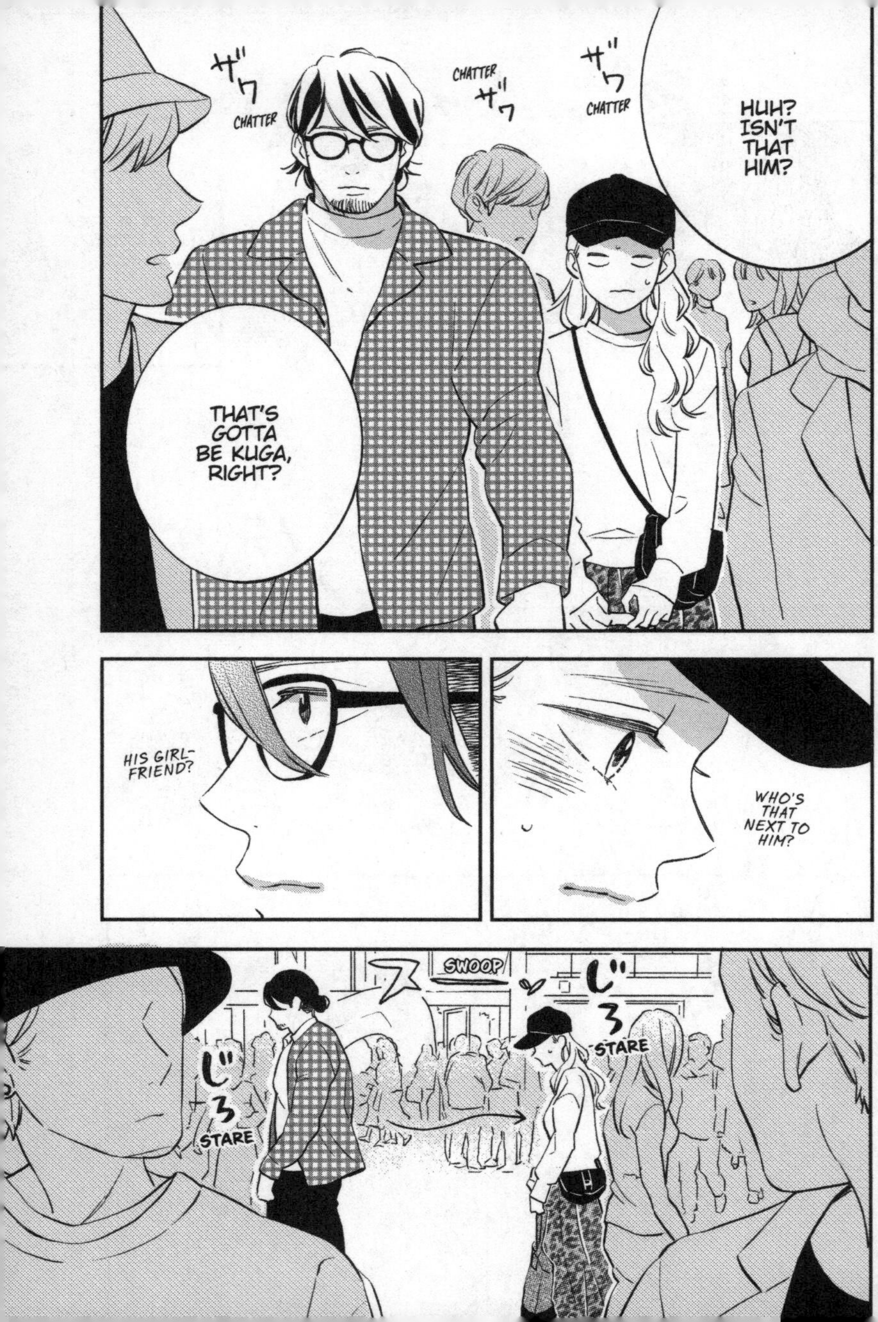
HUH? ISN'T THAT HIM?
ザワ CHATTER
CHATTER ザワ
ザワ CHATTER
THAT'S GOTTA BE KUGA, RIGHT?
WHO'S THAT NEXT TO HIM?
HIS GIRL-FRIEND?
じろ STARE
SWOOP
ス
じろ STARE

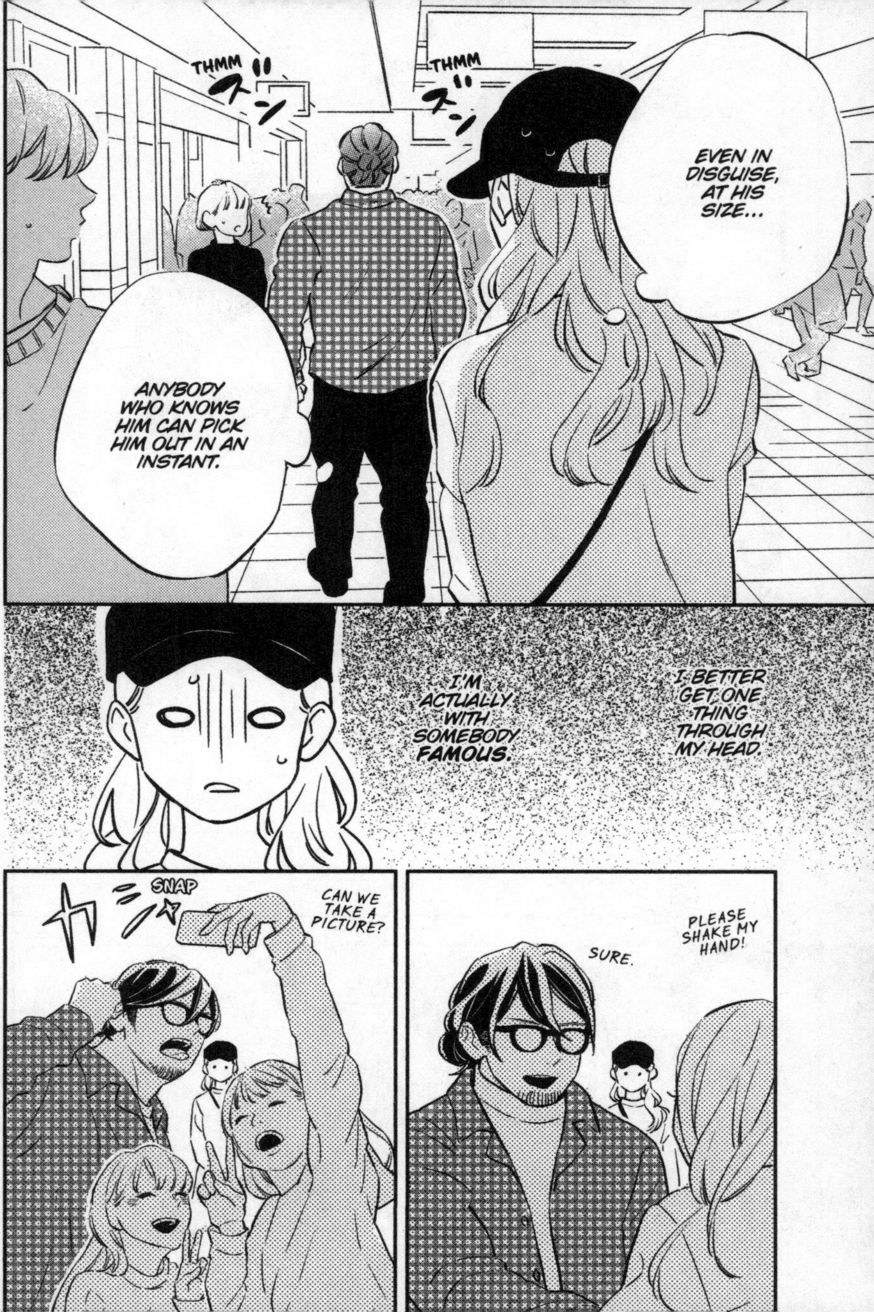
THMM
THMM
EVEN IN DISGUISE, AT HIS SIZE...
ANYBODY WHO KNOWS HIM CAN PICK HIM OUT IN AN INSTANT.
I BETTER GET ONE THING THROUGH MY HEAD.
I'M ACTUALLY WITH SOMEBODY FAMOUS.
PLEASE SHAKE MY HAND!
SURE.
CAN WE TAKE A PICTURE?
SNAP

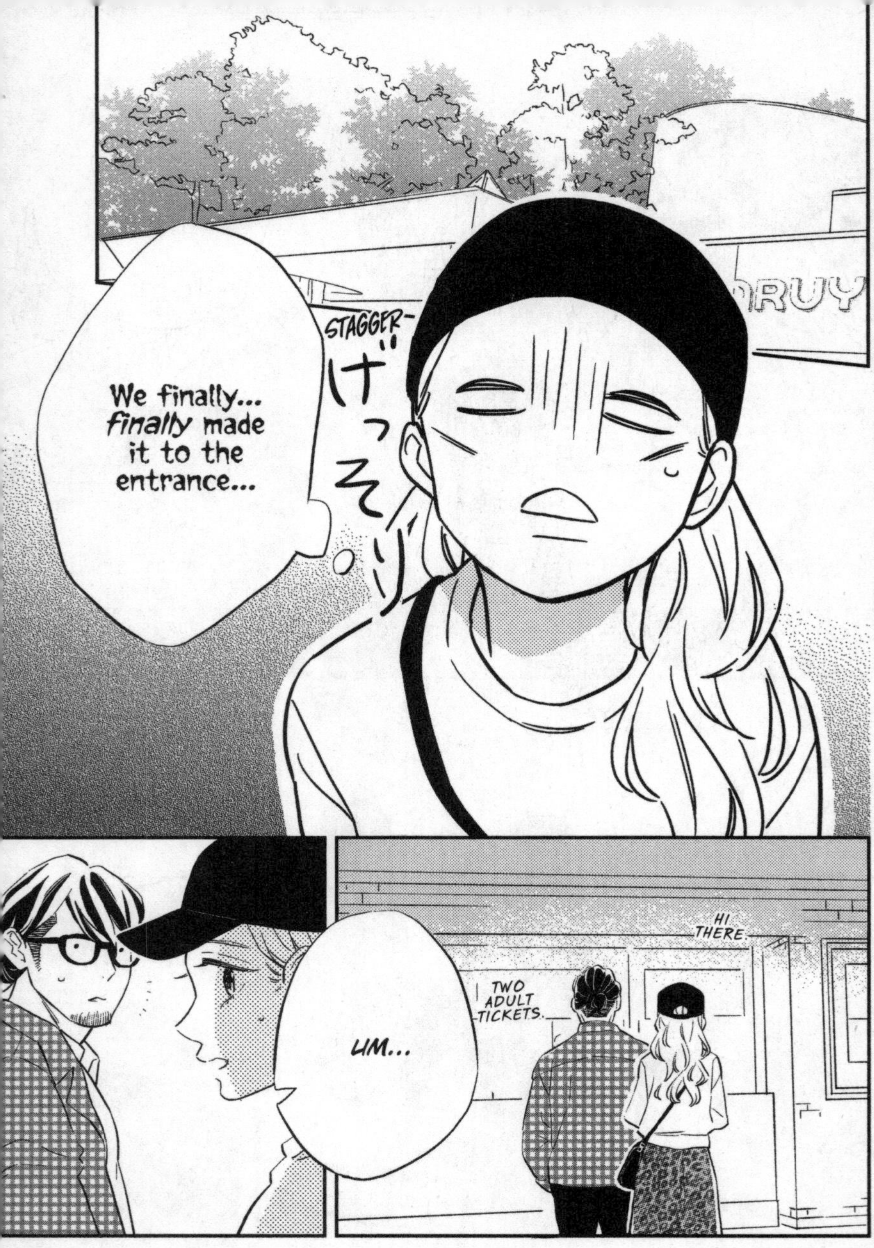
STAGGER-
げっそり
We finally... *finally* made it to the entrance...
HI THERE.
TWO ADULT TICKETS.
UM...

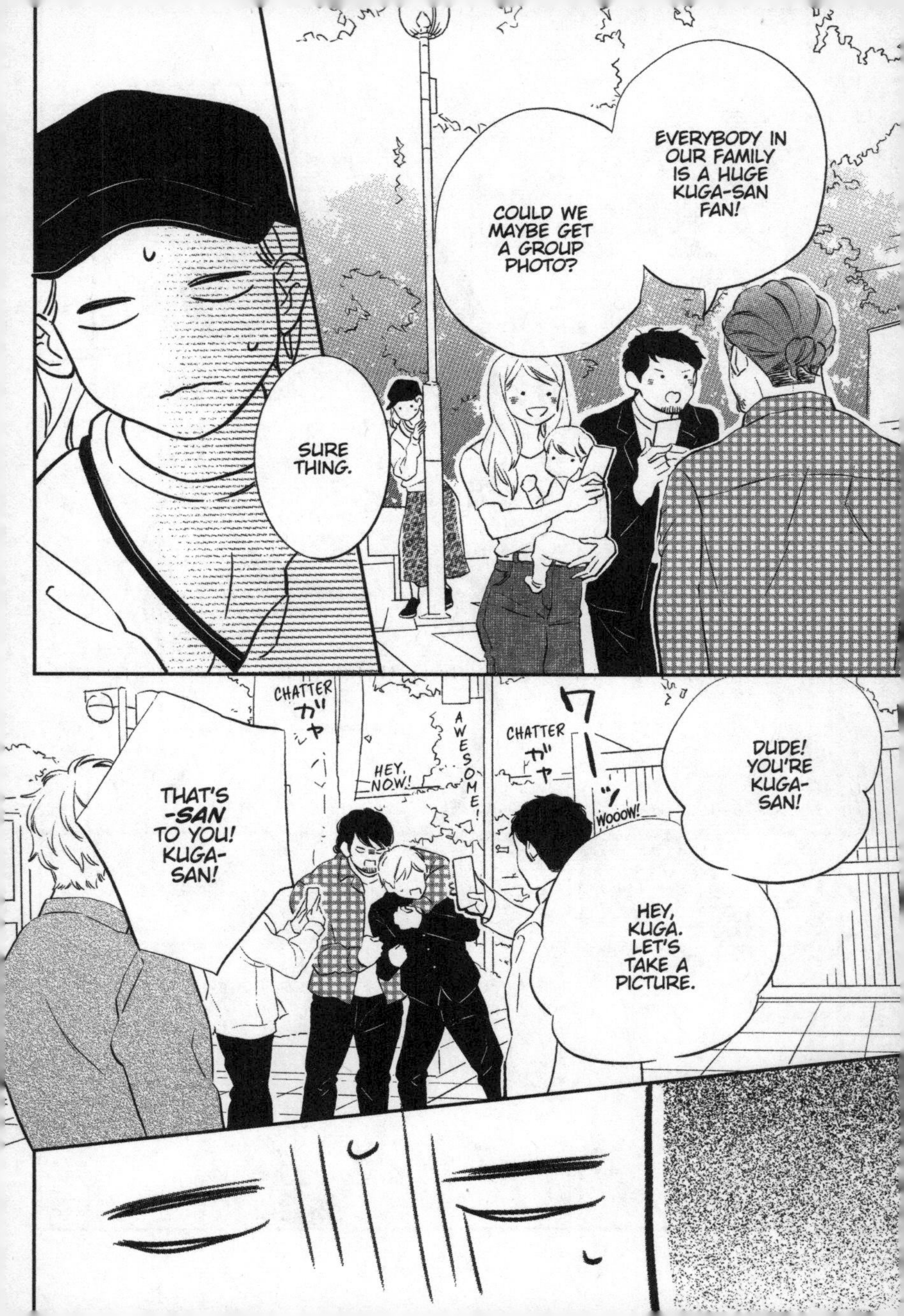
EVERYBODY IN OUR FAMILY IS A HUGE KUGA-SAN FAN!
COULD WE MAYBE GET A GROUP PHOTO?
SURE THING.
DUDE! YOU'RE KUGA-SAN!
ワーッ
WOOOW!
HEY, KUGA. LET'S TAKE A PICTURE.
CHATTER
ガヤ
AWESOME!
HEY, NOW!
CHATTER
ガヤ
THAT'S -SAN TO YOU! KUGA-SAN!

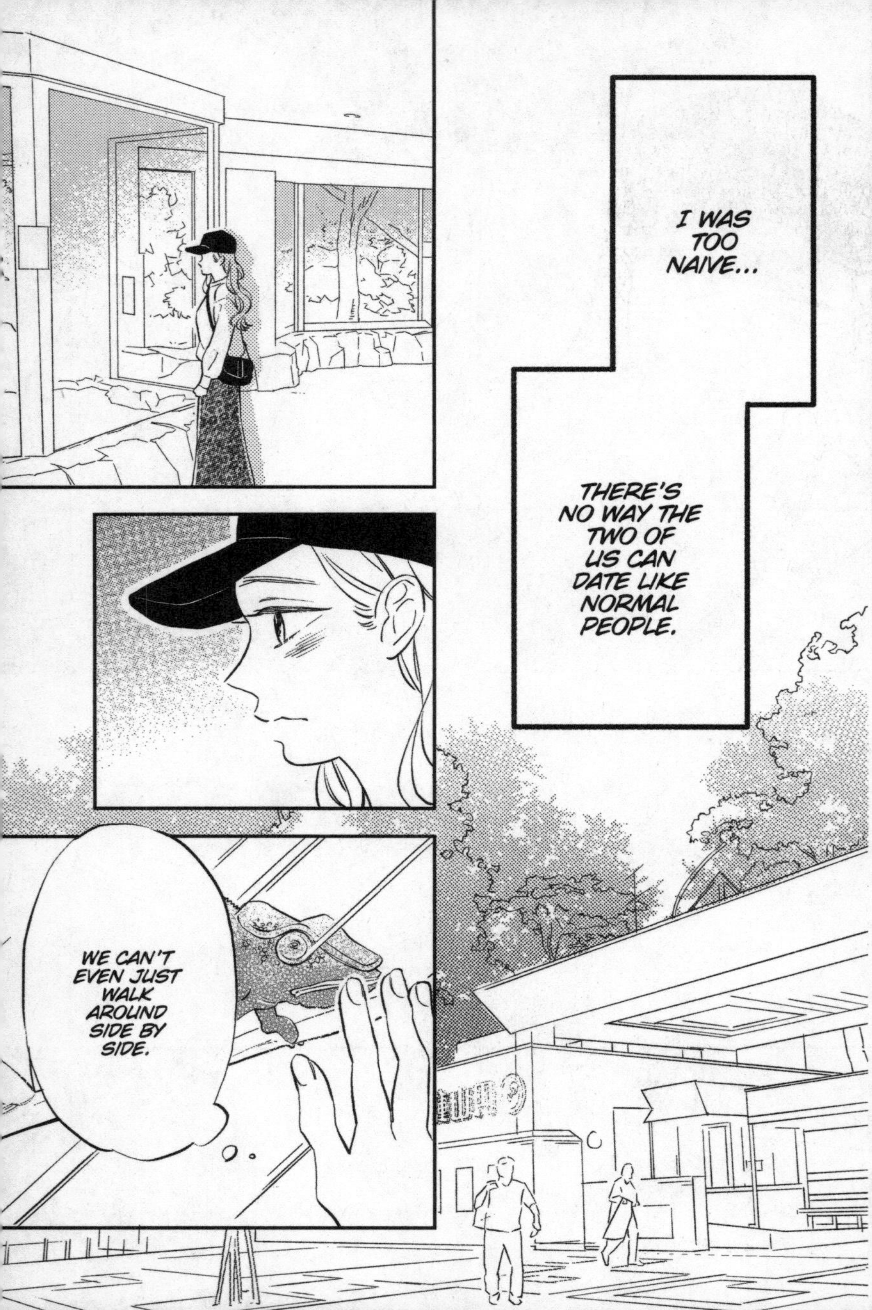
I WAS TOO NAIVE...
THERE'S NO WAY THE TWO OF US CAN DATE LIKE NORMAL PEOPLE.
WE CAN'T EVEN JUST WALK AROUND SIDE BY SIDE.

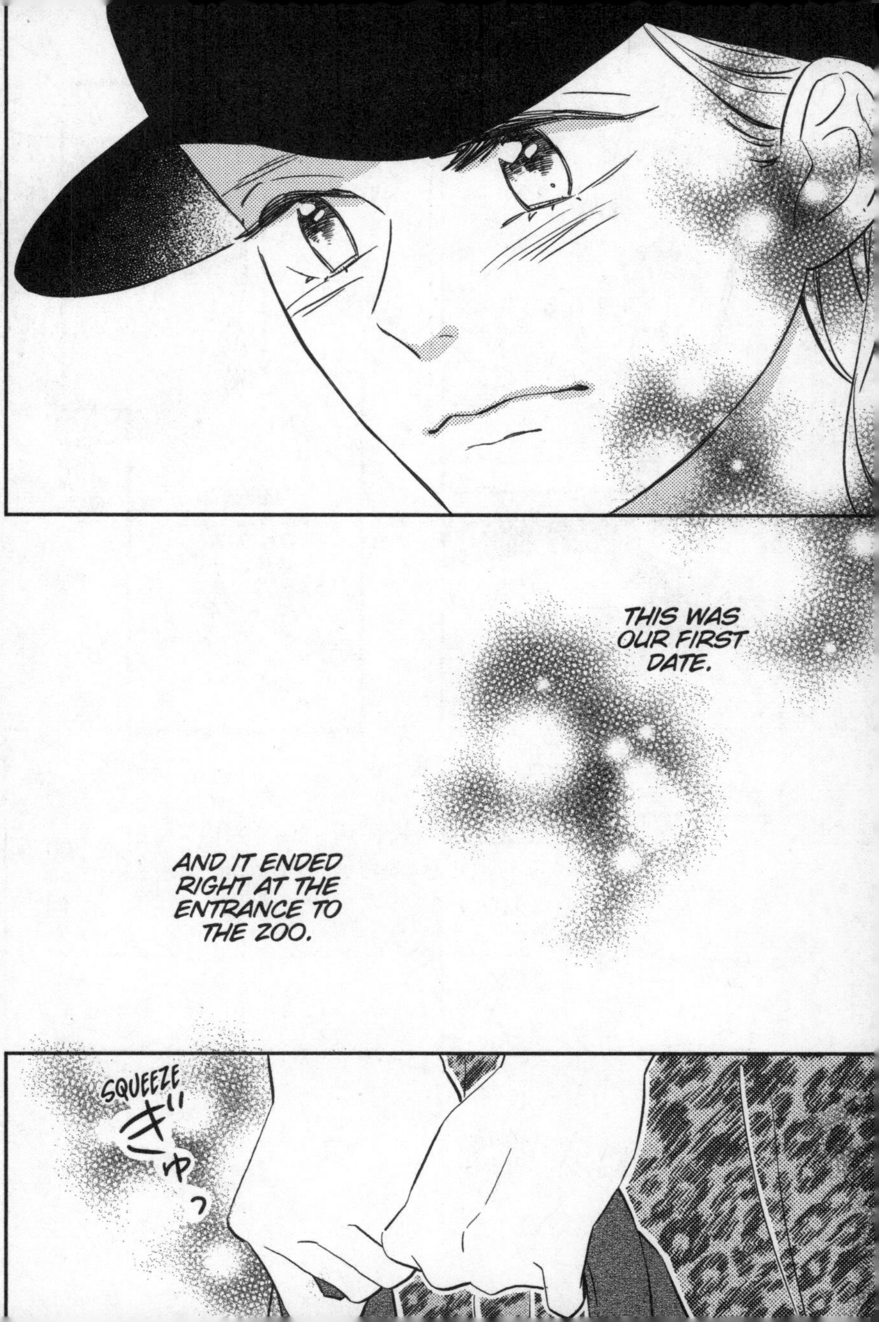
THIS WAS OUR FIRST DATE.
AND IT ENDED RIGHT AT THE ENTRANCE TO THE ZOO.
SQUEEZE
ぎゅっ

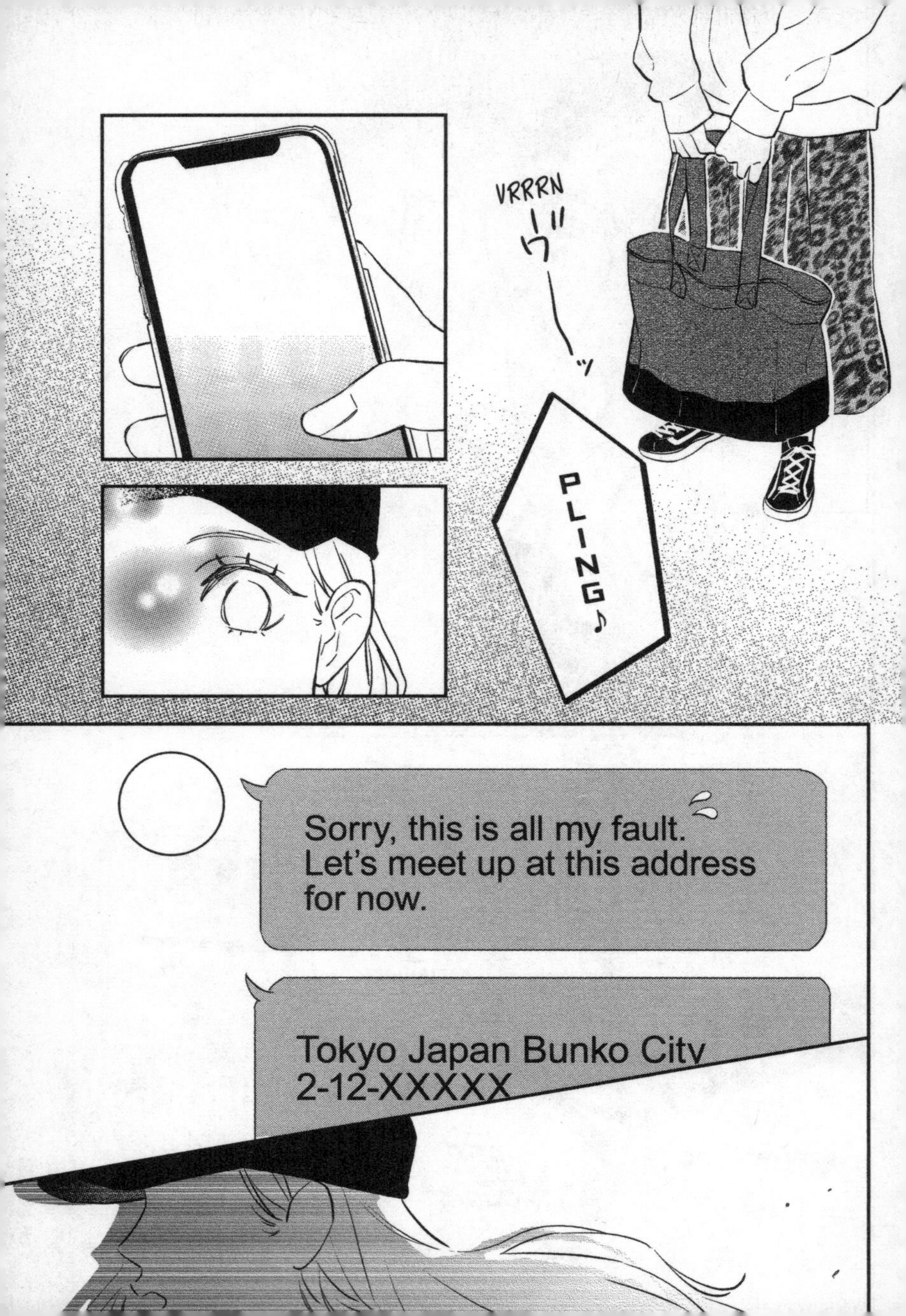
VRRRN
ヴーッ
PLING♪
Sorry, this is all my fault. Let's meet up at this address for now.
Tokyo Japan Bunko City 2-12-XXXXX

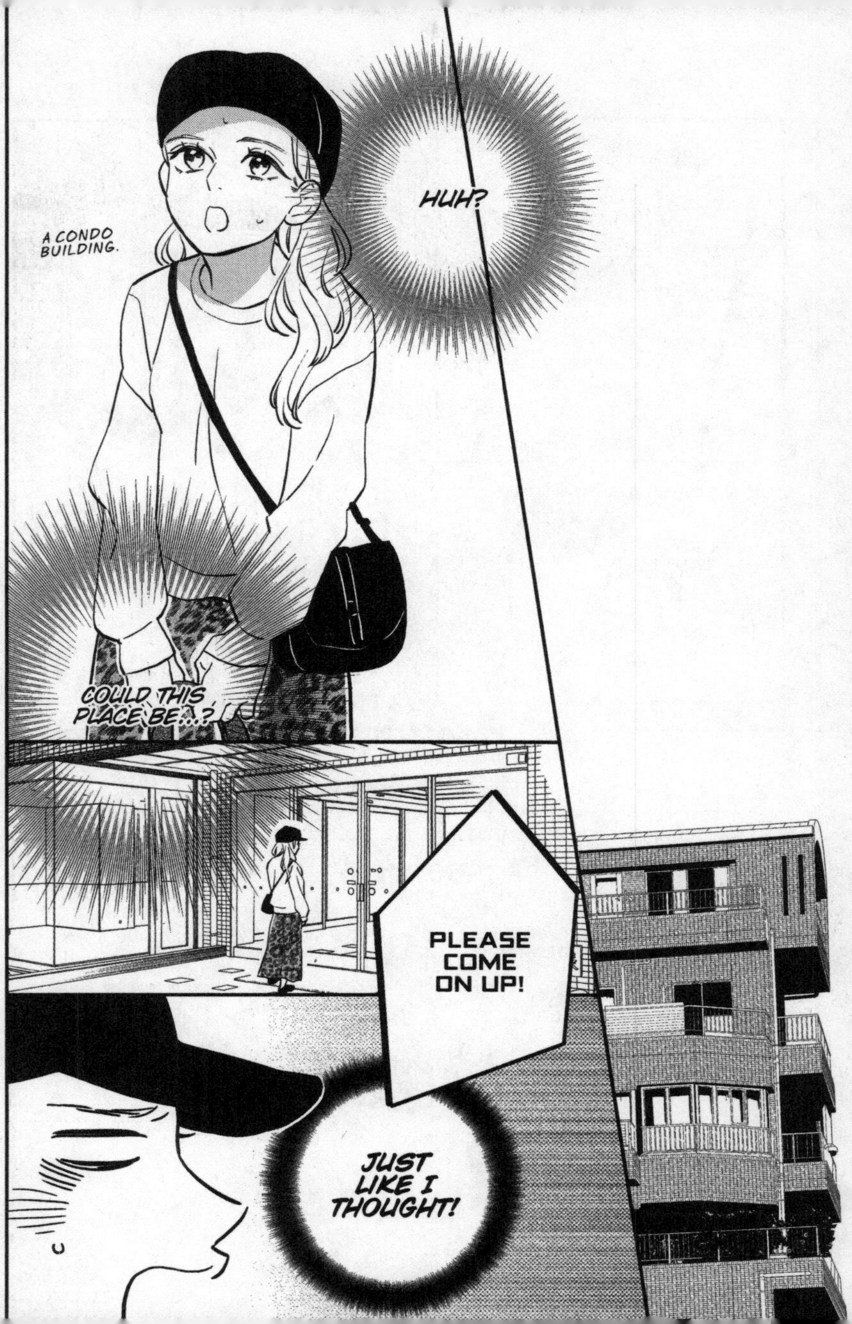
HUH?
A CONDO BUILDING.
COULD THIS PLACE BE...?
PLEASE COME ON UP!
JUST LIKE I THOUGHT!

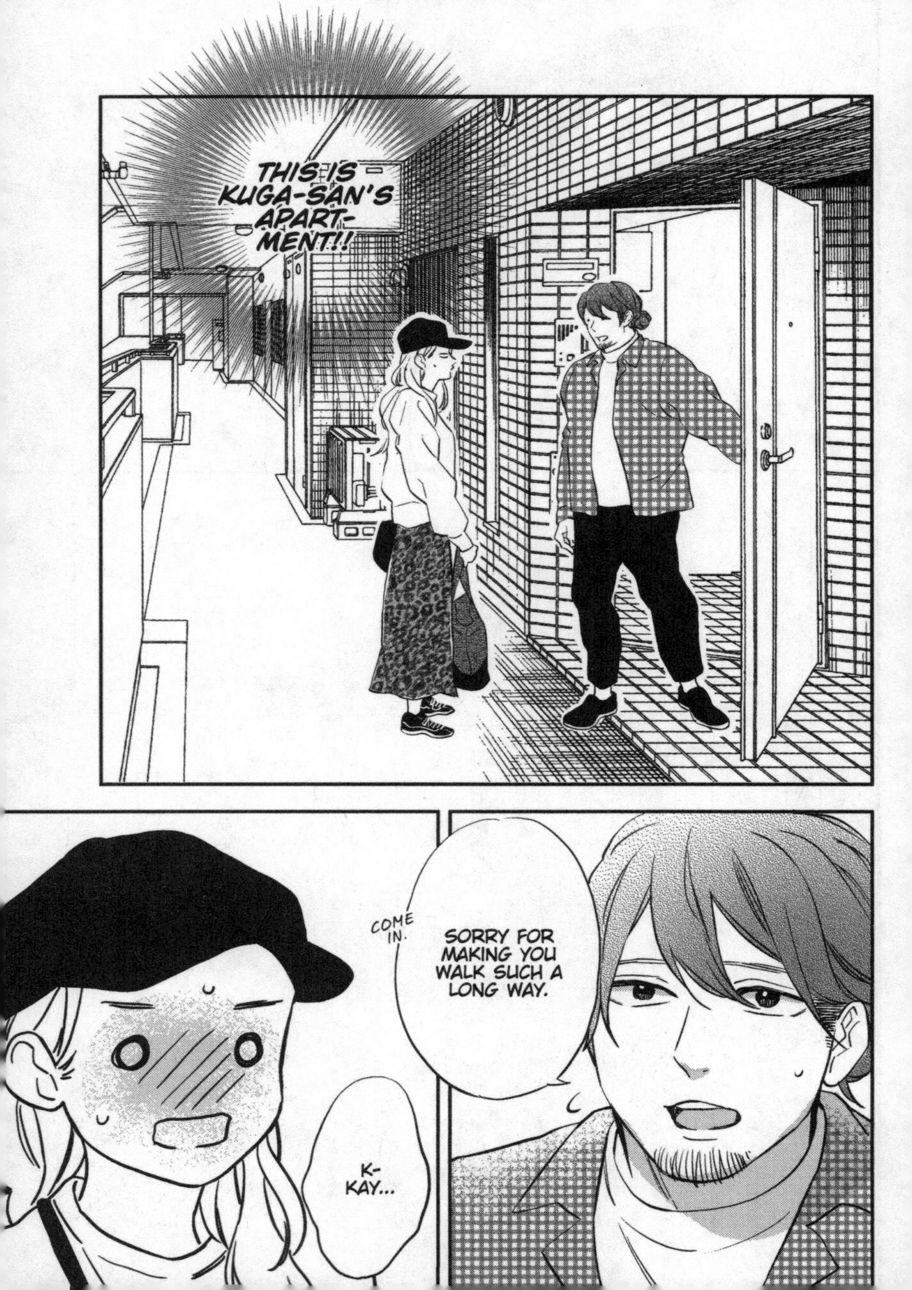
THIS IS KUGA-SAN'S APART-MENT!!
SORRY FOR MAKING YOU WALK SUCH A LONG WAY.
COME IN.
K-KAY...

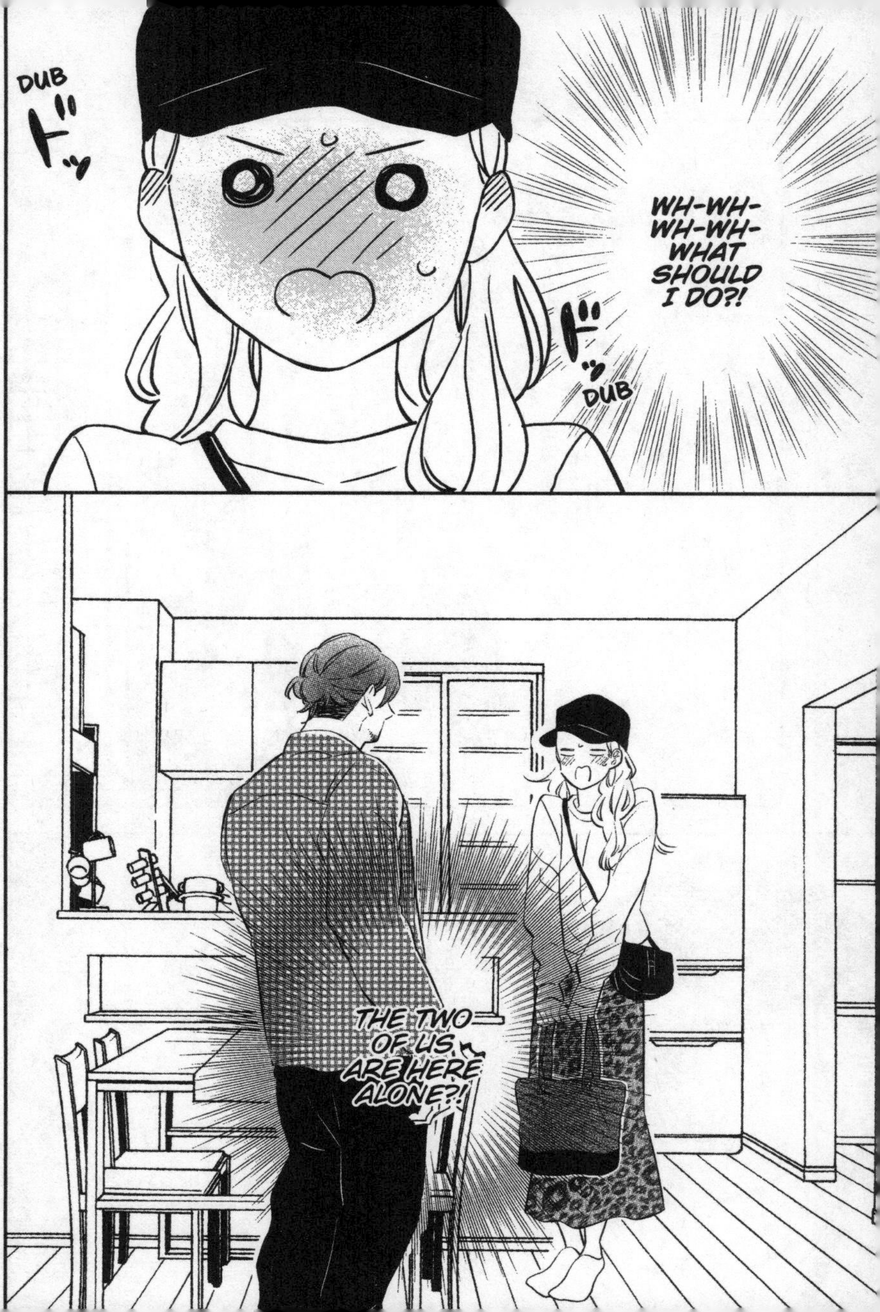
WH-WH-WH-WH-WHAT SHOULD I DO?!
ドッ
DUB
DUB
ドッ
THE TWO OF US ARE HERE ALONE?!

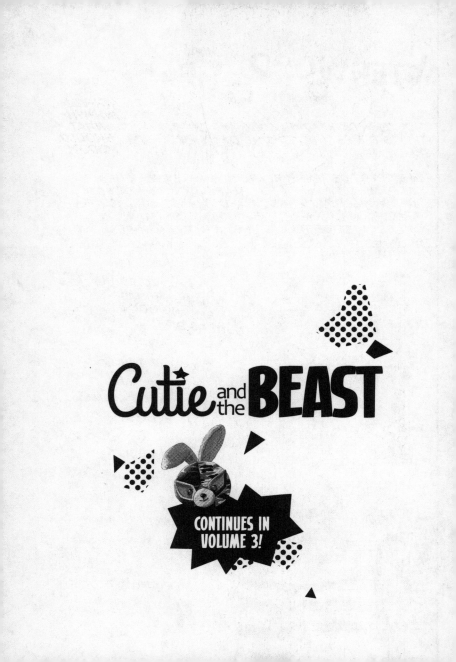

Cutie and the BEAST

CONTINUES IN
VOLUME 3!

AFTERWORD

THANK YOU FOR READING *CUTIE AND THE BEAST* VOLUME 2. THIS IS THE SECOND VOLUME OF MY FIRST-EVER SERIALIZATION! (ALL RIGHT—!!)

THE LETTERS I GET FROM READERS ALWAYS CHEER ME UP. IT MAKES ME VERY HAPPY TO KNOW THERE I'VE GOT BOTH READERS WHO ALREADY KNOW ABOUT WRESTLING AS WELL AS READERS WHO STARTED GETTING INTERESTED IN THE SPORT BECAUSE OF THIS SERIES. I CAN'T REALLY RESPOND TO EVERYONE, BUT I MAKE SURE TO READ THEM ALL! (I'M REALLY, REALLY GRATEFUL.)

I WILL WORK HARD SO THAT YOU CAN CONTINUE TO CHEER FOR KUGA-SAN AND MOMOKA. I'LL BE COUNTING ON YOUR SUPPORT!

TO WRAP THINGS UP:
* EDITOR-SAMA
* ASSISTANT-SAMA
* MY FAMILY
* EVERYONE WHO PICKED UP THIS BOOK

THANK YOU ALL SO VERY MUCH!!

I RECENTLY STARTED USING TWITTER AGAIN. MY LITTLE SISTER IS RESPONDING IN MY PLACE! PLEASE FEEL FREE TO FOLLOW ME THERE, TOO: @YUUHI_AZUMI

TO ALL THOSE WHO HELPED ME MAKE THIS MANGA A REALITY, THANK YOU VERY MUCH!!

YUHI AZUMI　安曇ゆうひ

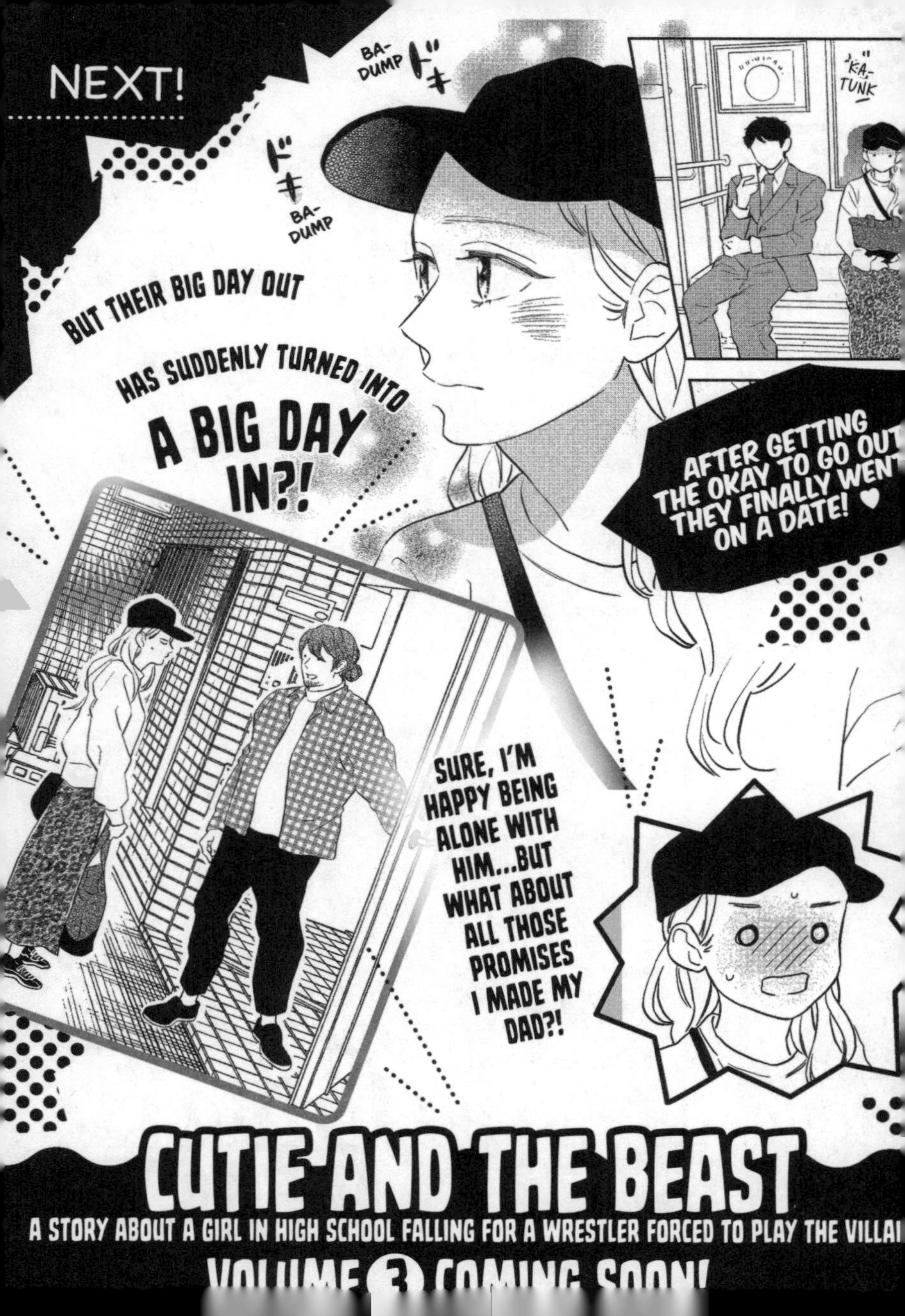
NEXT!
KA-TUNK
BA-DUMP ドキ
ドキ BA-DUMP
AFTER GETTING THE OKAY TO GO OUT THEY FINALLY WENT ON A DATE! ♥
BUT THEIR BIG DAY OUT
HAS SUDDENLY TURNED INTO
A BIG DAY IN?!
SURE, I'M HAPPY BEING ALONE WITH HIM...BUT WHAT ABOUT ALL THOSE PROMISES I MADE MY DAD?!
CUTIE AND THE BEAST
A STORY ABOUT A GIRL IN HIGH SCHOOL FALLING FOR A WRESTLER FORCED TO PLAY THE VILLAI
VOLUME 3 COMING SOON!

Cutie and the BEAST

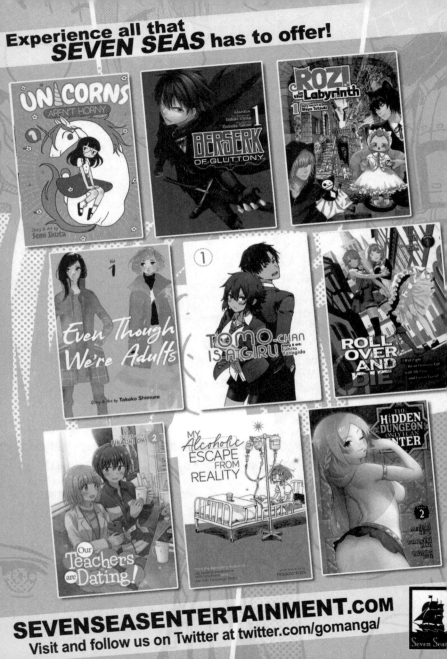

SEVEN SEAS ENTERTAINM

Cutie and the BEAST

story and art by **YUHI AZUMI**

VOLUME 2

TRANSLATION
Angela Liu

ADAPTATION
Andrea Puckett

LETTERING AND RETOUCH
Erika Terriquez

INTERIOR LAYOUT
Christa Miesner

COVER DESIGN
Nicky Lim
(LOGO) **George Panella**

PROOFREADER
Brett Hallahan
Dawn Davis

EDITOR
J.P. Sullivan

PREPRESS TECHNICIAN
Rhiannon Rasmussen-Silverstein

MANAGING EDITOR
Julie Davis

ASSOCIATE PUBLISHER
Adam Arnold

PUBLISHER
Jason DeAngelis

PUJO TO YAJU VOL. 2
©2019 Yuhi Azumi. All rights reserved.
First published in Japan in 2019 by Kodansha Ltd., Tokyo.
Publication rights for this English edition arranged through Kodansha Ltd., Tokyo.

Seven Seas press and purchase enquiries can be sent to Marketing Manager
Lianne Sentar at press@gomanga.com. Information regarding the distribution
and purchase of digital editions is available from Digital Manager CK Russell
at digital@gomanga.com.

Seven Seas and the Seven Seas logo are trademarks of
Seven Seas Entertainment. All rights reserved.

ISBN: 978-1-64505-949-3

Printed in Canada

First Printing: January 2021

10 9 8 7 6 5 4 3 2 1

FOLLOW US ONLINE: *www.sevenseasentertainment.com*

READING DIRECTIONS

This book reads from ***right to left***, Japanese style.
If this is your first time reading manga, you start
reading from the top right panel on each page and
take it from there. If you get lost, just follow the
numbered diagram here. It may seem backwards at
first, but you'll get the hang of it! Have fun!!

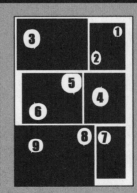